Massacre
of the
Dreamers

UNIVERSITY OF
NEW MEXICO
PRESS

Albuquerque

Massacre

ESSAYS

of the

ON

Dreamers

XICANISMA

ANA CASTILLO

Library of Congress Cataloging-in-Publication Data

    Castillo, Ana.
      Massacre of the dreamers : essays on xicanisma / Ana
Castillo.—1st ed.
      p. cm.
     Includes bibliographical references.
     Contents: Introduction—Countryless woman: the early
feminista—The 1986 Watsonville women's strike: a case of mexicana
activism—The ancient roots of machismo—Saintly mother and soldier's whore: the leftist/Catholic paradigm—In the beginning there
was Eva—La macha: toward an erotic whole self—Un tapiz: poetics
of conscientizacion—Brujas and curanderas: a lived spirituality—
Toward the mother-bond principle—Resurrection of the dreamers.
      ISBN 0-8263-1554-2
      1. Mexican American women.   2. Feminism—United States.
I. Title.
E184.M5C369   1994
305.48'86872073—dc20
94-3204
   CIP

Designed by Linda Mae Tratechaud
Calligraphy by Terry Kocon

In Memory of My Beloved Father,
Raymond Castillo
(1933–1990)
I thank him for giving me the gifts
of creativity and dreaming.

To my mother, Raquel Rocha Castillo,
whose life and example have taught me to persevere.

Also, to mi'jo, Marcel Ramón.

And, of course, to the trees.

CONTENTS

Acknowledgments   ix

Introduction   1

one   A Countryless Woman:
The Early Feminista   21

two   The 1986 Watsonville Women's Strike:
A Case of Mexicana Activism   43

three   The Ancient Roots of Machismo   63

four   Saintly Mother and Soldier's Whore:
The Leftist/Catholic Paradigm   85

five   In the Beginning There Was Eva   105

six   La Macha:
Toward an Erotic Whole Self   121

seven   Brujas and Curanderas:
A Lived Spirituality   145

eight   Un Tapiz:
Poetics of Concientización   163

nine   Toward the Mother-Bond Principle   181

ten   Resurrection of the Dreamers   205

Notes   227

Anyone dreaming anything about the end of the Empire was ordered to the palace to tell of it. Night and day emissaries combed the city, and Tenochtitlan paid tribute in dreams . . .

But finding no good in the thousands offered, Moctezuma killed all the offenders. It was the massacre of the dreamers, the most pathetic of all . . .

From that day there were no more forecasts, no more dreams, terror weighed upon the spirit world . . .
—*Laurette Sejourne,* Burning Water:
Thought and Religion in Ancient Mexico

Queen Xochitl . . . legendary queen of the Toltecs. During her reign women were called to war service. She headed the batallions and was killed in battle; legend has it that as she died, blood streamed from her wounds, foretelling the scattering of the Toltec nation.
—*Marta Cotera,* Profile on the Mexican American Woman

Perhaps the greatest harm patriarchy has done to us is to stifle, coopt, and deform our powers of imagination. Moralisms, dualistic dogmas, repressive prohibitions block our imagination at its sources, which is the fusion of sexual and spiritual energies.
—*Monica Sjöö & Barbara Mor,* The Great Cosmic Mother:
Rediscovering the Religion of the Earth

ACKNOWLEDGMENTS

My passion for my subject is understandable. But my aim here in offering my interpretations and analyses has been to have my view serve as a springboard for further intellectual discussion. Sensitive and introspective reflection is needed on the part of all those who desire to participate in the ongoing polemic of our five-hundred-year status as countryless residents on land that is now the United States.

I would formally like to thank the following:

First and foremost, I am indebted to the late Dieter Herms of the University of Bremen, Germany. Dr. Herms, former Dean of the American Studies Program at the University of Bremen offered me the rare opportunity to submit this manuscript to his university in lieu of a formal dissertation. Despite ill health, he served as a continuous ally to me in this work.

I would also like to thank the other members of my defense committee, with a special note to Ingrid Kerkhoff of the University of Wuppertal, Germany, who also served as a supporter of this project from its inception. Primarily through the relentless support of Drs. Herms and Kerkhoff I was conferred the Doctorate in American Studies by the University of Bremen in July, 1991, for this interdisciplinary work.

Because scholarship by U.S. people of color has often been questioned by white academia, I would like to add the following regarding the process by which I received my PhD. My dissertation project, by my own insistance, was unorthodox. That is, it crossed boundaries of cultural criticism, social sciences and creative literature. Moreover, it directed itself to the subject of its thesis rather than to the academy. However, it is to the great credit of those scholars on my defense committee that such an ambitious and unprecedented work was accepted and conferred the doctorate in Germany. It is also significant to point out that a woman of color with a reputation for writing on themes that largely concern her perspective as a second class citizen in the United States, was not given that same invitation to submit such work for scholarly review by any university in the United States. Those who are unable to dismiss the idea that revolutionary work and action is by its nature inferior to work that conforms to the standards of the status quo—in this case, the academy—may rest easy that neither I nor my thesis were given special allowances with regard to the criteria that German academia maintains for its doctoral candidates.

The writing of this manuscript has covered the years from Fall 1987 to Fall 1993, with interims during which I devoted myself to other writing and to earning my livelihood. During the early stages of this project, I received cash awards from the California Arts Council (fellowship in the category of fiction, 1989) and from the National Endowment for the Arts (fellowship in the category of poetry, 1990). Also, I was given time and room to complete this project as a Dissertation Fellow (1989–1990) with the Chicano Studies Department at the University of California, Santa Barbara.

My warm appreciation is extended to the staff of the Colección Tloque Nahuaque at the UCSB Library, with special thanks to its head librarian, Salvador Guereña, for their ready assistance.

The Archives of Ana Castillo are housed in the Special Collections Department at the University of California, Santa Barbara Library. Anyone interested in the early versions of this project as well as other documents pertaining to my writing may study them there.

After twenty years of writing, still

> . . . English syntax
> makes it way to my mouth
> with the grace of a clubbed foot.
> —Ana Castillo, *My Father Was a Toltec*

Because of this, one year, when I was feeling particularly fatalistic and india, I offered it to a friend to rewrite and sign his name to it, another year I considered throwing it over the Bay Bridge. But like the proverbial bad penny, it kept turning up. Without question, this project has been the most challenging one I have had to date. I would like to thank my editors at the University of New Mexico Press, Andrea Otañez and Barbara Guth and others who helped me with my "English" and for their patience.

As always, thanks Susan B.!

Over the years the list of friends, comadres, and scholars who generously gave me their time, feedback, and support for this project has grown. I would like to thank María Herrera-Sobek, Hector Torres, Luccia Chiabula Burnbaum, Betita Martínez, Ronnie Burk, Jennifer, Camille & Barbara, summer of '92, Dorothy, my George por su amore e intelecto, Rosalía, Elsa, and our comadre-brujas for their faith and Tuesday prayers. Also, those authors whose works I have cited here, mil gracias for writing. With heart in hand I thank everyone who shared these ideas, and most of all, believed that this work is worthwhile for all of us who dream.

A.C.

Tierra de los Seminoles

día de los muertos, 1993

Acknowledgements of publication: "The Watsonville Women's Strike, 1986: A Case of Mestiza Activism" appeared in *Gulliver* no. 26: Faeun—Arbeit, Kulter, Aktivismus, Germany 1989; "Toward an Erotic Whole Self" appeared in *Chicana Lesbians: The Girls Our Mothers Warned Us About* (Berkeley: Third Woman Press, 1991); and "Un Tapiz: Poetics of Conscientización" appeared in *Critical Fictions: The Politics of Imaginative Writing* (Seattle: Bay Press, 1991).

INTRODUCTION

I AM A BROWN WOMAN, from the Mexican side of town—torn between the Chicago obrero roots of my upbringing and my egocentric tendency toward creative expressions. Characteristically, as a poet I am opinionated and rely on my hunches. These have been my guides throughout this book. Because the critical essay format demands it, where possible I have attempted to corroborate some of my ideas with data from a variety of resources from U.S. Census Bureau reports to ethnographic studies.

The woman in the United States who is politically self-described as Chicana, mestiza in terms of race, and Latina or Hispanic in regards to her Spanish-speaking heritage, and who numbers in the millions in the United States cannot be summarized nor neatly categorized. I have applied my ideas as broadly as possible, ever mindful that at the same time they are my own reflections.

Throughout the history of the United States "I" as subject and object has been reserved for white authorship and readership. However, when I speak of woman within these pages, I speak very specifically of the woman described above, unless otherwise indicated. (This also holds true for the use of the word men, children, people, and so on. I refer at all times to Chicanos/as-mejicanos/as unless otherwise specified.) I distinguish terms such as Chicana, Xicanista, Mexican, according to the context of the discussion. Within the confines of these pages, "I" and the mestiza/Mexic Amerindian woman's identity become universal. It is to that woman to whom I first and foremost address my thoughts.

Due to a general viewpoint regarding our historical lack of formal education, money, poor language skills, and other reasons often given to explain the omission of non-whites from fully participating in this society, publishing companies have not considered us a viable book buying market. Therefore, major publishers have not traditionally published books reflective of our reality as mestizas. "Women's" books that have been enormously successful in recent years include, for example, *Backlash* by Susan Faludi, *The Beauty Myth* by Naomi Wolf, and Camille Paglia's *Sexual Personae,* not to mention the slew of self-books and new age literature that has made many a white woman a rich celebrity, such as Marianne Williamson, Lynn Andrews, Harriet Gold-hor Lerner, among others. Irrespective of the claims to certain sources, such as in Lynn Andrews' and Marianne Williamson's books, all of these texts are infused with Anglocentric perspective. Despite the dense pedantry of Paglia's study of women in Western Civilization, it was a best seller and an international success because it catered to the white male hegemony that still directs today's world. Moreover, much of the popularity of these books as well as those of other widely read authors who write formula fiction, such as Danielle Steel and Stephen King, is owed to intense promotion and media support that reinforces white America's reality.

Finally, there remains a tenacious insistence that all peoples resid-ing in the United States must eventually assimilate into dominant society and therefore should not be "pandered" to, as some representa-tion of our culture is often seen to be. Assimilation may have worked in the past and continues to work for white people regardless of their ethnic background, but people of color in the U.S. have not suc-cessfully blended into the infamous melting pot for a number of rea-sons: 1) historical, institutionalized and legislated racism in the United States does not permit it; 2) the fundamental ideology is protestant while most of Latin America and the Caribbean is overwhelmingly Catholic; 3) as for Spanish/European Catholic rule in Mexico, racial antipathy toward the indigenous population resulted in unbelievable horrors perpetrated on the "indio" and mixed bloods that is not for-gotten. For all the lip service in Mexico given to indigenismo, Mexic Amerindians remain on the bottom of the social strata and depending on one's *color* and class, so do many mestizo/as. The vast majority of Mexican descendants in the United States are mestizo/as and come from the lower classes; 4) it is erroneous to categorize Chicano/as as immigrants (which implies that we are newly arrived and equated with those groups from Europe and other countries) who must only pay our dues as European immigrants did and over time we too, will become part of the U.S. social fabric. While there is admittedly an ongoing growing population migrating from Mexico (as from other parts of the world today), a large percentage of Chicano/as are not immigrants. In fact, the ancestors of many are from the Southwest United States and were not solely Spanish or Mexican but also Amerindian. Further-more, the changing border that divides the U.S. and Mexico (another important distinction between our status and those from other coun-tries) has placed Mexicans in a continuous neocolonial state providing the U.S. with legislated surplus labor as needed. Finally, Chicano/as-Mexicans are the only people besides the Native Americans who have a treaty with the United States. As with many of the treaties between Native Americans and the U.S. government, ours, The Treaty of Guadalupe Hidalgo has been largely violated. This appropriation of territory came as a result of what is known on this side of the border as the Mexican-American war (1846–1848). In Mexico it is known as the North American Invasion. Again, we see that history depends on the view of the chronicler.

Despite our constant presence on these lands since before the establishment of this nation, the book-market industry in the United States continues to render us invisible. Our writing has been and remains confined mostly to academic circles and our frame of refer-ence reduced to pedagogic argument, if not simply a defensive (read: angry) diatribe. Therefore it would seem economically impractical for the publishing market to promote literature by and addressed to mes-tizas, United States citizens, numbering in the millions but not cus-tomarily known to read, let alone buy books.

Our work and words against racism are accused of being nothing more than litanies of hatred by those (for example, some white edu-cated males and white feminists, also, apolitical Hispanics) who don't realize, or refuse to see, the extent to which racism continues to affect U.S. people of color. By denying our right to express the ostracism—or not accepting our claims to the degree to which we are ostracized—that we experience in white society, they inadvertently contribute to it.

Early white feminists, such as Kate Millett and Germaine Greer, made arguments that resounded throughout the western world, re-garding their rage against white, male-dominated society and claimed their right to be angry. "Woman" had for too long been forced into quiet complacency. In the sixties, what was the purpose of the campus bra-burning, after all, if not to demonstrate their militant refusal to be continually sexualized by male culture. And yet, when feminists of color show their indignation and express intolerance of racism, some white feminists and intellectuals accuse us of being "too angry". Should we ask first what is "anger-appropriate" so as not to offend anyone by expressing our indignation and pain?

Or should we conclude that indignation, expressed eloquently or crudely, is the exclusive right of men and women who lay claims to being part of the mainstream? While Germaine Greer went on national television over fifteen years ago, expressing her desire for women and "little" men—knowingly shocking the viewing audience, African American activist, Angela Davis did not make public her lesbianism until the late 1980s. Our struggles as women of color have never been—and remain inherently tied to—issues of racism as they are with gender inequities. When we are politically active, our race/ethnic communities place demands on us that members of dominant society who are politically active don't have to undertake.

Equally crucial to consider is the well-known fact that most renowned white feminists have come from middle- to upper-class backgrounds. This fact of their own orientation into society can never be excluded from their understanding of it, despite the occasional recent attempts at "political correctness" when including women of color in their analysis. I would like to note that when I speak of "white feminists," I do not limit myself to North Americans but to the international white feminist movement, which includes Mexico, Latin America and Europe. Very, very, very few dark women from poor or working class backgrounds who have taken up the pen have ever been published anywhere to date. (In the United States, such publications have been mostly limited to African American women.) To enter into the ongoing international debate of women's issues poor, working women of color have had to rely on their representation by light-skinned or European descended women who identify with their ethnicity and/or nationality.

It is also assumed by the dominant culture that because we have been historically barred from the writing profession that we have nothing of interest, much less of value to contribute (since the cultivation of corn) to the world at large. In fact, there is an insinuation that we are incapable of it. African American writers have given illuminating arguments against this white supremacist censorship by recalling slavery in the United States. The slave is much more aware of the master than the master ever knows the thoughts of the slave. The slave's very survival depends on knowing the master. It stands to reason that because people of color in the U.S. are forced to succumb to white dominant society's rules, are educated in Western culture, and read the literature that gives white dominant society's viewpoint we understand quite a bit about the world we live in, in addition to our own unrecognized one. Our survival depends on it.

The facts are, as non-white readers in the U.S.: 1) we do buy books but because what is made available is about white people that is what we must mostly buy and read. Sometimes we identify with the non-WASP viewpoint of Latin Americans and African Americans, which up to now have been more available than the writings of U.S. Latino/as. 2) Like other readers we search for information about or affirmation of our life experience, but despite presumptions of white writers, their perspectives are not wholly applicable to us. 3) Our perspectives have yet to enter wholly into public discussion. However, we are not asserting that our perspective is the only legitimate one, that it is superior to or should replace, repress, or censure others. What we are conscious of is that our reality is vastly different from that of the dominant culture and by any measure worth considering.

Yet, white society insists that only European history and Greco-Roman civilization have intellectual importance and relevance to our society. The legacies of Amerindians from Alaska to Tierra del Fuego are considered primitive. The ignorance of white dominant society about our ways, struggles in society, history, and culture is not an innocent and passive ignorance, it is a systematic and determined ignorance. The omission in most literature of the history and presence of millions of residents who inhabited these lands long before European occupation forces us to read between the lines.

If reading between the lines is what white feminists have had to do with the "classics," it most certainly is what we do, as educated U.S. Mexic Amerindians with all that is handed to us through literature and the mass media. We exist in the void, en ausencia, and surface rarely, usually in stereotype.

This continuous U.S. intellectual and academic mind set that Western thought is superior to all else is commingled with the equal conviction that indigenous people in the Americas are intellectually naive. But many of us—starved for affirmation about who we are as Mexic Amerindian women—realize from strenuous research (usually having to go beyond the university classroom and certainly beyond our local bookstore) that we have descended from people with blood ties traceable on these continents for many thousands of years, people who left phenomenal records demonstrating artistic and scientific brilliance.

The repressive attitude that we have experienced is not only found in the United States but throughout the Americas and other places in the world where primal peoples reside and where white colonialism has reigned, such as with the native "Aborigines" in Australia. The black diaspora is a long, mournful wail reminding of us of the inhumane history of European and Euro-American greed. Off the mainland United States, from the Aluets and Inuits north of us to the Polynesian ancestors of the native Hawaiians have also been stripped of their Ways, almost completely annihilated, christianized, and relegated to the outposts of society to live impoverished and demoralized lives. This acknowledgement of our cultural legacies and our reclaiming of our indigenous blood-ties, I hope, is not simultaneously an assertion that our heritage is superior to that of peoples from throughout the world. We are not the only people who have been wronged by racism and conquest, whose records have been destroyed, who have themselves, in fact, been nearly all destroyed. Learning about our indigenismo is a way of learning about ourselves, an acceptance of oneself as an individual and of her/his people. Then we may educate the world, including our own communities, about ourselves. But more importantly, it will show us another way of seeing life and the world we live in now.

As Mexic Amerindians we must, to find a clue as to who we are and from whom we descend, become akin to archaeologists. These efforts must be strenuous and aggressive because indigenous perspectives are omitted from the ready material we are handed throughout our formal schooling and what may be found in the book market. Yet, when we assert this deliberate intent on our part to dig for information about ourselves, we are accused by Eurocentric intellectuals of being narrow minded and limiting ourselves intellectually. The fact remains that it is only they who remain narrow minded and virtually ignorant of *our* knowledge since in fact, we have been schooled in a Western perspective and immersed in it all our lives.

Along these lines, in daily life and in the mass media, our bilingualism is generally not seen as an asset. People with Spanish accents (and Native people's accents) are often treated as if they are simply not very smart, while on the other hand, people with European accents, such as French, or Australian (who are not directly European but British descended) but especially the British, are assumed by white people in the United States to be intellectually superior on the sheer basis of an accent.

WHILE I DESCEND FROM MEXIC AMERINDIAN LINEAGE, the fact that I was born and raised in the United States, a descendent of one and two generations of migrants from Mexico, and was raised in the inner city of Chicago (Place of Wild Onions), means that I have been completely alienated from my indigenous connection to the Americas. This led me as a graduate student at the University of Chicago to prepare a final thesis entitled: "The Idealization and Reality of the Mexican Indian Woman." I researched and used documentation from two fields: imaginative literature and anthropology.

Unfortunately the writings of mestizos, criollos,[1] Spaniards, and Anglos from the nineteenth century up to that time (1979) did not reveal anything more than stereotypes. At best I found ethnographic data that ultimately did not bring me closer to understanding how the Mexic Amerindian woman truly perceives herself since anthropology is traditionally based on the objectification of its subjects. Furthermore, to my mind, the Mexic Amerindian woman had been gagged for hundreds of years. I not only refer to the literal silencing of the Mexican indigenous population, economically impoverished and therefore powerless and voiceless, but also the censorship that results from double sexism, being female and indigenous. The Mexic Amerindian woman has inherited the sexism instituted by dominant Mexican and U.S. society compounded by the sexism within certain oppressed indigenous cultures. In neither the creative literature nor the ethnographic documentation, did I hear her speak for herself. Only in 1992, the quincentenary of European conquest, was the world delivered the voice of *one* Mesoamerican woman, the Mayan Rigoberta

Menchu who received the Nobel Peace Prize for her ongoing activism on behalf of her people's human rights.

In graduate school, perceiving myself as a Mexic Amerindian woman once removed, I wrote the autobiographical poem "Entre primavera y otoño." In poetry I have found the freedom to speak both from my mind and heart. In this poem, I liken myself to the silenced indigenous woman of México. It begins:

> La india carga su bandera
> sobre su cara
> manchada de sangre
> sus cicatrices corren
> como las carreteras viejas
> de su tierra
> y la india no se queja.[2]

The Indian woman carries her flag/over her face/blood stained/her scars run/like old roads through her land/and the Indian woman does not complain.

Most Mexicans are mestizo/as and by and large mostly Mexic Amerindian. However the denigration of our indigenous blood has been so pervasive that few of us, especially in the past, have claimed our lineage. During the Colonial period of Mexico, a mestizo with money could buy his whiteness, thereby also purchasing the privileges reserved for criollos and Europeans. While mestizo/as came to compose the majority in Mexico, in the United States, genocide of the Native American was the preferred alternative for the Anglo for establishing a new nation.

It has been said of me and of my writing that I am in search of identity, as indeed we all are, which is a fact of living in a world of fragmented selves. White men (and white women) have always attempted this through their writing; and because they are members of dominant society, their search was considered representative of all, therefore, universal. On the other hand, the search by those of us who come from marginalized cultures in the United States is categorized as a sociological dilemma or a schizophrenic self-perception.

In graduate school I did indeed search for some clue to a crucial part of my "identity" inherent in the Mexic Amerindian woman.

Unfortunately and not surprisingly, I certainly did not find her within the ivy halls of academia. In 1979 the first generation of college educated Chicanas was in the making and their investigations and publications were also difficult to come by. It was indeed a question of each one becoming a *re-conquistadora,* exploring herself as subject through scholarship. Although I had no interest in pursuing a doctorate after receiving my Master's Degree in Social Science (Latin American and Caribbean Studies), my informal investigations as a creative writer and my own analyses with regard to being Chicana continued to feed the search for my Mexic Amerindian woman sense of self.

PEDAGOGY OF THE OPPRESSED: I began teaching college right after receiving my Bachelor's Degree in 1975 at the age of 22. It was shortly thereafter that I was introduced to the writings of Paulo Freire, the renowned Brazilian educator who espoused a pragmatic teaching philosophy for the "masses." Along with a formal education, he proposed a raising of political consciousness which would enable the Brazilian population, the majority of whom live in poverty, to become empowered by understanding their social conditions. He called this consciousness raising process, *consientizaçao.* Throughout the rest of Latin America it was translated to *conscientización.* There is no single word equivalent for this verb turned noun and in the United States it was translated to consciousness raising. Like the internationally used term, *machismo,* it transcended translation.

Just as English-dominant speakers are by and large familiar with the meaning of consciousness raising, throughout Latin America, activists are familiar with the term *conscientización.* Because of this, in our Spanish translation of *This Bridge Called My Back,* Norma Alarcón and I chose it as our term of preference to discuss consciousness raising, which is the intent of that text.[3]

The majority of Freire's impoverished population in Brazil were mulattos, people of mixed European, indigenous, and African blood. In this country, too, the majority of the population that has traditionally been marginalized by poor and working-class status are people of color. However, the discussion that has traditionally taken place regarding the direct connection between the lower classes and people of color has been restricted mostly to the African American population. The Native American population, what has not been annihilated thus far, remains nearly non-existent in terms of this kind of discussion. The people from whom I descend as a Chicana, are mestizo/as. Our history is inextricably tied to United States history because of the Mexican-American war whereby half of Mexico's territory was appropriated by the United States over one hundred fifty years ago.

As a poet, writer, and educator, my own educational process led me to accommodate Paulo Freire's philosophy to my status as a mestiza in the United States. I will add that as a Chicana, my process has not been singular but indeed one shared collectively by Latino/a activists. Paulo Freire's significant book, *Pedagogy of the Oppressed* was not recommended to me by chance. His work was enormously popular among Latino/a activists in the seventies. The concept of the conscientización process was initially intended for all poor people.

By the beginning of the new decade, however, many Chicana/ Latina activists, disenchanted, if not simply worn down, by male dominated Chicano/Latino politics, began to develop our own theories of oppression. Compounding our social dilemmas related to class and race were gender and sexuality. For the brown woman the term feminism was and continues to be inseparably linked with white women of middle- and upper-class background. (This is also the case, by and large, in México.) Feminism, therefore, is perhaps not a term embraced by most women who might be inclined to define themselves as Chicanas and who, in practice, have goals and beliefs found in feminist politics. Therefore, I use the term *conscientización* as it has been applied among Spanish-speaking women activists.

Along those same lines, many women of Mexican descent in the nineties do not apply the term Chicana to themselves seeing it as an outdated expression weighed down by the particular radicalism of the seventies. The search for a term which would appeal to the majority of women of Mexican descent who are also concerned with the social and political ramifications of living in a hierarchical society has been frustrating. In this text I have chosen the ethnic and racial definition of Mexic Amerindian to assert both our indigenous blood and the source, at least in part, of our spirituality.

I also use interchangeably the term mestiza, which has been used among Mexican intellectuals as a point of reference regarding our social status since the Mexican colonial period. When discussing Mexican culture and traditions, I may use mejicana for both nationals and women born in the U.S. When discussing activism I often use Chicano/a. I introduce here the word, Xicanisma, a term that I will use to refer to the concept of Chicana feminism. In recent years the idea of Chicana feminism has been taken up by the academic community where I believe it has fallen prey to theoretical abstractions. Eventually I hope that we can rescue Xicanisma from the suffocating atmosphere of conference rooms, the acrobatics of academic terms and concepts and carry it out to our work place, social gatherings, kitchens, bedrooms, and society in general.

MOYOCOYOTZIN: SHE WHO CREATES HERSELF: At this point in our twenty plus years of Chicana concientización and activism, women have begun an ardent investigation in the many ways our spirituality and sexuality have been denied us by male legislature and religion. While, it is crucial for us to grapple with issues of racism, it is equally crucial to realize that the root of that racism is in a historical, worldwide mind-set of conquest and that abuse of material power is a result of a spiritual imbalance. Four to five thousand years ago, humanity began moving toward the deliberate omission of the feminine principle. We all have masculine and feminine within us, but only the masculine has been allowed to reign. Among those who identify as Chicano/as, we have traditionally looked to the Mexica, the people of the Aztec Empire for some connection with our Pre-Hispanic past. However, it is imperative to understand that the Aztec-Tenochtitlan Empire was firmly entrenched at the time of the Conquest in a phallocracy. All early societies seem to yield traces of Mother worship. The Mexica did as well. Tonantzin, Mother Earth, was worshipped on hills and mountains. Iztacihuatl, the volcano near Pueblo, was another version of Her. But by the time we get to the sixteenth century, the militant Mexica have transformed Coatlicue (another version of the Mother) into a ghastly, hostile deity. The death aspect of the dual power of Mother—fertility and death—had taken over. Around her neck a necklace of mens' hearts and hands was symbolic of her insatiable thirst for human sacrifice. Let's keep in mind that that image of Coatlicue was created in the context of a war-oriented, conquest driven society, that of the Aztecs.

Here is the juncture in our story where I believe Xicanisma is formed: in the acknowledgement of the historical crossroad where the creative power of woman became deliberately appropriated by male society. And woman in the flesh, thereafter, was subordinated. It is our task as Xicanistas, to not only reclaim our indigenismo—but also to reinsert the forsaken feminine into our consciousness.

The goddesses of the Mexica pantheon was transformed from one deity to another—from being numinous to an earthly or male version of her original self—never losing her significance for the important historical symbolism she has in any given part of the story. Like the Ixcuiname—the four sisters-sex goddesses—each represents a phase of the moon—all the names we employ as tools to educate others and each other about our various stages of development, our reality, intent, and purpose remain relevant. A crucial distinction between labels we have been given by officials of the state and our own self-naming process is that only doing the latter serves us. The very act of self-definition is a rejection of colonization.

All this notwithstanding I am inclined to object to the claim that we are simply in search of identity but rather asserting it. The polemic as I see it, has to do with terminology and semantics not with the facts of our existence.

A COUNTRYLESS WOMAN: The Chicano/Latino Movement of the late sixties to mid seventies served as the catalyst for the Xicanista's sociopolitical perspective. I have added to the Chicano/Latino Movement theme an examination of how Catholicism has shaped our identity as well as our political activism. In the first and last chapters, I introduce and hopefully, conclude my reflections along these lines.

El Movimiento as it was influenced by Marxist-oriented ideology (which was overshadowed admittedly by nationalism) focused on our economic and class struggles as a people. While that socialist influence rightly understood the connections between institutionalized religion with a surplus-based society and therefore, rejected the Church (at least on principle)—el Movimiento simultaneously confused spirituality with the Church. In practice, the majority of activists did not give up Catholicism.

Spirituality and institutionalized religion are not the same thing.

Spirituality is an acutely personalized experience inherent in our ongoing existences. Throughout history, the further man moved away from his connection with woman as creatrix, the more spirituality was also disconnected from the human body.

In the following pages I argue that we have been forced into believing that we, as women, only existed to serve man under the guise of serving a Father God. Furthermore, our spirituality has been thoroughly subverted by institutionalized religious customs. The key to that spiritual oppression has been the repression of our sexuality, primarily through the control of our reproductive ability and bodies.

Woman's ability to give birth to a human being was acknowledged as sacred in the earliest traces of human history. And indeed, what greater act can we as human beings perform if not that one of further replenishing the Earth which sustains us? If not with children, then with ways that regenerate the Earth's resources. As male dominated societies moved further away from woman as creatrix, the human body and all that pertained to it came to be thought of as profane.

The ways in which human sexuality has been repressed, distorted, and exploited both by the leftist ideology of el Movimiento and the Catholic Church are examined throughout this book, but specifically in four chapters that take up our political activism as Chicanas and our inherited religious practices. They are "The Ancient Roots of Machismo"; "Saintly Mother and Soldier's Whore: The Leftist Catholic Paradigm"; "In the Beginning There Was Eva"; and "La Macha: Toward an Erotic Whole Self."

Inasmuch as woman's religiosity directs her life, la Xicanista is creating a synthesis of inherited beliefs with her own instinctive motivations. In the essay on our spirituality, "Brujas and Curanderas: A Lived Spirituality," I have explored this topic with personal viewpoints. Spirituality that departs from institutionalized religion is very popular at present among conscienticized women but is by no means practiced by the majority of women of Mexican background, who continue to adhere to Catholicism.

Concientización in Mexico, as well as in the United States among Latino activists, has usually meant a move toward socialism. However, efforts at socialism have not given women the kind of humanitarian restitution predicted by the designers of communist doctrine in the past century. We can cite the cases of the Soviet Union, Cuba, and China to show how women continued to struggle for equal social status after their respective social revolutions. In the "Watsonville" chapter I used the successful cannery strike of 1986 to demonstrate how the conscientización process can be activated through a specific social struggle. What I have highlighted in the account of the strike and with interviews of women activists of Watsonville is how conscientización does not fully recognize the extent of the ramifications of sexism that permeates not only dominant society but also the attitudes of political activists.

Machismo was another important subject for me to explore within the context of our personal and public lives. As a writer who is professionally introduced with the labels "Chicana" and "feminist," I am inevitably asked (often, by Mexican men, sometimes white men) to define "machismo." White men seem to associate machismo with a kind of Mexican, male killer instinct. They cite examples of Mexican toughness in prisons, of street gangs, the stereotypical knife-toting vato loco. In response I point out to them that machismo is an exaggerated demonstration of male virility that is inherent in most cultures, but is exemplified most in the United States by their own Anglo leaders, who in the past decade maintained an olympic trillion-dollar defense budget.

Mexicans (Latinos, in general), ask me about machismo because they are subordinate to Anglo men and feel that by accusing them of oppressing women, I expose them unfairly to Anglo supremacist society. I reply to them in the same fashion as I do to white men, which usually ends the discussion. Of course we do experientially understand that Anglo machismo dominates everyone.

Chicana feminists often look no further than the Mexican Catholic Church when tracing the origins of machismo. We are reluctant to acknowledge male supremacist practices of the Mexicas (Aztecs) because of our own romantic ideas of pre-Conquest society, nationalist bias, or lack of information but mostly because European culturicide has rendered Mexica practices ineffective to our lives. But it seems to me that the influences on our social behavior go way beyond the legacy of Catholicism, Spanish culture, and our indigenous background. In the chapter, "Ancient Roots of Machismo," I have attempted an investigation into our Arabian heritage and made comparisons with the early North African clan practices (that have influenced Iberian, Mediterranean, and subsequently Latin American and Caribbean cultures because of Islamic conquests) and our own Mexican culture.

In the essay entitled, "Un Tapiz: The Poetics of Conscientización," I suggest that we look at our particular use of language to see how it can limit the way we see ourselves by perpetuating learned concepts of who we are and how we should live. On the other hand, breaking with traditional use of language allows us to explore new possibilities.

In the kaleidoscope viewing of how woman is allowed to manifest in our culture, I concluded that no role has been viewed as more important than that of Mother. While the concept of *mother* is idealized, mother in society is denigrated.

In early societies throughout the world, since the entire population depended upon the products that harvests yielded many religious rites were practiced around fertility. Over the millennia, woman's fertility, therefore her sexuality, was controlled by society and regulated by religion. While she is abandoned by society, woman as Mother continues to have the monolithic task of preserving the human race.

In the chapter entitled "Toward the Mother-Bond Principle," I propose that by using the Mother as our model to guide us in place of an abstract, amaterial, distant Father God (that all Christians are called to obey, if not to attempt to emulate in his incarnation as Jesus), it may be possible to have a vision of a truly nurturing society.

DREAMERS AND MAGICIANS, BRUJAS Y CURANDERAS: As descendants of Mexic Amerindians, ours *is* a formidable and undeniable legacy. Among our most ancient ancestors are the Olmecs, whose origins in the Americas predate 1000 B.C. and who "we might possibly call Magicians," as Frederick Peterson refers to them in his book *Ancient Mexico: An Introduction to the Pre-Hispanic Cultures.*[4] The "Magicians" cultivated the use of rubber and tobacco and were masters of stonework. What has been concluded from the tremendous sculpture legacies left by the Olmecs is that theirs was a sophisticated, powerful, and mystical society. Frederick Peterson speculates regarding the religious beliefs system of the Olmecs that "coincidence of the dreams with actual happenings" may have given an individual (whose dreams seemed to prophesize occurrences) a reputation as an oracle with a privileged position in society. I interpret this to mean that within indigenous primal cultures, the *dreamer* has been heeded since very ancient times.

More than two millennia later in Tenochtitlan, Moteuczoma called upon the thousands of dreamers who were sharing the same premonition: the prophesied arrival of Cortés and the subsequent annihilation of the Empire. Moteuczoma's order to have the dreamers murdered en masse did not stop the landing of those alien ships that were already on their way with those whose intentions were to take whatever riches found at any cost.

Moteuczoma, who relied heavily on mysticism and having received various ominous omens about the fall of his empire, also consulted with his greatest wizards and magicians. These, unable to advise Moteuczoma as to how to prevent what had already been divinely decreed were imprisoned. But being magicians they mysteriously escaped. Moteuczoma avenged them by having their wives and children hung and their houses destroyed.[5]

Dreams may provide vision, knowledge, guidance. Moteuczoma knew that the dreamers and magicians were not responsible for the awaited demise of his kingdom but he murdered them out of his own sense of despair and because of his abuse of power, which had already been demonstrated in many other shameful ways during his rule. And when the time came to act, it was Moteuczoma's fatalism that debilitated him and caused the end of the Mexica world.

The dreamer, the poet, the visionary is banished at the point when her/his society becomes based on the denigration of life and the annihilation of the spirit for the sake of phallocratic aggrandizement and the accumulation of wealth by a militant elite. This is accompanied by a fierce sense of nationalism and "ethnic pride." This was the case of the "Massacre of the Dreamers" in the Mexica Empire and is happening again throughout the globe.

But we, the silenced dreamers rendered harmless, see these patterns. After extricating our imaginations from the tight reigns of patriarchal imperialism, our next step is to bring others into the fold. Quite the contrary to our so-called assimilation as "Hispanics," I firmly believe, along with many women of conscientización in the Americas, that U.S. society must eventually acculturate our mestiza vision. Our collective memories and present analyses along these lines hold the antidote to that profound sense of alienation many experience in white dominant society.

I was unable to unearth the female indigenous consciousness in graduate school[6] that I am certain is a part of my genetic collective memory and my life experience. Nevertheless I stand firm that I *am* that Mexic Amerindian woman's consciousness in the poem cited above and that I must, with others like myself, utter the thoughts and intuitions that dwell in the recesses of primal collective memory. However, in this book about us, for us, I have not relied on my poetry or story-telling (that is, fiction), nor written—with the exception of rare anecdotal references—a personal testimony to describe our social reality. Any of these vehicles might have made our perspective more palatable to the taste of readers (not limited to the U.S.) who are accustomed to literature that includes them in a direct way, if not as subjects, then emotionally. Otherwise, they are disinterested, and even feel threatened when excluded. Instead, I stand by my premise that a general discussion of our various experiences as conscienticized U.S. mestizas (descendants of Mexic Amerindians) is relevant to anyone trying to understand the world he or she lives in. Although dominant society has rendered us powerless and silent, it does not naturally equate that we are indeed powerless (inconsequential) and silent (stupid).

In the following pages I have reflected upon our recent history of activism, our spiritual practices, sexual attitudes, artistic ideology, labor struggles, and education-related battles. I hope I've done so in a straightforward manner. Without pretensions to producing empirical analyses, I offer my reflections to perhaps serve as reference work for other laborers in the vineyard. Lest all our dreams become self-fulfilling prophecies of doom, together we must form the vision that all dreamers share, 'though ever so briefly, as in the following pre-Conquest canto which invokes the moon goddess:

. . . So Coyolchiuqui left it said:
Soon we come out of the dream,
we only come to dream,
it isn't true, it isn't true
that we come to live on Earth.[7]

Massacre of the Dreamers

one

A COUNTRYLESS WOMAN
THE EARLY FEMINISTA

I would have spoken these words as a feminist who "happened" to be a
white United States citizen, conscious of my government's proven capacity
for violence and arrogance of power, but as self-separated from that govern-
ment, quoting without second thought Virginia Woolf's statement in The
Three Guineas *that "as a woman I have no country. As a woman I*
want no country. As a woman my country is the whole world." This is
not what I come [here] to say in 1984. I come here with notes but without
absolute conclusions. This is not a sign of loss of faith or hope. These notes
are the marks of a struggle to keep moving, a struggle for accountability.
—*Adrienne Rich, "Notes toward a Politics of Location,"*
  Blood, Bread, and Poetry

I CANNOT SAY I AM A CITIZEN OF THE WORLD as Virginia
Woolf, speaking as an Anglo woman born to economic means, declared herself; nor can I make the same claim to U.S. citizenship as
Adrienne Rich does despite her universal feeling for humanity. As a
mestiza born to the lower strata, I am treated at best, as a second class
citizen, at worst, as a non-entity. I am commonly perceived as a
foreigner everywhere I go, including in the United States and in
Mexico. This international perception is based on my color and features. I am neither black nor white. I am not light skinned and cannot
be mistaken for "white"; because my hair is so straight I cannot be
mistaken for "black." And by U.S. standards and according to some
North American Native Americans, I cannot make official claims to
being india.

Socioeconomic status, genetic makeup and ongoing debates on
mestisaje aside, if in search of refuge from the United States I took up
residence on any other continent, the core of my being would long
for a return to the lands of my ancestors. My ethereal spirit and my
collective memory with other indigenas and mestizo/as yearn to *claim*
these territories as homeland. In the following pages, I would like to
review our socioeconomic status, our early activism and feminismo,

and to begin the overall discussion that moves toward a Xicanista vision.

IN THE 1980S, LEFTISTS AND LIBERALS recognized the atrocities of U.S. intervention in Central America, as similar sympathizers did with Viet Nam in the 1960s. Their sympathy is reminiscent of North American leftists and liberals who in the 1930s struggled against fascism during the Spanish Civil War. In each instance, there is the implication that these liberal individuals are not in any way responsible for the persecution, and that it is all their government's fault. These same humanists have vaguely and apologetically acknowledged the injustice done to the descendants of their country's former slaves and to the Native Americans who have been all but obliterated through genocide and dispossession.

Yet, mestizo/as, those who are Mexican citizens as well as those who are U.S. born, are viewed less sympathetically. We are advised to assimilate into white dominant society or opt for invisibility—an invisibility that we are blamed for because of our own lack of ability to take advantage of the supposedly endless opportunities available through acculturation.

Racism has been generally polarized into a black-white issue. U.S. mestizo/as of Mexican background, therefore, are viewed by many white people, by many African Americans and yes, by some Native Americans as having the potential to "pass" for white, in theory, at will. This general view is based on the assumptions, lack of information and misinformation that accompanies policies, media control, and distorted historical documentation disseminated to the general populace by the white male dominated power system that has traditionally governed this country. The United States cannot deny its early history of importing Africans as slaves, which explains the presence of African Americans throughout the Americas. However, censorship continues regarding the extent of genocide of Native Americans. As for mestizo/as, we were identified as a mongrel race, a mixture of the dispensable Amerindian race and the lowly Spaniard. Little is known by the general public regarding how these attitudes caused ongoing persecution of Mexic Amerindians and mestizo/as in what was once Mexico and later became United States territory. For example, while it is well known that in the South there were lynchings and hangings of African Americans, it isn't common knowledge that Mexicans were also lynched and hung in Texas and throughout the Southwest.

Most people in the United States have little awareness of this government's ongoing dominant-subordinate relationship with Mexico since, of course, this is not taught in schools as part of United States history. The general public assumes that all Mexicans are immigrants and therefore, *obligated* to assimilate just as European immigrants did and do.

Most members of dominant society have very little understanding of the numerous ways a country, especially one supposedly based on the free enterprise system and democracy, systematically and quite effectively disenfranchises much of its population. While some white members of society have an understanding of this from an economic and historical standpoint, they do not or will not recognize that there are, to this day, economic inequities based on racism. Many more do not understand or refuse to accept that today all women suffer, in one way or another, as a result of the prevalent misogyny legislated and expounded in this society.

For the last twenty years the leaders of the U.S. government have tried to convince its population that the Civil Rights Movement succeeded in creating a true democracy and that increasing poverty and unemployment are primarily a question of world economics. If indications of the growing frustration on the part of women and people of color who cannot overcome job and educational inequities based on race, gender, and limited economic resources were not evident enough to the federal government, the national riots after the Rodney King verdict serve as the final argument.

WHILE I HAVE MORE IN COMMON WITH A MEXICAN MAN than with a white woman, I have much more in common with an Algerian woman than I do with a Mexican man. This opinion, I'm sure, chagrins women who sincerely believe our female physiology unequivocally binds all women throughout the world, despite the compounded social prejudices that daily affect us all in different ways. Although women everywhere experience life differently from men everywhere, white women are members of a race that has proclaimed itself globally superior for hundreds of years. We live in a polarized world of contrived dualisms, dichotomies and paradoxes: light vs. dark and good vs. evil. We as Mexic Amerindians/mestizas are the dark. We are the evil . . . or at least, the questionable.

Ours is a world imbued with nationalism, real for some, yet tenuous as paper for others. A world in which from the day of our births, we are either granted citizenship or relegated to the netherstate of serving as mass production drones. Non-white women—Mexicans/Chicanas, Filipinas, Malaysians, and others—who comprise eighty percent of the global factory work force, are the greatest dispensable resource that multinational interests own. The women are in effect, represented by no country.

Feminists of color in the United States (and around the world) are currently arduously re-examining the very particular ways our non-Western cultures use us and how they view us. We have been considered opinionless and the invariable targets of every kind of abusive manipulation and experimentation. As a mestiza, a resident of a declining world power, a countryless woman, I have the same hope as Rich who, on behalf of her country aims to be accountable, flexible, and learn new ways to gather together earnest peoples of the world without the defenses of nationalism.

I WAS BORN, RAISED, AND SPENT MOST OF MY LIFE in one of the largest cities in the United States. Despite its distance from México, Chicago has a population of approximately a quarter of a million people of Mexican background. It is also the third most frequent U.S. destination of Mexican migrants after El Paso and Los Angeles. The greatest influx of Mexicans occurred during the first half of this century when the city required cheap labor for its factories, slaughterhouses, and steel mill industry.

In an effort to minimize their social and spiritual alienation, the Mexican communities there developed and maintained solid ties to Mexican culture and traditions. This was reinforced by the tough political patronage system in Chicago, which was dependent upon ethnically and racially divisive strategies to maintain its power. Thus I grew up perceiving myself to be Mexican despite the fact that I was born in the United States and did not visit México until the age of ten.

Assimilation into dominant culture, while not impossible, was not encouraged nor desired by most ethnic groups in Chicago—Mexicans were no exception. We ate, slept, talked, and dreamed Mexican. Our parishes were Mexican. Small Mexican-owned businesses flourished. We were able to replicate Mexico to such a degree that the spiritual and psychological needs of a people so despised and undesired by white dominant culture were met in our own large communities.

Those who came up north to escape destitution in México were, in general, dark-skinned mestizos. In the face of severe racism, it's no wonder we maintained such strong bonds to each other. But even those who were not as outwardly identifiably Mexican were usually so inherently Mexican by tradition that they could not fully assimilate. Not a few refused to "settle in" on this side of the border with the pretense that they would eventually return to their home towns in México.

As I was growing up, Mexicans were the second largest minority in Chicago. There was also a fair size Puerto Rican community and a fair amount of Cubans and other Latin Americans. But in those years, before the blatant military disruption of Latin American countries such as Chile and El Salvador, a person with "mestiza" characteristics was considered Mexican. When one had occasion to venture away from her insulated community to say, downtown, impressive and intimidating with its tremendous skyscrapers and evidently successful (white) people bustling about, she felt as if she were leaving her village to go into town on official matters. Once there she went about her business with a certain sense of invisibility, and even hoped for it, feeling so out of place and disoriented in the presence of U.S. Anglo, profit-based interests, which we had nothing to do with except as mass-production workers. On such occasions, if she were to by chance to run across another mestiza (or mestizo), there was a mutual unspoken recognition and, perhaps, a reflexive avoidance of eye contact. An instantaneous mental communication might sound something like this:

I know you. You are Mexican (like me). You are brown-
skinned (like me). You are poor (like me). You probably live in
the same neighborhood as I do. You don't have anything, own
anything. (Neither do I.) You're no one (here). At this moment
I don't want to be reminded of this, in the midst of such lux-

ury, such wealth, this disorienting language; it makes me
ashamed of the food I eat, the flat I live in, the only clothes I
can afford to wear, the alcoholism and defeat I live with. You
remind me of all of it.

You remind me that I am not beautiful—because I am
short, round bellied and black-eyed. You remind me that I will
never ride in that limousine that just passed us because we are
going to board the same bus back to the neighborhood where
we both live. You remind me of why the foreman doesn't move
me out of that tedious job I do day after day, or why I got fe-
verish and too tongue-tied to go to the main office to ask
for that Saturday off when my child made her First Holy
Communion.

When I see you, I see myself. You are the mirror of this
despicable, lowly sub-human that I am in this place far from
our homeland which scarcely offered us much more since the
vast majority there live in destitution. None of the rich there
look like us either. At least here we feed our children; they have
shoes. We manage to survive. But don't look at me. Go on
your way. Let me go on pretending my invisibility, so that I can
observe close up all the possibilities—and dream the gullible
dreams of a human being.[1]

AT SEVENTEEN, I JOINED THE LATINO/CHICANO MOVE-
MENT. I went downtown and rallied around City Hall along with
hundreds of other youth screaming, "¡Viva La Raza!" and "Chicano
Power!" until we were hoarse. Our fears of being recognized as lowly
Mexicans were replaced with socioeconomic theories that led to political radicalism. Yet our efforts to bring unity and courage to the
majority of our people were short lived; they did not embrace us.
Among the factors contributing to this were the ability of some to
assimilate more easily on the basis of lighter skin color and the
consumer-fever that overrides people's social needs. The temptations
of the rewards of assimilation and the internalization of racism by the
colonized peoples of the United States was and is devastating. Society
has yet to acknowledge the trauma it engenders.

THE HISPANIC POPULATION IN THE U.S., totalled 22,354,509,
according to the 1990 U.S. Department of Commerce report. 13,495,938

of that total were of Mexican origin. (We can estimate therefore that when we are discussing the woman of Mexican origin we are referring to a population of about seven million women in the United States.) According to the 1989 report immigration constituted half of the recent Hispanic population growth. I am personally glad to see the U.S. Department of Commerce gives this reason to explain the disproportionate growth of Hispanics as compared to non-Hispanics, as opposed to the 1987 Department of Labor Report, which states that there are so many Hispanics because Hispanic women tend to be more fertile than non-Hispanic women. These figures, of course, do not include the undocumented Latino population. The U.S. Immigration and Naturalization Service estimated 1.2 million apprehensions at the border in 1986.

Hispanic as the ethnic label for all people who reside in the U.S. with some distant connection with the culture brought by the Spaniards during the conquest of the Americas is a gross misnomer. The word promotes an official negation of people called "Hispanic" by inferring that their ethnicity or race is exclusively European rather than partly Native American (as are most Chicano/as), or African American (as are those descendants of the African slave trade along the Caribbean coasts).

The term Hispanic is a misnomer because one-fifth of South America—Brazil—does not speak Spanish. A large population of Guatemala speaks indigenous dialects as a first language and maintains its own indigenous culture. Chicano/as and Puerto Ricans may have little or no fluency in Spanish having been brought up in an English-dominant society, having attended its monolingual schools, and having been discouraged, in general, from pursuing the language of their ancestors. In fact, despite the provisions made by the Treaty of Guadalupe Hidalgo of 1848 to allow Spanish speakers in the Southwest to retain their native tongue, Spanish was prohibited in schools and workplaces. The debate rages on among educators and government alike.

If Hispanic refers to all natives and descendants of Latin America, it is including no less than twenty countries—whose shared patterns of colonization may allow them to be called Pan-American, but whose histories and cultural attitudes are nevertheless diverse in very particular ways.

How can people from the Caribbean states, whose economies depended on slave trade be generically called Hispanic? Is it because they are from states that are presently Spanish speaking or were once colonized by the Spaniards, although they may presently be under another country's dominion? In the Caribbean, Hispanic includes Puerto Ricans, Cubans, and Dominicans. While Cuba's official language has remained Spanish since Spanish rule, many of its people are of African ancestry. Citizens of the Dominican Republic are considered Hispanic because they speak Spanish, but the residents of the other side of their island, Haiti, speak French (and more commonly, as I understand, patois). Are there enough major racial differences between these two nationalities on the same island to justifiably classify one as Hispanic but not the other? The Philippines were once colonized by Spain and now have English as a dominant language, but they are not classified as Hispanic. They are placed in another catch-all group, Asian.

Hispanic gives us all one ultimate paternal cultural progenitor: Spain. The diverse cultures already on the American shores when the Europeans arrived, as well as those introduced because of the African slave trade, are completely obliterated by the term. Hispanic is nothing more than a concession made by the U.S. legislature when they saw they couldn't get rid of us. If we won't go away, why not at least Europeanize us, make us presentable guests at the dinner table, take away our feathers and rattles and civilize us once and for all.

This erroneous but nationally accepted label invented by a white supremacist bureaucracy essentially is a resignation to allow, after more than two hundred years of denial, some cultural representation of the conquistadors who originally colonized the Southwest. Until now, in other words, only Anglo-Saxons were legitimate informants of American culture.

To further worsen the supposition that we can be Hispanic— simply long forgotten descendants of Europeans just as white people are—is the horrific history of brutal and inhuman subjugation that not only Amerindians experienced under Spanish and other European rules in Mexico and throughout Latin America and the Caribbean, but all those of mixed blood. Indeed, shortly after the Conquest of Mexico, Spanish rule set up a complex caste system in which to be of mixed-blood virtually excluded you from full rights as citizens and protection by the law. Jews and Moors in that Catholic society also experienced racist attitudes.[2] Just as with today's African-Americans, among mestizo/as and Amerindians, the result of such intense, legislated racism throughout centuries is demoralization. As one historian puts it regarding the Mexic Amerindian people, "Trauma and neuroses linger still, and may not be entirely overcome. For the Spaniards, in Mexico, did not commit genocide; they committed culturcide."[3]

Among Latino/as in the United States today there is a universe of differences. There is a universe of difference, for example, between the experience of the Cuban man who arrived in the United States as a child with his parents after fleeing Castro's revolution and the Puerto Rican woman who is a third generation single mother on the Lower East Side. There is a universe of difference between the young Mexican American aspiring to be an actor in Hollywood in the nineties and the community organizer working for rent control for the last ten years in San Francisco, although both may be sons of farmworkers. There is a universe of difference between Carolina Herrera, South American fashion designer and socialite, and a Guatemalan refugee who has hardly learned to speak Spanish but must already adapt to English in order to work as a domestic in the United States. Picture her: She is not statuesque or blonde (like Ms. Herrera). She is short, squat, with a moon face, and black, oily hair. She does not use six pieces of silverware at the dinner table, but one, if any, and a tortilla. There is a universe of differences among all of these individuals, yet Anglo society says they all belong to the same ethnic group: Hispanic.

A study by the University of Chicago shows that deep divisions based on race exist between black Hispanics and white Hispanics in the United States. The black/white dichotomy of the United States causes black Hispanics to relate more to African Americans than to non-black Hispanics. It is also revealed that "black Hispanics are far more segregated from U.S. whites than are white Hispanics."[4] *Color,* rather than saying simply ethnicity, in addition to class and gender, as well as *concientización,* all determine one's identity and predict one's fate in the United States.

EXCEPT FOR THE HISTORICAL PERIOD CHARACTER-IZED BY "MANIFEST DESTINY" fate is not part of United States Anglo Saxon ideology. But the United States does have a fate.

Sir John Glubb in his book *A Short History Of The Arab Peoples* suggests reviewing world history to see how frequently great empires reach and fall from their pinnacle of power, all within two hundred to three hundred years. According to Glubb, for example, the Greek Empire (330 B.C. to about 100 B.C.) lasted two hundred and thirty years; the Spaniards endured for (1556 to 1800) two hundred and forty four years; and the British Empire lasted two hundred and thirty years, (1700 to 1930). It is sobering to note that no great power simply lost its position as number one slipping into second or third place, nor has any former great power ever resumed its original, unchallenged position. They all have ceased to exist as a world power. After the fall of the Roman Empire, Italy has been little more than the home of the Pope for the past fifteen centuries. Moreover, regarding his figures Glubb tells us, "It is not desired to insist on rigid numbers, for many outside factors influence the fates of great nations. Nevertheless, the resemblance between the lives of so many and such varied empires is extremely striking, and is obviously entirely unconnected with the development of those mechanical devices of which we are so proud."[5] "Mechanical devices" means military might.

Signs of the decline of the United States as the leading world power are most apparent in the phenomenal growth of the public debt in the 1980s: during the Reagan-Bush years, the public debt of the United States went from 907.7 billion dollars in 1980 to over 3 trillion dollars in 1990 (as reported by the United States Department of the Treasury).

The United States, being a relatively young, therefore resilient country, can and eventually will allow for the representation of people of color in the institutions that influence and mandate peoples' lives— government, private industry, and universities, for example. It will gradually relent with its blatant refusal to fulfill its professed democratic ideals and include the descendants of its slave trade, the Native Americans, mestizo/as, and Asians (who also come from a wide variety of countries and social and economic backgrounds and who, due to various political circumstances, are immigrating to the United States at an exorbitant rate). It will do so because the world economy will not permit anything short of it. Nevertheless, most assuredly among those who will get further pushed down as the disparity between the few wealthy and the impoverished grows, will be our gente.

THE LARGEST MOVEMENT IN THE HISTORY OF THE UNITED STATES ever to force the government to reckon with its native Latino population was the Chicano/Latino Movement of the late 1960s and 1970s. Because of its force there is today a visible sector of Latinos who are college degreed, who have mortgages on decent houses, and who are articulate in English. (In Spanish, when a person has facility in a language to get by, we say we can "defend" ourselves; we now have a substantial number of Latinos who are defending themselves against Anglophile culture.) The generation that came of age in the 1980s was given the general message that acculturation can be rewarding. Yes, the status quo will always reward those who succumb to it, who serve it, and who do not threaten its well being.

In 1980 when the Republicans and the Reagan administration came to office, their tremendous repression quashed the achievements of the Chicano/Latino Movement, which has been based on collectivism and the retention of our Mexican/Amerindian culture. Community projects and grassroots programs dependent on government funding—rehabilitation and training, child care, early education and alternative schooling, youth counseling, cultural projects that supported the arts and community artists, rehab-housing for low income families, and women's shelters—shut down.

In their place the old "American Dream"—a WASP male philosophy on which this country was founded at the expense of third world labor—was reinstated. As in U.S. society before the Civil Rights Movement, material accumulation equalled self-worth.

The new generation of Chicanos and Latinos who came of age in the 1980s, had a radically different attitude than the collective mentality of the 1970s activists, believing that after two hundred years of racist and ethnic exploitation, the age of the "Hispanic" had finally come. Their abuelos, tíos, parents (some who had been in the Chicano/Latino Movement) had paid the dues for the American Dream. Now they could finally claim their own place in society. They had acculturated.

Encouraged by media hype announcing our arrival in the 1980s as the "Decade of the Hispanic," for the first time in U.S. history, ad campaigns took the Latino/a consumer into consideration. Magazines, billboards and even television commercials (Coors comes to mind) showed young, brown, beautiful Latina models in flashy wear reaping some of the comforts and pleasures of a democracy based on free enterprise. Also, there was the unprecedented tokenism of Latino/as in visible and high level government posts and private industry that further convinced many among the new generation that each individual indeed had the ability to fulfill his or her own great master plan for material success. The new generation was not alone. The previous generation became more conservative along with immigrating Latinos who also believed in the Republican administration and the trickle down theory of Reaganomics.

It is difficult to generalize why so many Latino/as moved toward conservative, if not overtly right wing, views. Personal disillusionment with leftist ideology may explain in part the change in attitude and goals for some. But for many, I believe it is basically a matter of desiring material acquisitions. It is difficult to maintain a collective ideology in a society where possessions and power-status equal self-worth.

Unfortunately, the continuous drop of the U.S. dollar in the world trade market caused the economy to worsen each year. In the 1980s, jobs were lost, companies closed down and moved out of the country, banks foreclosed on mortgages, and scholarships and grants once available to needy college students in the 1970s were taken away. These were only a few of the losses experienced not only by Latino/as but by much of the population.

Simultaneously, the cost of living went up. The much coveted trendy lifestyle of the white yuppie moved further away from the grasp of young and upwardly mobile Reagan-Bush generation. The nineties ushered a new generation cognizant of the white hegemonic atmosphere entrenched in colleges and universities and with a vigor reminiscent of the student movements of two decades earlier, have begun protests on campuses throughout the country. The acceleration of gang violence in cities, drug wars, cancer on the rise and AIDS continue to be the backdrop, while the new decade's highlights so far for living in these difficult times were the Persian Gulf War Espectáculo and the Rodney King riots that resounded throughout the world— sending out a message that this is indeed a troubled country.

EL MOVIMIENTO CHICANO/LATINO saw its rise and fall within a time span of less than two decades on these territories where our people have resided for thousands of years. El Movimiento (or La Causa) was rooted to a degree in Marxist oriented theory (despite the strong ties activists felt to their Catholic upbringings) because it offered some response to our oppression under capitalism. Socialist and communist theories which were based on late nineteenth century ideas on the imminent mass industrialization of society, did not foresee the high technology world of the late twentieth century—one hundred years later—or fully consider the implications of race, gender, and sexual-preference differences on that world. Wealth accumulation no longer simply stays within the genteel class but our aristocracy now includes athletes, rock stars, and Hollywood celebrities.

THE EARLY FEMINISTA, as the Chicana feminist referred to herself then, had been actively fighting against her socioeconomic subjugation as a Chicana and as a woman since 1968, the same year the Chicano Movement was announced. I am aware that there have been Chicana activists throughout U.S. history, but I am using as a date of departure an era in which women consciously referred to themselves as *feministas.*

An analysis of the social status of la Chicana was already underway by early feministas, who maintained that racism, sexism, and sexist racism were the mechanisms that socially and economically oppressed them. But, for reasons explained here, they were virtually censored. The early history of la feminista was documented in a paper entitled, "La Feminista," by Anna Nieto Gómez and published in *Encuentro Feminil: The First Chicana Feminist Journal,* which may now be considered, both article and journal, archival material.[6]

The early feminista who actively participated in the woman's movement had to educate white feminist groups on their political, cultural, and philosophical differences. Issues that specifically concerned the feminista of that period were directly related to her status as a non-Anglo, culturally different, often Spanish-speaking woman of lower income. Early white feminism compared sexism (as experienced by white middle class women) to the racism that African Americans are subjected to. But African American feminists, such as those of the Rio Combahee Collective,[7] pointed out that this was not only an inaccurate comparison but revealed an inherent racist attitude on the part of white feminists who did not understand what it was to be a woman *and* black in America.

By the same token, brown women were forced into a position in which we had to point out similar differences as well as continuously struggle against a prevalent condescension on the part of white middle-class women toward women of color, poor women, and women who's first language is Spanish and whose culture is not mainstream American. *This Bridge Called My Back,* first published in 1981, as well as other texts by feminists of color that followed serve as excellent testimonies regarding these issues and the experiences of feminists of color in the 1970s.

At the same time, according to Nieto Gómez, feministas were labeled as *vendidas* (sell-outs) by activists within *La Causa*. Such criticism came not solely from men but also from women, whom Nieto Gómez calls Loyalists. These Chicanas believed that racism not sexism was the greater battle. Moreover, the Loyalists distrusted any movement led by any sector of white society. The early white women's movement saw its battle based on sex and gender, and did not take into account the race and class differences of women of color. The Loyalists had some reason to feel reluctant and cynical toward an ideology and organizing effort that at best was condescending toward them. Loyalists told the feministas that they should be fighting such hard-hitting community problems as police brutality, Viet Nam, and La Huelga, the United Farm Workers labor strike. But white female intellectuals were largely unaware of these issues. While the Chicana resided in a first world nation, indeed the most powerful nation at that time, she was part of a historically colonized people.

I am referring to the approximate period between 1968 through the 1970s. However, more than twenty years later, the Chicana—that is a brown woman of Mexican descent, residing in the United States with political consciousness—is still participating in the struggle for recognition and respect from white dominant society. Residing throughout her life in a society that systematically intentionally or out of ignorance marginalizes her existence, often stereotypes her when she does "appear," suddenly represented (for example by mass-media or government sources), and perhaps more importantly, relegates her economic status to among the lowest paid according to the U.S. Census Bureau, the Chicana continues to be a countryless woman. She is—

I am, we are—not considered to be, except marginally and stereo-typically, United States citizens.

Nevertheless, according to las feministas, feminism was "a very dynamic aspect of the Chicana's heritage and not at all foreign to her nature."[8] Contrary to ethnographic data that portrays Chicanas as submissive followers who are solely designated to preserve the culture, the feminista did not see herself or other women of her culture as such. While the feminist dialogue remained among the activists in el Movi-miento, one sees in *Encuentro Feminil* that there indeed existed a solid initiative toward Chicana feminist thought, that is, recognition of sexism as a primary issue, as early on as the late 1960s. Clarifying the differences between the needs of the Anglo feminist and the feminista was part of the early feminista's tasks.

And if the focus of the Chicano male-dominated movement with regard to women had to do with family issues, the feminista zeroed in on the very core of what those issues meant. For instance, the femi-nistas believed that women would make use of birth control and abortion clinics if in fact they felt safe going for these services; that is, if they were community controlled. Birth control and abortion are per-tinent issues for all women, but they were particularly significant to the Chicana who had always been at the mercy of Anglo controlled institutions and policies.

Non-consenting sterilizations of women—poor white, Spanish speaking, welfare recipients, poor women of color—women in prison among them—during the 1970s were being conducted and sponsored by the U.S. government. One third of the female population of Puerto Rico was sterilized during that period.[9] The case of ten Chicanas (*Madrigal v. Quilligan*) against the Los Angeles County Hospital who were sterilized without their consent led to activism demanding re-lease of the Health, Education and Welfare (HEW) guidelines for sterilizations. During that period, HEW was financing up to 100,000 sterilizations a year.[10]

The feminista also wanted a bicultural and bilingual child care that would validate their children's culture and perhaps ward off an inferi-ority complex before they had a chance to start public school; tradi-tionally, monolingual and anglocentric schools had alienated children, causing them great psychological damage.[11]

The early feminista understood the erroneous conceptions of the White Woman's Movement that equated sexism to racism because she was experiencing its compounding effects in her daily life. The feministas were fighting against being a "minority" in the labor market. According to Nieto Gómez, more Anglo women had jobs than did women of color. We must keep in mind that most women of color in this country have always needed employment to maintain even a level of subsistence for their families.

According to the 1991 U.S. Dept. of Commerce Census Bureau Report, income figures for 1989 show that "Hispanic" women are still among the lowest paid workers in the United States, earning less than African American women:

WEEKLY INCOME

Hispanic women	$269.00
Black women	301.00
White women	334.00
Hispanic men	315.00
Black men	348.00
All Other Women	361.00

The mestiza still ranks in the labor force among the least valued in this country. In Susan Faludi's best-selling *Backlash,* which focuses on the media's backlash against the white feminist movement, the only noteworthy observation of women of color refers to our economic status in the 1980s. Faludi states that overall income did not increase for the African American woman and for the Hispanic woman, it actually got worse.

CLASHING OF CULTURES We need not look very far back or for very long to see that we have been marginalized in every sense of the word by U.S. society. But an understanding of the U.S. economic system and its relationship to Mexico is essential in order that we may understand our inescapable role as a productive/reproductive entity within U.S./Mexican society for the past two hundred years.

The transnational labor force into which most of us are born was created out of Mexico's neocolonialist relationship to the United States.[12] Throughout the history of the United States, Mexicans have served as a labor reserve controlled by U.S. policy. Mexico encourages the emigration of this labor force to alleviate its own depressed economy, and the United States all too willingly consumes this labor without giving it the benefits enjoyed by U.S. residents.

Contrary to the ideological claim of the United States that insists that all immigrants (which by legislature and action meant European) pay their dues before being able to participate fully in its melting pot economy, the underpaid Mexican worker is crucial to the survival of the profit-based system of the United States. The maquiladoras illustrate this point.[13]

Since the late sixties, U.S. production has undergone a transfer of manufacturing to less industrialized nations, such as México.[14] The U.S.-Mexican border has been an appealing site for such assembly operations. Unskilled women pressed with dire economic necessity serve as a reserve for these industries. A continuing influx of labor from the interior of México provides competition and keeps wages at a base minimum. Daily wage for a maquiladora *rose* to a mere $3.50 per day in 1988.[15] An unofficial border source told me that that figure had risen to $3.75 per day in 1992. The outrageously low wages for working in dangerous and unregulated conditions are among the strongest arguments against the free-trade agreements between United States, Mexico, and Canada.

The cultural and religious beliefs that maintain that most Latinas on either side of the border are (and should be) dependent on their men for economic survival are not only unrealistic, evidence shows they do not reflect reality. On this side of the border, according to the 1987 Department of Labor Report, one million "Hispanic" households were headed by women. Their average income was $337.00 per week. Fifty-two per cent of these households headed by women survive below poverty level.

Any woman without the major support of the father of her children and who has no other resources, must, in order to survive, commodify her labor. Even most Chicano/Latino men do not earn enough to support their families; their wives must go outside the home to earn an income (or bring it home in the form of piece work). Furthermore, statistics show that many mothers do not live with the father of their children and do not receive any kind of financial assistance from him.

MOST CHICANAS/LATINAS ARE NOT CONSCIENTICIZED. The majority of the populace, on either side of the border, in fact, is not actively devoted to real social change. That sense of inferiority, as when two people were confronted with their mexicanidad on the streets of downtown Chicago, permeates most Chicanas' self-perceptions. Lack of conscientización is what makes the maquiladora an ideal worker for the semi-legal, exploitative operations of multi-national factory production.

At an early age we learn that our race is undesirable. Because of possible rejection, some of us may go to any length to deny our background. But one cannot cruelly judge such women who have resorted to negation of their own heritage; constant rejection has accosted us since childhood. Certain women indeed had contact early on in their lives with México and acquired enough identification with its diverse culture and traditions to battle against the attempts of white, middle class society to usurp all its citizens into an abstract culture obsessed with material gain.

But many women born in the United States or brought here during childhood have little connection with the country of our ancestors. The umbilical cord was severed before we could develop the intellectual and emotional link to México, to the astonishing accomplishments of its indigenous past, to its own philosophical and spiritual nature so much at odds with that of the WASP. Instead we flounder between invisibility and a tacit hope that we may be accepted here and awarded the benefits of acculturation.

Looking different, that is, not being white nor black but something in between in a society that has historically acknowledged only a black/white racial schism is cause for great anxiety. Our internalized racism causes us to boast of our light coloring, if indeed we have it, or imagine it. We hope for light-skinned children and brag no end of those infants who happen to be born güeros, white looking, we are downright ecstatic if they have light colored eyes and hair. We sometimes tragically reject those children who are dark.

On the subject of color and internal conflicts there are also those who, despite identification with Latino heritage are light-skinned because of their dominating European genes or because one parent is white. For some this may be an added reason for internalizing racism, particularly when young (since it is difficult to explain the world to yourself when you are growing up). But for others, while their güero coloring may cause them to experience less racial tension in broad society, it may cause tension for a variety of reasons in their home, chosen communities, and when politically active against racism.

Let us consider for a moment a woman who does not necessarily desire marriage or bearing children, and works instead to attain a higher standard of living for herself. She must still interact with and quite often be subordinate to white people, and occasionally African Americans. I do not want to elaborate on the dynamics of her relationships with African Americans since it is understood here that institutionalized racism has not allowed either race to have real domination over the other. My own experience has been one of cultural difference rather than a racial one since there are also "black hispanos." But I will note that she will in all likelihood still feel "foreign" with African Americans who have an acknowledged history in the United States. Because of slavery, white people *know* why African Americans are here. They also *know* why Native Americans are here, yet they *assume* mestizos have all migrated here for economic gain as their own people did.

To compound our anxiety over our foreign-like identity in the United States is the fact that Mexican Americans are also not generally accepted in México. We are derogatorily considered *pochos,* American Mexicans who are either among the traitors or trash of Mexico because we, or previous generations, made the United States home. Unlike the experiences that many African Americans have had in "returning" and being welcomed in Africa,[16] many U.S.-born mestizo/as have found themselves more unwelcomed by mexicanos than white gringos.

Aside from skin color, language can add to the trauma of the Chicana's schizophrenic-like existence. She was educated in English and learned it is the only acceptable language in society, but Spanish was the language of her childhood, family, and community. She may not be able to rid herself of an accent; society has denigrated her first language. By the same token, women may also become anxious and self conscious in later years if they have no or little facility in Spanish. They may feel that they had been forced to forfeit an important part of their personal identity and still never found acceptability by white society.

Race, ethnicity, and language are important factors for women who aspire to a decent standard of living in our anglocentric, xenophobic society. Gender compounds their social dilemma and determines the very nature of their lifestyle regardless of the ability to overcome all other obstacles set against them.

Feminism at its simplest has not ever been solely a political struggle for women's rights, i.e., equal pay for equal work. The early feminista's initial attempts at placing women-related issues at the forefront were once viewed with suspicion by Marxist-oriented activists as The Woman Question was seen to be separate from or less significant than race and class issues by most activists, and along with gay issues, even thought to be an indication of betrayal to La Causa. Along those lines, in the 1990s, while issues of sexuality have come to the forefront, most recently with the national debate of permitting gays in the military, there remains a strong heterosexist bias among Chicano/Hispanic/Latino based organizations and our varying communities.

With the tenacious insistence at integrating a feminist perspective to their political concientización as Chicanas, feminist activistas, and intellectuals are in the process of developing what I call Xicanisma. On a pragmatic level, the basic premise of Xicanisma is to reconsider behavior long seen as inherent in the Mexic Amerindian woman's character, such as, patience, perseverance, industriousness, loyalty to one's clan, and commitment to our children. Contrary to how those incognizant of what feminism is, we do not reject these virtues. We may not always welcome the taxing responsibility that comes with our roles as Chicanas. We've witnessed what strain and limitations they often placed on our mothers and other relatives. But these traits often seen as negative and oppressive to our growth as women, as well as having been translated to being equal to being a drone for white society and its industrial interests, may be considered strengths. Simultaneously, as we redefine (not categorically reject) our roles within our families, communities at large, and white dominant society, our Xicanisma helps us to be self-confident and assertive regarding the pursuing of our needs and desires.

As brown-skinned females, often bilingual but not from a Spanish speaking country (not a Mexican citizen yet generally considered to not really be American), frequently discouraged in numerous ways from pursuing formal education, usually with limited economic means, therefore made to compete in a racist and sexist lower skilled work force, we continue to be purposely rendered invisible by society except as a stereotype and in other denigrating ways. The U.S. Women's Movement, which in fact began long before the Civil Rights Movement and the ensuing Chicano Movement, is now incorporating a more expansive vision that includes the unique perceptions and experiences of all peoples heretofore excluded from the democratic promise of the United States. Until we are all represented, respected, and protected by society and the laws that govern it, the status of the Chicana will be that of a countryless woman.

two

THE WATSONVILLE
WOMEN'S STRIKE, 1986
A Case of Mexicana Activism

I

*I worked for 23 years for this company. I came to the United States in
1962. I was following my father, who had been here for 25 years. I settled
in Watsonville. I've been fighting to maintain my family, to give them an
education. It is more difficult for a single woman to maintain the family.*
—Gloria Betancourt, strike leader

Included in the ongoing analysis among feminists and activists regarding the politics of gender, sexuality, race, and economic inequities has
been the theory of socialist feminism, that is, the possibility of merging
Marxist ideology with a critique of patriarchy.[1] Obviously, this discourse is essential with regard to working class women of color, but
especially those in low-skilled labor.

In 1993, at the time of this writing, this discussion is even more
crucial when considering that mejicanas and Chicanas, who are the
majority serving in low skilled labor jobs on both sides of the border,
will be directly affected by the North American Free Trade Agreement. They are directly affected in that they are among the vast world
labor pool that NAFTA supporters rely on for what they refer to as
economically efficient production. In other words, for very little pay
and with little regard to health and safety conditions and no benefits
for maquiladoras and other low skilled workers, multinational investors can produce more by spending less and making bigger profits from
world consumers. The workers—in this case, mejicanas/Chicanas—
are not the consumers of these products, of course, since they can't
afford them, which renders them further inconsequential in terms of
economic efficient strategy.

While the present Clinton Administration aggressively attempted
to pass the NAFTA agreement,[2] it was apparently unpopular in Can-

ada, among many people in the United States, and Mexican workers being most exploited can voice little public opinion about such policy decision making. Therefore to refer to it as an agreement of North American peoples appears erroneous. Furthermore, NAFTA was not a proposal for free trade, but a way to enable the transfer of multinational production to where it will be more economically efficient.

The misleading naming of this proposal gives the impression that as a result of it we will be opening the gateway at the Mexican/U.S. border and enjoying a friendly cultural exchange that promises eventual economic benefits to everyone. As the workforce in the United States continues to be put out of work, its hostility toward people of color—in this case, Latino/as (U.S., Mexican, Central American, Caribbean) whom they believe they are losing their jobs to, grows. Moreover, the truth about NAFTA is that it aims to benefit only the very few very wealthy multinational investors while the abominable conditions under which low-skilled laborers are forced to work and the ghastly communities they live in grow more devastating.

Unfortunately, the lives of most women, and specifically women of Mexican heritage, are not affected on a daily basis by intellectual debate. Juliet Minces reminds us:

> Let us not forget that in terms of both rights and actual behavior, women's condition in the West is still recent. It is worth recalling that, in France, women only secured the vote in 1945; that equal pay for equal work is still an expectation rather than a fact [certainly, this is the case in the U.S.]; that women participate far less in political and trade union activities than men do, not because they lack rights but because it is not yet *customary* [my italics] for them to be fully integrated.[3]

This essay provides an illustration of how labor activism among women may catalyze political conscientización by showing how the economic inequities that pervade their working lives are specifically related to race and gender. Understanding our women in the work force is one step toward the illumination of our whole sense of self, but despite Marxist claims, a degree of economic relief has not ended the limits on women's participation in society. This has been proven in the latter half of the twentieth century in various countries throughout the world, including the United States. To think otherwise in the late 1960s when these discussions began, was a gross underestimation of the phallocratic world in which we still live today. To illustrate this I will discuss here a case in point, a successful labor strike led mostly by mexicanas in 1986 in Watsonville, California and an interview I conducted with Chicana/mejicana activists in that same town the following year.

WATSONVILLE, a growing city of approximately 28,000, became the first town north of Fresno, California, with a Latino majority. It is the fertile region of cannery row painted by John Steinbeck in the 1930s. Whereas, years ago, its workers who labored packing fruit and vegetables were of Slavic and Portuguese origins, today most are Mexican.

Driving through Watsonville, it is easy to see that it has become predominantly Mexican—Mexican food stores, brown youth on the streets, Spanish heard everywhere. In 1992 Watsonville received its official sanction as a town of Guadalupanos—a term synonymous to being Mexican—with an apparition of the Virgin of Guadalupe. Her image appeared to a fifty-four year old mexicana cannery worker on an old oak tree in the state park. Since then hundreds of peregrinos—I among them—have gone to pay homage to Tonanztin/Guadalupe at the site.

Along with the glad feeling I have received from familiar cultural associations in Watsonville, there are also the many social problems that accompany poverty and the working class—drugs, gang and domestic violence, and a substandard educational system. Watsonville was hard hit during a major earthquake in 1989 and it has been slow in recovering because of the economic disparity that exists in that area.

My interest in Watsonville was first catalyzed with a visit there in 1987 when I conducted a twelve hour long writing workshop one Saturday with writer Cherríe Moraga. The workshop was sponsored by the local city college and the participants received credit. It was organized by a Chicana who worked at the college and also participated in the workshop.

All the women who attended, about a dozen, many activists, were Chicanas, with the exception of one Native American woman—

married to a Mexican and part of the Chicano community of Watsonville for many years. Their ages ranged from eighteen to sixty. Except
for the Native American woman, they were all fluent in both languages, with Spanish often being the first language. Their education
ranged from being junior college students to post-graduates. Most
were mothers, some breast feeding at the time; others had grown
children. In the case of one participant, she attended during the day,
then relieved her daughter of her own small children so that the
daughter could participate in the evening session. All these women
maintained jobs outside the home. All were from the working class or
the underclass of the working poor. All had an inherent sense of their
cultural difference from that of mainstream society. With the exception of two—the Native American woman and one older Protestant
Chicana—all were Catholic. The presence of the Native American
was significant in this instance, making the tie of Christian beliefs to
Mexican culture markedly apparent as compared to her own orientation with Amerindian philosophy.[4] Except for one woman, all presented themselves as heterosexual. All, with no exception, desired to
express themselves through writing.

It is important at this point, for the non-Chicana reader to keep in
mind the sense of familia that exists among women who identify
themselves as Chicanas throughout the United States and that crosses
the U.S./Mexican border. Therefore, our reputations as Chicana writers
preceded us and the invitation to conduct this workshop was based on a
sense of belonging to this group bound by Xicanisma. We were both accepted readily by the women and as a result, at the end of the workshop
I was able to interview four of the workshop participants for this essay,
which was originally published in Spanish in *Esta Puente, Mi Espalda*.

The interview included two women from México and two native
to the area. I selected these women because of their unquestionable
commitment to Chicana activism and their wide range of commitments. While we conversed quietly in Spanish, the other women
listened and made occasional supportive comments so that at no time
did I feel that the women who were actively responding were not
representative of the group.

At the start of our discussion, it was first established that a woman
without conscientización nevertheless perceives certain societal dis-

crimination directed *at her.* With conscientización, she begins a deliberate process of questioning this discrimination, but she may not yet
know how to grapple with its effects. With deliberate orientation
toward conscientización—which may come by way of higher education, the unusual experience of some social/political catalyst (such as
the Watsonville Strike which will be elaborated on in the second half
of this essay, or the Chicano Movement of the 1970s), or through a
personal deliberate effort to seek help from other women—she may
find she has no recourse but to finally take radical action.

The concept of the American Dream—an illusion long fostered
by the system to maintain its work force—was an overwhelming factor
that played with the hearts and minds of the Watsonville residents, the
women in the workshop informed me. People in Watsonville truly
believed they could improve their material conditions through hard
work. In fact, in comparison to the conditions they lived in México,
the material lives of mexicanas *had* improved. Simultaneously, in order
to achieve the goals of the American Dream, the Mexican tradition of
an extended family, including community, was deemed a hindrance
and relinquished within the time span of a single generation. In a
nation that strongly motivates people toward competition, individual
achievement, and, above all, material acquisitions, collectivity and
spiritual aspirations are anachronistic. That is, grandparents and otherwise unemployed relatives outside of the nuclear family would become
a burden on the way to material goals.

This dilemma is compounded for women of conscientización who
prefer to work for the common good of their ethnic community and to
oppose individual profit that often comes in conflict with the personal
ambitions of their family of origin, spouses, and their grown children and
goes in direct opposition to some Mexican traditions and gringo values:

Shirley: I think that people help each other more in other parts of
the world. In this country, you won't get help from your family, for
example, if you don't work. You won't get help from your community. One is forced to become part of the working class because if
you don't participate, you will die. The other side to this is that the
cost of living is so high, not only are you forced to be part of the
working class, but the working class is established such that even if

you do go to work every day, you can't exist in the economy due to the fact that inflation, housing, food, transportation, medical expenses are all much more costly than what the majority of the people can afford. Therefore, everyone lives at the substandard level.

Shirley's point is exemplified in the case of Arabian society, steeped in clan-oriented customs, in which one can see parallels between its traditions and those of Mexican culture, and how they have been affected by urbanization. Minces states, "The family group, in the broad sense, is the keystone of society." She continues, "Even when urban conditions have forced the family to become a nuclear unit (father, mother and direct descendants), people still think in terms of the extended family, with all the rights and duties that implies."[5] However, urbanization as a result of the transformation of the economic base of Arab countries has subsequently affected the ancient tribal tradition of the extended family.

THE CATHOLIC CHURCH AS AN INSTITUTION supported by the Mexican community in the U.S. seems to be a cultural norm rather than a source for real spiritual comfort for these women. The rituals of the church bring a sense of order to women's lives but not much personal tranquility because they do not alleviate her practical concerns. The response of mexicanas to the apparition of the Virgin's image on the oak tree is, to my mind, an indication of a need for spiritual consolation and material relief. Again, it is not so much a manifestation of the church but of the women's culture and ethnic identity. Above all, I see the Guadalupe cult as an unspoken, if not unconscious, devotion to their own version of Goddess.

However, it is the church that represents authority in her life, especially over her sexuality and reproductive ability. The complexities of how society as a whole does not concern itself with the best interest of woman begin to unravel for the activist. The life she has led has been an arduous one, based on hard work, little material compensation, subservience to all (except to other women like herself and their children), and with very little leisure. If she is married, as many women are at a relatively young age, her life may be dictated by her husband's domination. However, when she has some analysis as to the unnatural oppressiveness she experiences because of her home life, endorsed by family, community, and church, she may look for a way out. As María states here, speaking hypothetically of such married women:

María: And they [the former Watsonville strikers] begin to question the religious values of . . . "I don't think that God would like me to be in the position that I find myself with this cabrón, so I am not going to continue this way . . . !"

The "cabrón" to whom María refers to is the hypothetical woman's husband. Culture and religion exalt the value of motherhood, but given her societal status the mejicana struggles endlessly to fulfill the practical necessities of raising children. Therefore, she begins to repudiate the church's firm stance against contraception. Contraceptives are more acceptable in the United States, and consequently she is apt to go against this doctrine (usually not without having had children first) and limit her childbearing. It must be added here however, that medical care is to some degree of better quality in the U.S. than what is available to poor women in México:

AC: Is there certain pressure from the man or Mexican culture that says to be a good wife or a good woman you have to have all the children that God sends you?
María: Definitely, of course. My mother, for example tells me: You can be as professional as you want, you can be as perfect as you want, however you want it, BUT if you don't have a child, you will not be complete, you will never fulfill the role that God gave you.
AC: Do you have a child?
María: None. And I won't have any. It's a conviction.

How a conscientisized woman concludes that she is going to tear herself away from the fabric of her traditions as mandated by the church is her own process and largely dependent upon the degree of her "political" education.

FORMAL EDUCATION IS ELUSIVE AND LOFTY, difficult to manage, and sometimes unheard of for many women from poor to working class families:

Shirley: In this society you have to have at least four distinct things before you can obtain an education: You have to be oriented within your family that tells you that education is good. Second, you have to have freedom: freedom from child care, other such responsibilities, mobility . . . Another thing you must have are the abilities—your parents must help you through that system. It isn't an easy system to enter [financially]. The other thing that you must be is comfortable in that environment . . .

Moreover, education for the most part and for the large majority of these women has not been seen by the family as a necessity toward the improvement of the family as a whole. This has been unfortunate, since women have traditionally been wage earners perhaps even the principle wage earner of the family when the husband is absent, ill, stricken with alcoholism, or for any number of reasons is not able to contribute sufficiently to the maintenance of the family. Often the woman is expected to be the devoted wife and model mother and bring home a wage. But *how* she manages to provide for the material needs of her family is only a secondary consideration to the expectation that she do so.

If her family and community acknowledged that along with the mandate of motherhood, she quite often is the only one to feed, clothe, house, and maintain all of her children's needs (and sometimes those of her husband's and other relatives as well), then perhaps the pressures for her to be married and to have children might at least be postponed until she can acquire skills to improve her employment opportunities.

But it's not easy for the Mexican woman to go to school. First and foremost she must feel that she is *educatable*—that she can learn, that she may be a valuable contributor to society as a result of educating, in other words, that she is worthy of such a luxury as formal schooling. If the impoverished woman of color does not receive encouragement in this direction from home, but by some stroke of luck is persuaded by an outside influence—a scholarship or a friend within the institution— she must also contend with the other obstacles. If she is already a mother, who will care for her children while she goes to class and when she needs to study? If she must work to support her family, where does she find the time for all the responsibilities?

If she is not a mother by a certain age (I would guess from personal observation, between the ages of 25 and 30), as María stated above, all else pales in comparison to the only accomplishment expected from her: motherhood. But few women who do not have children and struggle for an education are ever convinced of the merit of their own achievements:

Shirley: See, what happened was that I began to see the problems in society and I began being an activist. I realized that I could not tackle all areas when I began trying as an activist in the community to do it all—education, voter registration, women's issues, everything. I found that in reality I was burning out. So I made the decision to choose, to choose geographically, with what population, and what problem. So I chose Watsonville. I chose to work with women and in the area of education. Thus, I do what I can within the system to achieve social change.

AC: You're married. Have you received support from home for what you do?

Shirley: I have obtained support after I have demanded it, never before.

THE RUDE AWAKENING FROM THE AMERICAN DREAM jolts Chicana activists toward their displaced Mexican customs. The reason is that assimilation into Anglo society is rarely completely successful. The need to belong to some specific culture brings them full circle to their Mexican heritage, which they once rejected. As Octavio Paz states in his book *The Labyrinth of Solitude,* "[The United States is] a country full of cults and tribal costumes, all intended to satisfy the middle-class North American's desire to share in something more vital and solid than the abstract morality of the 'American Way of Life.'" In attempting to assimilate into the "American Dream" the edges of woman's own personal sense of identity are blurred; she ultimately fits nowhere, is accepted nowhere:

Cruz: Until I was twenty-four years old, I thought I was white, that I was American. I had lost my Mexican values. Just now I am recovering them . . . some, I don't think ever all of them. For me, there was never the hope of going to college. I was the only one in my family that continued studying and finished college until this next generation now that my daughter is attending. I, with children (I am divorced), decided to educate myself . . . At that time there was economic help and I could do it [she refers here to the seventies when there was funding available to minority students in the way of grants, loans, and scholarships]. And I didn't want to go on to the university—I was afraid—but I went. I achieved it. I came out and I didn't learn a lot, but I achieved it.

The inability of parents, who themselves have little formal education, to instill in their children—especially daughters—the desire for education is an aspect of why many mexicanas and Chicanas may not see themselves as educatable. Another aspect is that early on, in primary school, children begin to experience a sense of disorientation within Anglo culture, language, values, and its system of competition:

Gabriela: It's an underlying discrimination that we can only see when we have certain conscientización, education, but that you don't see when it has been happening to you. I can't exactly explain it because I grew up here and in Mexico. I know, with my students at school, that those who have been with Mexican teachers most of the time, that have been treated well and have been in a well implemented bilingual education program in school, who have the self-esteem for who they are and have their models—those children are going to get very far . . .

For most Watsonville women, the responsibility of just caring for the daily needs of their children makes it difficult for them to even worry about finding quality education and bilingual programs for their children. Yet, the awareness achieved by the organizing success of the strike of 1986—a pragmatic learning process in itself—caused some of these women to understand how all of these issues are interrelated and how they, as mexicanas, are not given consideration by this society.

This particular member of our U.S. society has been raised to believe at best, she must obey the mandates of her culture—not to question the institutions deemed sacred (the church, her parents, her husband); to bear and care for children; and to maintain the order of her immediate environment as it is dictated to her. It is no wonder that her only personal aspiration may be to acquire commodities, marketed as indispensable necessities, conveniences, or comforts. A person born into very humble economic means learns to yearn for material acquisitions. Products ultimately become the only way to elevate her status within her community, among her family and friends, and within the world at large.

BUT COMMODITIES DO NOT SATISFY THE XICANISTA. She realizes that she is only a worker who is aiding the very system that keeps her from making any real economic progress; that she is a member of a group that because of race has been relegated to the lower social strata in the United States; and that as a woman, she has been subjugated both outside and inside her home. If she decides to act upon her awareness, she finds that for a while she must disassociate from any solid ties to North American *and* Mexican values, which, for her are more similar than they are dissimilar.

The philosophy of the male-dominated Chicano Movement was akin to the theories of Frantz Fanon, who professed that revolutionary struggle for "national independence" would suffice to change people's attitudes toward women's subordinate status. The participation of women in the national struggle would prove their equality to the men and at the same time change women so that they would demand their own "liberation." However, in the case of the Algerian revolution where the people freed themselves of 130 years of colonization in 1962 this indeed did not happen.[6] Each struggle for national freedom must be evaluated in its own historical context but national struggles continue to disregard the reality that women ultimately remain subject to male authority. By male I do not restrict myself to actual men but to the system.

In the case of the Chicano Movement in the United States, Chicanos as a whole have been divided into such diverse positions—from complete cooptation by Anglo society to (and this is much less the case) militant separatism. The difficulty of unifying such a movement *within* the United States on the basis of ethnicity is clear: the promise of the unattainable "American Dream" in a country ridden with commodity fever focuses the individual on elevating the self not on general improvement of society as a whole. Competition not community is the motivation.[7]

Nevertheless, while most women activists are bound to the community of their ethnic background (with the exception of some lesbian activists who may find a closer kinship to a women's community), women's consciousness today is forcing them toward a unique perspective. While socialism may be their point of departure, women's issues remain the core of their struggle.

The tragedy of mexicanas in the United States lies not in the entrenched notion that woman exists only to propagate the species and to be a man's "mother" throughout his adult life, but that women are conditioned to *desire* this status *despite* the reality of their experiences. Her experience as propagator may give her little personal satisfaction, but she is conditioned to accept it from the day of her birth. At the same time, if she publicly acknowledges the contradictions of her reality she risks adverse reaction from the complex network that represents society:

Cruz: I work organizing in my community, it is my life. I feel a lot of pressure sometimes, because people tell me, well, "You should dress differently, you should do this, or that, buy yourself a car!" But no. I have my path and I am on it. Perhaps in the future I'll change how I'm doing it but right now I feel very clear. But yes, I see that pressure.
AC: You are estranged from your parents, your family?
Cruz: I can't tell them what I do.
AC: You live alone?
Cruz: Yes.
AC: Who is your family?
Cruz: Here, this community.[8]

II ━━●━━

IN THE SUMMER OF 1985, THE WATSONVILLE CANNING AND FROZEN FOOD COMPANY, a major frozen food processor in the U.S., cut the wages of its 1,100 workers by up to 40 percent.

It also demanded serious reductions in health benefits and stopped deducting union dues from the workers' paychecks. The Richard Shaw Company, another local cannery, also demanded similar cutbacks. As a result, over 1,600 workers went on strike in September of that year.

In February 1986 Richard Shaw broke rank with Watsonville Canning and convinced his workers to accept a settlement of better wages, plus a profit-sharing incentive, with restoration of some benefits. Watsonville Canning decided to press for its slashed hourly wages.

Teamsters Local 912, a small and predominantly white union, had organized the freezer plants and canneries during World War II. In 1986 its membership was five thousand; nine out of ten were Latino, and most of them were women. The union was not prepared for the strike. Furthermore, Watsonville Canning hired a law firm known for union busting and the union feared that if it were ousted it would have to fight its way back into every plant in Watsonville. The gap between the leadership and the membership of the union was so great that many of the workers believed that Watsonville Canning had been out to break their union altogether.

The workers formed a strikers' committee to handle the daily conduct of the strike. Court injunctions reached such proportions that strikers who lived near the plants were arrested for simply standing on their front porches. Few had savings and their fifty-five-dollars-a-week strike benefits could hardly feed their families, much less withstand the strike's growing legal expenses. But the word of the strike spread throughout the state during the following eighteen months before it was settled and they received much outside support, "especially from the Chicano Movement" according to the periodical *Forward: Journal of Socialist Thought*.[9]

Not surprisingly, the Watsonville women's strike took on Mexican cultural overtones. The women were fiercely conscious of their race—shocked at and even aggressive toward Mexican scabs whom they perceived as traitors to la raza. "We just couldn't believe it when we saw other mexicanos crossing the picket lines. In México, when they put out those red and black flags [denoting a strike], if you cross the line, you're dead," stated Gloria Betancourt, a strike leader.[10] Although some were handcuffed and arrested, it was only their lack of

financial resources for posting bond that deterred the striker's determined attempts at discouraging scab labor.

When the company offered wage concessions but refused restoration of health benefits, the strike leaders went on a hunger strike.
Finally, the strikers secured the publicity they needed by conducting a
Catholic pilgrimage on their knees to a local church where they prayed
for justice. On March 11, 1987 the strike was over. Their medical
coverage was to be restored within three months. As reported by the
press, "the strikers now, after 18 months on strike, know that they can
take their children to the doctor when necessary."[11]

As a result of this successful effort, the numbers and organizing
power of the Latino population of Watsonville became known to its
city officials. However, economic improvement for the Latino population when and if it were to come, would be gradual since government
representatives remained nearly exclusively Anglo. Development and
the high cost of real estate continued to force Mexican workers to live
in sometimes deplorable conditions, as was sharply proven at a county
housing hearing when the fire chief at that time told of grossly over-
crowded buildings and recounted finding field workers living on the
roofs of downtown buildings.[12]

For one and a half years the women strikers were up against what
would be presumably insurmountable institutionalized opposition. In
addition to the economic disadvantage of being women, some mothers,
there were the added disadvantages of language, little formal education
and social orientation, and sometimes lack of support from male partners.

The strike spotlighted the obvious reality for them as women:
their duty to maintain two jobs at once—with little compensation for
either—at work and at home. Women who were married sometimes
received little, if any, emotional support from home for their participation in the strike.[13] They also grew to have some understanding of the
legal system and their rights. Moreover, this understanding decreased
their fear of laws. As individuals being called upon to speak publicly
throughout the state, they had become persons with acknowledged
and legitimate opinions and lives.

While they learned the worth of their bargaining power, however,
the women's gains from the strike should not be overestimated. The
losses a woman activist experiences as a consequence of such rebellion

compared to men's are devastating. If her marriage, for example, breaks up as a result of her husband's intolerance of her insurgent behavior, she loses his income (which is usually higher than her own), as well as the status she receives from society as a married woman. Her status actually drops when she gets divorced or becomes an abandoned woman. She is usually left with their children; she most likely will have to provide for material and emotional care alone.

The principle lessons the Watsonville women strikers learned is that there is no separation between their private and their public worlds, from their wage earning world and their world of kitchens and bedrooms, from their pregnancies and their priests, from the education they never had and from the education their children may be deprived of.

LEFTIST ORGANIZATIONS RALLIED AROUND THE STRIK-ERS, bringing with them the added stigma of the label *communist*. Already these women were behaving in a way completely uncharacteristic of their tradition. While the strike leaders accepted support from wherever it came, they acknowledged that the socialist ideology that they were exposed to at that time seemed in accord with the strike's goals.[14]

Early socialist oriented activistas theorized that capitalism would undermine the hierarchy of patriarchy by requiring women to join the labor force and eventually become "independent" of men and become an equal participant in society. We now see that in the long run patriarchy and capitalism actually accommodated each other, in fact undermining any possibility for the woman in the labor force to break from her traditional role as subservient to man's personal needs. Women provide the bulk of domestic services in the home, care for the children, and create a warm, nurturing atmosphere for men, who still see themselves as entitled to refuge and solace because they believe they alone battle in the outside world. Women, of course, battle as wage earners in the outside, while they are the principle caretakers of the home.

In addition, a visible and growing new underclass largely consisting of single mothers has developed during this post-industrial era. The underclass also includes the working poor. When we understand a growing number of families that belong to this underclass are headed by working mothers, it is not at all surprising that the Watsonville Strike, consisted of and was led mostly by women.[15]

However, white supremacist patriarchy (not restricted to the U.S.) recognizes the participation of its non-white, female citizens in the work force and our sizable population, only insofar as it can continue to use their labor while it subverts women's potential to contribute to the transformation of society. This subversion is firmly entwined into each facet of our lives. It is not a struggle against the "bourgeois patrones" alone. It is not a misunderstanding with one's husband when he walks out or becomes abusive because his wife insists on attending a labor or community meeting. It isn't the idiosyncratic nature of one individual who underestimates a woman's intelligence and undermines her work at meetings, nor the behavior of one lecherous individual who becomes sexually aggressive with the same woman because he can only see her gender rather than her whole being.

Like clockwork, these reactions not only go into play at the onset of a woman's activism, they complement each other to the extent that she can justly regard them as a conspiracy. The domineering husband, the sexist activist, and el patrón all conspire against her participation. Moreover, the profit-hungry interests of global corporations depend on the human resources of impoverished populations (predominantly of women) at all costs.

The socialist communism of some male activists within el Movimiento has always been a clear cut case of us vs. them; the enemy is always outside the men themselves. When a woman, who is not supported by any institutions that exist in society, attempts to struggle for better wages, she systematically finds herself confronting more than just the holder of the purse strings. Male activists have had a reputation of being unable to separate their view of woman as worker from their general perception of woman as wife, mother, lover, whore, laundress, cook, dishwasher, mother to men and, generally, his inferior.

If they attempt to split their perception of woman, accepting the ideology of the female as "compañera" within the context of activism and social reform as a worker, the tendency has been to shortchange her when engaging in a personal relationship with her, defeating the whole premise of their socialist ideology. At least, this is to a large extent true within the Chicano/Latino Movement. I do not mean to imply that no male activist ever contributed to the housework or child care on a regular basis. I do suspect, however, that it did not usually happen without much determination on the part of his female partner for him to think along those lines. This is because patriarchy in Mexican traditions and Catholicism overrides the male activists' identities as "workers," which Marxism so narrowly focuses upon in its economic analysis of society.

GIVEN THE HISTORY OF UNION ORGANIZING IN THE U.S., (despite the monumental achievements of the late Cesar Chávez and the continued efforts of Dolores Huerta and their forebears) the Mexican woman laborer would seem an unlikely candidate to challenge a system that has never recognized her as a force to whom it should be accountable. The concept of the union—historically white and male—did not include providing for the labor force that is non-white, female, and single mothers. Therefore, the women who participated in the Watsonville strike learned how their entire lives are depersonalized for the benefit of mass production.

The Watsonville case may recall the novels of John Steinbeck and his working man's theme of the thirties. However, the Watsonville Strike did not take place a half-century ago when—if white people were living at subsistence level due to the stock market crash—Mexicans were being deported in cattle cars to México so that the U.S. government would not have to contend at all with their no longer needed labor nor with their American born offspring. I must reiterate: unions have traditionally benefitted white male workers; while women of color, mestizas, Native Americans, Chinese, Filipinas, Puerto Ricans, and African-Americans have always worked the fields, factories, and kitchens of the United States, alongside their unionless, unrepresented husbands, fathers, and brothers. At the tail-end of the twentieth century, someone is still working in the fields at minimum or below minimum wages, someone is still packing, and that someone is *still* a Mexican woman—except that *now,* if she has proof of U.S. citizenship, she might be allowed in a union.

Regarding the Simpson-Rodino Immigration Reform and Control Bill that was passed in 1986 and has been touted as an "amnesty" bill, it in fact allows for a "guest worker" plan similar to the Bracero

Program implemented in the 1940s. Growers are allowed to hire as many as 350,000 seasonal workers per year who are not granted amnesty. Without staying vigilant to the kinds of legal agreements made between the Mexican and United States governments, often with multinational interests in mind, we cannot understand how, one way or another, we will continue to serve as a source of cheap labor. We must be attentive to these policies not for the sake of a few hundred immigrants coming into the United States in the last few years, or thousands of Mexicans over decades, but for the *millions* of mestizas today who have no choice if they and their families are to survive at all. As maquiladoras they earn about three dollars a day and in Los Angeles garment sweat shops as little as seven cents a garment.

For the undocumented worker her troubles are compounded beyond most of our imaginations. There are horrifying reports from the border of cases of women who never make it across the border when attempting illegal crossing. Rape is often expected by these women, who begin taking birth control to prevent an unwanted pregnancy in anticipation of being raped when trying to cross over. Illegal crossing includes risking no less than their lives by the method that they may be forced to cross. In addition, in recent years some women were murdered for the purpose of having their organs sold by organ brokers.[16] Once on this side of the border, their deplorable experiences may range from below minimum wage earnings to being kept on ranches in indentured servant conditions.

In January 1993 the recently elected Democratic Clinton administration nominated Zoe Baird for the top-ranking government post of Attorney General. However, her nomination was challenged when it was made public that she had hired undocumented workers to care for her children. While she admitted awareness of the illegality of this act, her defense was that she was acting out of concern to provide child care for her children and was motivated as a mother more than anything else. In July 1992 13.2 percent of the labor force was unemployed or underemployed. There was no shortage of legal residents in this country who care for children. However, they would require minimum wages and other legal benefits , such as payment of social security and unemployment taxes. A person of Zoe Baird's professional stature must surely earn sufficient income to pay such a salary. In view of her motherly concerns, it would appear that her children are worth whatever fee is within her means to insure their security and well being. After much controversy over this matter, Ms. Baird withdrew from nomination.

The exploitation of poor working women of color knows no boundaries on either side of the border. From a global perspective, abuse of women of color in the labor market throughout the world, has had no limits. The average wage of workers (mostly women) in Indonesian production plants subcontracted by Nike in 1991 was *$1.30 per day*. Filipina workers for Mattel, the toy manufacturer, are offered prizes for undergoing sterilization. In addition to slowing down the population growth, corporations, such as Mattel feel that sterilization of women ensures a less demanding labor force in the free trade zone.[17] These inhuman abuses of women will surely continue into the twenty-first century. Only drastic measures taken on their behalf by government policies and corporate interests can protect them.

As Xicanistas who may or may not find ourselves in garment sweatshops in Los Angeles, earning seven cents a garment, or working in indentured servant conditions in the fields with our children for twelve hours a day, or in any number of other heinous labor conditions akin to feudalism that millions of women are forced to endure today, every day in order to feed our children—we must not forget our hermanas who do. We must support them and observe their strikes, even if only by refusing to purchase the products of the company they are fighting against. Just as importantly, we can no longer delude ourselves that while our lives may not be directly and immediately affected by such disregard for humanity as that shown by those who exploit the women who work in low skilled labor, everyone is affected by the kinds of products major industries mass market. We should remember, for example, that the same pesticides that have caused birth defects in the children born to women working in the fields are in the produce at our local supermarkets. The UFW Strike against grapes is not only about pressuring farmers and ranchers who take advantage of their laborers. The grape boycott now—yes, the boycott is still on—is representative of a need for all consumers to be conscious of the poison mass-marketed produce is sprayed with. We must not put it on our tables and serve it to our loved ones. This is almost impossible to avoid in some areas in this country because organic farmers are kept out of the agricultural industry's competition. Moreover, there is little land that has not been contaminated already.

The goal of socialist ideologies was liberation—liberation of the worker. For the feminist socialist, it was liberation of woman within post-industrial society. However, the ultimate liberation is that of enlightenment. Through conscious decisions guided by being informed about the intricate clockwork of industrial destruction of lives and natural resources, each of us is not only being responsible to others, but we are being accountable to ourselves. Most importantly, we are being there for the children who will inherit what we make of this world.

three
THE ANCIENT ROOTS
OF MACHISMO

BECAUSE OF THE SEVERE ATTACK ON THE SOPHISTI-
CATED INDIGENOUS CULTURES of México and the annihilation of their beliefs, pre-Conquest history is probably deemed irrele-
vant to our daily lives by most of us. Save for scholars, most of our
people can recite the Apostles' Creed but would be hard pressed to
identify the Mexica (Aztec) sun god, Huitzilopochtli, or the earth
goddess and mother of Huitzilopochtli, Coatlicue.

By the same token, many would also feel quite unconvinced that
the Islamic faith of North Africa has any more to do with us than the
theology of the Mexica. We may acknowledge a certain degree of
obvious Arab influence in Mexican culture. To be sure, traces of
Arabic are found in our Spanish language. When we put our hands up
in desperate hope, for instance, and utter, ¡Ojala! we are doing no
more than reiterating an Arab expression used in the same context:
Oh, Allah! But our connection with our ancient cousins is much
deeper than many of us in the Americas imagine.

More significantly to us as women, ancient Arab practices are a
part of our Spanish Catholic heritage. This is due to our historical ties
with Spain. Until shortly before Spain's explorations and exploitation
of the Americas Spain had been conquered and ruled by the North
African followers of Muhammad for nearly eight hundred years. It is
impossible to dismiss the tremendous influence Arabs had on Spanish
culture after a period of domination that lasted over three times the
duration of the United States's existence as a nation.

Once we recognize this fact of our history, we may more closely
examine how this early and adamant culture has contributed to our
social relations between the genders and how it has influenced the
particular way in which woman has been commodified by Mexican
culture. When acknowledging our kinship with the Arab world, we
find uncanny similarities in both our peoples' social behavior and
attitudes toward women that may be traced back thousands of years to
the African continent.

My point here is not to argue whether Islamic patriarchy is more dominant than Christian patriarchy; and I certainly would not argue that the Mexica males' dominance was less oppressive of women than that imposed by the Spaniards.[1] There is little point in debating which is the lesser of the evils.

Because of the importance of the Mexica society to Chicano/a ideology, however, I think it is worth commenting on women's status at the height of the Aztec Empire. As I have stated elsewhere in this book, as capitalism intensifies so has the oppression of women, who come to be seen as property, producers of goods and reproducers. Therefore, while there are indications of Toltec women having power (at least as queens and warriors) in the tenth century and there are indeed matrilineal societies throughout the indigenous Americas, such as among the Zapotec people of the Oaxaca region, the great Tenochtitlan held women in no higher regard than the traditions I believe we have inherited from the Arab world that will be discussed here. This is aptly summarized in the following passage:

> Girls were hardly schooled at all, since females played no civic, military, or political roles in Mexica society. Young girls were required to learn religious duties and domestic arts, and they were taught most of what they were expected to know as mothers. Women were under strict supervision all their lives. The Mexica were enormously puritanical, as most societies overwhelmingly devoted to social purpose tend to be. Females were normally chaperoned, and they were expected to never interfere in the warriors' business. One Mexica proverb indicated that the men preferred women with both ears plugged and their mouths stopped up. . . . The revered speaker and the lords of Mexico were permitted huge harems, but sexual license, and even sexual liberty, did not extend to the common people.[2]

At one point, the court doctors reported no less than 150 of Moteuczoma's women in the palace were expecting babies from him. Prostitution was illegal but tolerated to reduce rape and adultery. Divorcées were repudiated by their communities. They were considered nymphomaniacs and hence, went away, to be sold into slavery as concubines.[3] These brief examples illustrate that at the time of the

Conquest women were already living out the blueprint for the following generations of Mexican women. However, because of culturcide, that same patrimonial blueprint came to us more directly vis à vis the Spaniards.

My intent in this chapter is first to make a direct association between us and those women in the world who have been controlled in similar ways. Second, I want to show how these controlling attitudes toward women predate the religions that our cultures subscribe to and suggest that when the new religion did not accommodate the older custom, the religious law has been ignored.

ISLA DE MUJERES is an island off the coast of the Yucatan. I am told that it has most recently become a favorite vacation spot for lesbians, in all likelihood because of its name (as well as its natural beauty), a kind of an American Lesbos. But when I first happened upon it in 1976, while there was still little tourist appeal to the place, voyeuristic adolescents peered at my woman friend and me through our bathroom window. We were the subjects of defaming lies spread by the men of the island; they said they had had their way with us. We narrowly escaped a gang rape.[4]

Those experiences were to us an echo of the legends that surrounded Isla de Mujeres. For one, there is a tiny ruin that is said to have been a *mirador*, a belvedere. The island residents said that the native Mayan women built the *mirador* after their men went out to sea and disappeared. They hoped to sight the men's return. We were also told that when the Spaniards arrived they found a great many statues of female deities, hence, the island's name. Imagine for a moment, these Mayan women left on their idyllic isle, self-sufficient, constructing their own society, erecting icons in their own image at the time of the invasion by strange men of another race: bearded, filthy, scurvied, and otherwise diseased. What a shock this must have been to those smooth skinned, dark women living in their quiet tropical tranquility.

The most disturbing relics on Isla de Mujeres, however, are spider-webbed gratings that lead to dungeons in which the native women were said to have been kept by the invaders. Are these dungeons on Isla Mujeres any different than the bars through which the many wives of a Muslim in Spain were allowed to peer to catch the light of day?

What purpose could there have been for imprisoning women physically and spiritually who were incapable of being a threat to armed soldiers?

Recognizing the tremendous influence of North African customs and not solely questioning the virgin/whore dichotomy of the Catholic faith, I began to suspect the true origins of our notorious cultural trait known as *machismo,* and hence the particular ways in which patriarchy manifests itself in Mexican culture.

With regard to Anglo dominant society, which we have experienced to an extent as residents in the United States, there is evidence that many aspects of machismo discussed here have also manifested throughout Northern European history and in the present North America. Examples of preoccupation with female virginity appear from the chastity belts of the Crusades to restrictions placed on white middle-class girls in the United States (before the "free love" motto of hippy culture and the availability of the birth control pill in the late sixties overturned them) to the pre-wedding medical exam the future wife of Prince Charles of England—heir to the throne—underwent in 1981. In a comparative study between Anglo and Latino culture the question might be legitimately posed: What was worse, the Puritan ethic on Anglo women or concepts of machismo among Latinas? However, the focus of this essay is to explore direct influences on Mexican male-female relations, however historically remote.

THE ARGUMENT ON BEHALF OF MACHISMO: The word *macho* means to be male or masculine. Machismo, therefore is that which is related to the male or to masculinity. Machismo, as associated with Mexican culture for the social scientist, is the demonstration of physical and sexual powers and is basic to self-respect. Political scientists specifically interpret this characteristic of exaggerated virility as a defensive response to the racist and classist hierarchy under which most of modern civilization lives. On the basis of this explanation, of course, one could not define machismo as idiosyncratically Mexican, or Latino for that matter. According to our social pyramid, all men who feel displaced racially, culturally, and/or because of economic hardships will turn on those whom they feel they can order and humiliate, usually women, children, and animals—just as they have been ordered and humiliated by those few privileged who are in power. However, this definition does not explain why there are privileged men who behave this way toward women.

It is dangerous to rationalize the existence of machismo through a romantic and personal perspective. For example, in *Borderlands/la Frontera: The New Mestiza,* Gloria Anzaldúa agrees with the above explanation; she sees it as a result of the Mexican man's "loss of a sense of dignity and respect." However, she refers to this behavior as *false machismo* (italics mine). She states, "for men like my father, being 'macho' meant being strong enough to protect and support my mother and us, yet being able to show love."[5] The existence of machismo seems to be justified here if in fact, the macho in question can dictate his authority through affection.

The basic question for women regarding machismo is not only what are men protecting us from, but why? One might respond since laws and society have been created on behalf of men and not in the interest of women, only men can intercede on women's behalf. Indeed, some ways in which a "good macho" protects a woman may be:

1. Through marriage:

Until the 1970's, an unmarried, pregnant woman was not eligible for prenatal medical insurance furnished by employers. Today, live-in partners, heterosexual, homosexual and lesbian, are for the most part not covered by their partners' health insurance. Most insurance companies still maintain the policy that only legally married spouses are eligible for coverage.

Laws have usually "protected" women through marriage.

The historical and societal importance placed on the father role makes marriage the preferred option for women who want children.

Heterosexism and sexist laws reinforced with the nuclear family construct a world in which a woman finds herself financially, sexually, and/or emotionally dependent on a man.

2. Economics:

The ancient tradition of men being viewed as the primary providers for women and children found its way to the first unionizing activities when

Male as traditional, principal provider.

men in the United States were given family wages and women were seen as surplus labor and were paid less. Thirty years after the Equal Pay Act was passed, women today earn only seventy cents for every dollar a man makes. If the media reported sky-rocketing salaries for women in the 1980s, it was a misleading comparison to mens' wages that dropped during that period because of inflation. In any case, those figures affected above all white, educated women. Middle income women's wages hardly changed while lower income women's salaries dropped.[6]

3. Physical:

The quality that men used to get control of humanity more that 2000 years ago, is one of their most important assets today.

Women throughout the world in most urban and rural settings cannot venture out alone without the risk of being preyed upon by men and being subjected to their violence. Worse, they are also at times unsafe in their own homes.

4. Romance:

Still highly prized in our culture, although less practiced on both sides of the border is courtly behavior. Chivalry (if we only recall Rudolph Valentino as prototype of the Latino lover, the gallant cavalier, and the conquering, sheik all in one) was imported to Europe via Arab culture.

Although romance today has been grossly commercialized, women still are made to feel, primarily through mass media, that their lives may be enhanced and higher valued by the chase. This kind of romance further commodifies and objectifies the female as "object of desire", since her social worth appears dependent on the lover's courtly gestures and gifts.

There is no justification for machismo. Morally there never was, although given the economic system that civilization developed, society depended on patriarchy to uphold its political and economic principles of exchange. Machismo, has lost its raison d'être, as has the very nature of the way that present society functions. We must not feel inclined to long for a mythical time when man, in the form of father (God), protected women.

TRANSCONTINENTAL AFFINITIES. Although born and raised in the United States, I feel more affinity with the feminist writings of Egyptian Nawal el Saadawi than white American feminists, such as the famous American radical, Kate Millett. I find more in common with post-revolutionary Algerian women than the women who were part of the sexual revolution of the 1960s in the United States and Northern Europe. Spanish culture and my indigenous blood are at the root of my empathy. The immediate reasons for my connections are racism and classism. Due to my mestisaje I descend from a labor force long exploited by Anglo capitalism; therefore, it is true that I have certain social bonds with women of "third world" countries.

But confrontations with present day colonizers did not satisfy my quest for the origins of the particular machismo that informs our gender roles within our social networks, the nuclear family, extended family, and the community at large. The Catholic Church and the impossible dichotomy of Virgin Mary who was both chaste and a mother have long contributed to the formation of our attitudes as Mexicans. However, a historical overview informs us that the conquistadors who brought their faith to the Americas were freeing themselves from eight hundred years of Islamic domination. The Spanish conquistadores, who were not all doctors of theology to be sure, must certainly have brought with them customs not directly dictated by their Catholic faith that were nevertheless supported by the church. A prime example of what I mean that followed both Conquests, the Conquest of Spain and the Conquest of México, would be the Muslim and Catholic obsession with female virginity. Woman as property controlled by male society predates both religions throughout the Mediterranean for centuries.

By the same token not all Arab conquerors of Spain and the Mediterranean were theologians. Many beliefs and mores brought to Spain and instated in the name of Islam were a legacy from ancient Moorish society. Many customs historically attributed to Muslims predate Muhammad's teachings by centuries. The Muslim practice of circumcision, which is almost synonymous with baptism, is an exam-

ple of this; there is evidence that circumcision was practiced throughout the Mediterranean world one thousand years before the birth of
the Prophet.

The same period of the Reconquest of Spain was that of the
Spanish Conquest of the Americas. Spaniards today acknowledge the per-
vasiveness of Moorish influence in their culture, especially in the south
of Spain. But in the Americas, particularly those of us who are born in
the United States, who know so little of Mexico, less of Spain, and
even less of Spain's history, would not identify our kinships as having
anything to do with North Africa.

What we, who are oriented in Mexican Catholic culture have in
common, above all, with the people of North Africa whose cultures
predate both religions, is the historical seclusion/exclusion of woman
from society's economic system of exchange and a longer tradition of
female seclusion/exclusion at all levels of society. This ancient system
includes the early bartering of women and infiltrated every level of
society as it evolved.

Today, we consider much of our behavior resulting from those old
traditions to be human nature. Jealousy is a good example of this. We
often perceive that it exists in all of us to one degree or another and
generally accept it as part of the "Latin temperament." But jealousy, as
we will discuss more fully later in this chapter, is also a manifestation of
a philosophy and economy based on ownership, and woman has been
long counted as man's property. In some cases, when certain behavior
must be regulated or justified, monogamy, for example, religion has
mandated it to be sacred. The regulation of female fidelity from a
historical economic viewpoint had more to do with man's view of
woman as property and his children as heirs to his property than a
transgression of love and morals. These examples, along with others
that I will discuss all have their roots in the early tribal societies, which
predate Catholic and Islamic religions and which were practiced for
thousands of years by our "ancestors," los moros, on the continent of
their origins, Africa.

Nawal El Saadawi, the Egyptian Marxist-feminist who has written extensively on the oppression of Arab women and whose books
were banned in her Egyptian homeland, claims that the "unnatural
oppression and super-exploitation" of woman for centuries evolves

from the fact that indeed woman *is* powerful and as such, men have reason to fear her.[7] For like the Christians, the Muslims also are told to believe in the origin of the first man and woman in the story of Adam and Eve. Woman is the embodiment of evil because of her pursuit for knowledge or more likely, because of her desire to retain her knowledge as the mother goddess.

The version of the myth taught to Christians and Muslims alike for centuries, was that woman is the embodiment of evil as a result of her disobedience to God/Allah. But just as Nawal El Saadawi and certain white feminist Christian theologians have noted, the plot is full of holes. It is thought by these scholars, who believe that humanity's origins may be found in the pre-recorded history of matriarchy and Goddess worship, that the Book of Genesis was and remains woman's strongest document to establish once and for all when patriarchy was installed as the modus operandi for the whole of humanity.[8]

What one is left to consider, therefore, is that there were specific customs formulated and adhered to since early recorded history in a particular part of the globe that were passed down and spread to peoples across continents over the centuries. The anthropologist Germaine Tillion puts forth the hypothesis that much of what constitutes Mediterranean and Latin cultures, traditions, and even religious beliefs originated out of a geographical region and civilization known as the Maghreb. The ancient culture of the Maghreb originated in North Africa, spread throughout the Mediterranean, and as a consequence of the conquest of the Americas via the Spaniards, to the Southwest United States, Latin America, and the Caribbean.[9]

My own hypothesis regarding the connections we have as Mexican Catholics with ancient strains in North Africa predating Islamic religion, will be scaffolded by Tillion's argument as an ethnographer. By scaffolding I mean a provisional structure from which we may try to see across the centuries and continents how humanity has evolved and connected through migration and time. The Maghreb since ancient times have been divided into two groups, agricultural and nomadic. Their society is defined by two main features, preferential marriage between cousins in the paternal line and a politics of natality, "race" and conquest. Geographically they have resided along the area in the world that we term today as the "Cradle of Civilization," not necessarily including Egypt. Their ill defined territories are west of Egypt, while those people known as the Levants are east of Egypt, and Egypt serves as the border country between these two cultures. The Maghreb people include all those whose language and culture are Berber-Arab. They reside in five states on that continent including Morocco, which is where we have a direct connection with the Moorish Conquest of Spain.

Records of the Maghreb may be traced to Egyptian inscriptions 3,000 years prior to our era. They still exist today, although because of urbanization and immigration, as is the case throughout the post-industrial world, many of the Maghreb practices that I will discuss here in connection with our own Catholic orientation and Latin traditions, are in the process of degeneration.[10] Because of similar reasons, in addition to the influence of feminism, these "traditions" in our own culture are also in the process of change.

As a consequence of our Spanish Catholic heritage, connections we have with the ancient North Africans (not necessarily Muslim) are:

1. (nuptial) jealousy
2. (family) vendettas
3. privilege (and responsibility) of first born male
4. brother's (male cousin's) defense of sister's honor
5. the patrimonial ties to incest
6. male sexual obsession as a result of female seclusion (making women forbidden) at the same time obliging males to "come on" to any female they are alone with
7. romance: the objectification of the female as enigma and aggrandizement of the male's prowess and virility
8. brotherhood society
9. the origins of a certain type of "racism"

These commonalities are also found in Greece, Italy, parts of France, Spain, Latin America, and the Caribbean. My hypothesis regarding our own culture is based on our historical socioeconomic practice of patrimony (the passing down of property through the father). Patrimony predates both Muslim and Christian religions. I will elaborate on the list above in the following pages by way of explaining my hypothesis.

ANCIENT ROOTS OF MACHISMO

IN ALL COUNTRIES INFLU-
ENCED BY THE ANCIENT
CUSTOMS of the Maghreb, in
some cases, even into the twentieth
Century, a man, whether father,
brother, or husband, who has murdered a woman suspected of adultery was automatically acquitted by
public opinion.

In Italy, for example, a law of a
minimum three-year prison sen-
tence for such killings was finally
passed.

The Commandments forbid murder (Holy Wars notwithstanding)
and the Koran prohibits the slaying
of an adulterous wife unless there are
several witnesses who saw the adultery committed. Yet, both Christians
and Muslims have ignored those
mandates of their holy books when
it comes to woman. With the subject of adultery, that is, "a violence
against man," comes jealousy. The
crimes of passion it visits upon
women might also be traced to the
ancient culture of the Maghreb.

While vacationing in Mexico in 1988,
I was overcome by fitful sleep. Each
night my innermost thoughts about
the patriarchy of Mexican society
manifested themselves in nightmares.
One such dream was of a primaher-
mana of mine. I shall call her here
"Ifigenia." She and I were like sisters
during our childhood. In the dream
she is telling me about a woman
whose husband has slit her throat
because she was discovered to have
been unfaithful to him. In the dream,
everyone feels bad for the slain
woman, but we understand that her
fate was predictable given society's
mandates.

The jealousy a Mexican man may have for his wife finds its roots
in a time when women were counted as man's property, much as a
cow was. Since women are bipedal and quick witted, unlike the cow
or other beasts of burden, certain "laws" sacred and secular, were
invented by man to control women's behavior.

Many women of our culture find jealousy in their male lovers
flattering. Regardless of its perversity and sometimes psychotic manifestations, jealousy demonstrates to some women their value. It assures
them of a secure position in society. Since women have had no real
social status in and of themselves; they have had to count on whatever
status they may receive as possessions of men.

AKIN TO THE TRADITION OF JEALOUSY and "crimes of passion" is the family custom of the vendetta. When I was in my early teens the cousin of a good friend was murdered by her husband. The husband, whom I also knew, worked at the local Y.M.C.A. as a teen counselor. He was young, handsome, and charming, and I was quite shocked by the whole thing. He spent about three months in prison and was released. The murdered cousin was an only child. It was to the mother's great sorrow that she had no sons and that her husband was too old to avenge her daughter's death by going after the murderer and getting the justice that the law did not provide. The customary question that comes to mind is, what did the murdered woman do . . . to deserve to die? And yet, we know that there is no justification for murder.

Physical and verbal abuse particular to our communities are only now being openly confronted. Such crimes against women have long been attributed to jealousy. In *Mejor Sola Que Mal Acompañada*[11] the standard definition of machismo has been reiterated: as the result of losing his self-esteem, a man turns his wrath on his wife and children.

Again, it is an erroneous assumption that a man who is not degraded on the basis of racism or other social prejudices is not capable of abusing those "beneath" him. I think of the Argentine film, *The*

Ifigenia as a young girl worked while in high-school and her out-going personality and natural beauty had promised her a life much different than the one led in the twenty years of her marriage. Instead, she stayed, by her husband's orders, behind closed doors. She was not allowed visitors, at least not without the permission and presence of her husband. She could not go out to earn wages, but has stayed home to raise their seven children. She keeps her home spotless, or at least gets it that way before her husband comes home from work. She must not go anywhere without permission and certainly not without all of her children. For several years, she was not allowed to have a telephone. On cold winter mornings, she warmed his trousers on the radiator before he stepped into them, when he was employed. On Christmas Eve, she alone kneaded pounds of cornmeal for the traditional holiday tamales. When her eldest daughter was old enough, she became the indispensable assistant. She is heir to her mother's household duties. She cooks, cleans, tends to the younger siblings under the strict supervision of her mother, like the new wife in a polygamous household. Ifigenia's husband has beaten her and abused her in public, as well as in front of her own relatives. He threatened her with a gun on at least two occasions. Her mother, my tía, says of her daughter's life: With so many children now, she is better off staying with the husband. Both Ifigenia and her husband were born in the United States and live there.

Official Story. In the film, the pro-
tagonist, a middle-class, white
woman, both educated and modern,
the wife of a government official,
enjoys a harmonious marriage. Her
husband is the authority figure and
shows his affection by providing
protection and a comfortable lifestyle. Discovering her husband to
be a torturer in the government's
dictatorship, she threatens to expose
him, and in that instant he brutally
turns on her.

Male control of women manifests
itself in many ways and to varying
degrees in any given society. My
point here is that the issue lies in an
archaic system of patrimonial culture, not in "good" or "bad" forms
of male protection, "good" or
"bad" providers, that is, "good"
or "bad" machismo.

Let us review. A man, defeated by the limitations of success in
Anglo culture, may "rationalize" his abuse of his wife and justify it
with psychotic accusations of betrayal. This jealousy is a symptom of
our hierarchical "civilization," but it is also a trait permitted by society
and handed down to us throughout the millennia. It has been methodically woven into our culture, customs, and social norms. Likewise, the
custom of vendetta, justice for crimes committed against one's family,
is shared by the descendants of the Maghreb civilization. And who
must assume the responsibility for such vendettas? Again, it is the men.
What is the purpose of the vendetta? Usually to save family honor, that
is, to regain some material loss; women are counted as man's material
property. The male members of a family are responsible for a vendetta;
in the case of an absent father, the task usually falls on the eldest
brother.

SONS

*The Muslim household is made up of the king, the queen, the pig, and
the beast of burden. The king is the baby, the queen is the mother, the
beast of burden is the father, and the pig is the elder brother.*
—*Tlemcen proverb*

Let us first look briefly at the similarities throughout the regions
influenced by the Maghreb in regard to the privileges of the first born
male, the preference of sons, the making of future *paterfamilias,* in other
words, machos. All women of Mexican background would agree that
1) there is a propensity in families to give preference to first born sons,
2) these sons enjoy a degree of privilege and power over all other
siblings, and 3) the mother of such sons becomes subordinate to them
as children grow into men.

Although *primogeniture* (the practice whereby the oldest son is the
exclusive heir) was abolished in France by the French Revolution, into
the early part of this century the custom of referring to the eldest
brother in the formal "vous" instead of "tu" was still prevalent. In
México, a custom also no longer widely practiced, was to refer to one's
elder brother with the "usted" form.

Throughout the Mediterranean, in Latin America and the Southwest, if a son experienced birth-given privileges, it traditionally was
also his responsibility to see to the welfare of younger siblings. Unfortunately, this latter custom is rarely carried out by first sons.

An example of such customs may
be cited in the well known novel
Bless Me Ultima by Rudolfo Anaya.
A revealing passage that demonstrates this point is at the end when
the young Antonio has overcome
the major philosophical conflicts
that plague his rites of passage.
When it is clear he will soon replace his father as head of the family, he sends his older sisters to their

Growing up, Ifigenia was often subject to poundings by her older
brother. When Ifigenia complained
to her mother, she was always told
that it was her brother's right to
"discipline" her.

room and he also gives his mother an order speaking to her "as a man for the first time." He is ten years old. Antonio is not the first born male but he is the only son left at home therefore such rights are defaulted to him.

Among the Arabs, as in Mexican culture, the last born male is not without certain privileges as well. However, such special treatment has its drawbacks when the child is displaced by the forthcoming birth of another child.

Until then, among his siblings he enjoys the most attention from the mother. Imminent displacement of the mother's doting affection, which may include being weaned, may cause the child to get sick. This illness in a region known as "Bône" in North Africa is known as "bouba-ran". Ba'ran means anus, and jealousy for the forthcoming child causes the anus to protrude.[12] Among Mexicans, this illness with similar symptoms also exists. It is known as chipil. Chipil is an emotional state of being that effects a small child, male or female. A child is said to be chipil when a new baby is brought into the household. Symptoms may vary but most commonly there is clinging to the mother and constant crying.

Ironically, years later when Ifigenia was married and the victim of her husband's violence, it was not the older brother who came to her defense but the younger. Her "baby" brother, a teenager, had become the head of the household due to the fact that although the father was present, he had become an alcoholic, dysfunctional, and therefore unable to contine in his role as authority and the older brothers had left home.

BROTHER'S DEFENSE OF SISTER'S HONOR Throughout the Mediterranean and wherever Iberian culture surfaces in the Americas, a great preoccupation

When Ifigenia was seventeen she was forced to quit high school to marry a young man her mother believed she had slept with. (The suspicion was based on Ifigenia's riding is still placed on female virginity, which given its absolute uselessness, more than ever, is a social neurosis. Virginity, like marriage and the monogamy it demands, have outlived the particular political circumstances that instated them. Woman, still essentially perceived as man's property, as well as the sacred model of Virgin Mother, continues to reinforce the moral standard of female chastity before marriage.

Through recorded history to the twentieth century, there have been many cases in Mediterranean, North African, and Latin American history where it has been up to the brother to regain family honor after a sister has supposedly lost her virginity out of wedlock. Muslim and Catholic families alike have not been strangers to murders of sisters by brothers who have accused them of shaming their family name with supposed disgraceful behavior.

alone with him in his car.) After a brief unsuccessful marriage, Ifigenia was back home. During the short interim between her first and second marriages, when she began dating the young man whom she subsequently married, Ifigenia could not go out to meet her new amor (who became the abusive husband mentioned above) without her younger brother as chaperon (the eldest had already left home). The family was protecting Ifigenia's honor as divorcée.

Even women who have been violently raped by a family member, have been murdered by brother or father, sometimes with the aid of the rapist-relative. The "honor" in question, however, is little more than a guise for the fact that the victim lost her monetary worth when she lost her virginity.[13]

In their article, "Women and Corsican Identity," Anne-Marie Quastana and Sylvia Casanova, state of Corsican society today,

> . . . 'protection' of women's virtue is a family matter mobilizing not only the father and mother but all the brothers, uncles, and cousins . . . the purity of women and the virility of men are the cardinal virtues that govern relations between the sexes in a traditional society. But when you say virility, you are saying

power, that is the capacity to protect the women in one's group from other men.[14]

In this article on traditional Corsican society, which is French and Catholic, the points I am making here regarding Maghrebian influences are exemplified. In another article in this same text, Maria Minicuci describes the case of an unmarried pregnant woman who is deserted by her fiancé, " 'Dishonor' and shame will strike the woman and her family who will choose to remove the 'guilty' woman to another village . . ."[15]

In our own culture, too, men's concern with women's virginity and faithfulness in marriage stems from an ancient time when the family's possessions—which included women—were of utmost concern. As with all the components of machismo discussed in this essay, the family's preoccupation with its women's "honor" has its roots, according to Tillon, in early tribal Maghreb society.

A tribe was related by blood. Women were saved for marriage to their cousins in order to preserve property and territorial claims. In endogamous (marrying within the tribe) societies, certain incest was not taboo. For example, in Egypt, Cleopatra was married to her brother. (She also murdered him, but that's another discussion.) In Israel, during the time described in Genesis, a distinction was made between the father's sister and the mother's sister. A man's father's sister was a potential wife for him, as were her daughters.

Woman, as an object of ownership, was and is always susceptible to being "conquered" by someone outside the family. For this reason, "good girls," (while they may not wear veils or be covered from head to foot on the street) must not behave so as to elicit aggressive male behavior that would jeopardize family honor, or as more popularly put today: "get them in trouble." By the same token, honorable men do not enter the home of a married woman when she is alone. Again, all of these customs can be traced beyond our own Mexican culture and our Catholic beliefs, to our early patrimonial roots which we share with women in other parts of the world.

THE BROTHERHOOD In all of this, a bond between men has existed that overrides all pretensions to protect woman and guard her honor. This bond refers to male ownership and dominance over all things. For things to have value in man's world, they are given the role of commodities. Among man's oldest and most constant commodity is woman.

It was necessary for man to dispense with endogamy as a socially accepted form (therefore making incest taboo) in order to advance the evolution of today's commercial system. Meanwhile, woman's role as man's possession to exchange according to his needs, has remained basically the same.

French feminist Luce Irigaray proposes that the historical system of brotherhood to which I refer, is in fact, "hom(m)o-sexual" in nature.[16] Heterosexuality, the only acceptable sexual relationship in our society, "is nothing but the assignment of economic roles . . . For in this culture the only sex, the only sexes, are those needed to keep relationships among men running smoothly." While incest has been deemed unnecessary for today's commerce, and therefore forbidden, she notes "the exemplary case of father-son relationships." While an older male and young male may display pederastic love in every way but sexually, to make them explicit would disrupt our commodity based system. That is, the labor force and all its products are commodities to be given value by men and exchanged by men, but men themselves cannot enter into the present system as commodities. Overt homosexuality would disrupt the system in which men are not commodities but agents of commerce and is therefore made a social taboo.

In this system of brotherhood, all transactions are done by man, and women are among their bartering products. The woman does not exist except as an object of transaction to serve the present market. Since woman in and of herself does not exist in society except through male perception, Irigaray argues, then all acknowledged relations are between men. "Reigning everywhere, although prohibited in practice, hom(m)o-sexuality is played out through the bodies of women, matter, or sign, and heterosexuality has been up to now just an alibi for the smooth workings of man's relationships with himself, of relations among men."[17]

"POR LA RAZA TODO, AFUERA DE LA RAZA, NADA":
EARLY ROOTS OF RACISM AMONG THE BROTHERHOOD
Endogamy, practiced in the ancient world of clan alliances, offered a

mysterious bond of blood that to this day, in our familias, implies by birthright the unconditional support of relatives.

In New Mexico, many of the original hispano Catholic families share this type of socioeconomic history. Erlinda Gonzáles-Berry, a native nuevo mejicana and professor of Spanish and Chicano literature at the University of New Mexico, affirms this with regard to her own paternal line. Her paternal grandfather, she remembers, was once a large landowner who was considered a benevolent patrón, parcelling land out to other familias for homesteading. He and his wife were first cousins who received dispensation in order to be married by the church. In Northeastern New Mexico where Gonzáles-Berry grew up, she notes that there were basically five to seven families who owned most of the land and who intermarried for generations.

As endogamy throughout the world was replaced by exogamy with the spread of capitalism, which necessitated exchanges beyond the narrow geographical spheres of certain families, marriages to "foreigners" or that is, those not bound by the clan by blood, became acceptable, even preferable. Through marriage, of course, there is an eventual blood bonding. This along with claims to territories, developed the fraternalism of nationalism.

While a growing nation suppresses the conquered one, an ethnocentric (that is, racist) attitude has traditionally accompanied it. The power that the new nation acquires as a result of the combination of stolen knowledge and resources of the conquered race, geographical advantage, historical timeliness, technological or other material benefit—and always justified with a healthy dose of self-righteousness and divine conviction—has been justified by race supremacy.

As for the exploited populations of a given nation, strong blood bonding also persists. This bonding gives rise to resistance. This sense of nationalism, at both ends of the hierarchical spectrum, serves the perpetuation of ideas that espouse a world in which domination and subordination is an ineradicable fact of life. We see indications of this tendency within the early Chicano Movement. As mestizo/as the denigration we had been subjected to since the Conquest of México provoked a resistance that included racial pride. However, "La Raza," as we have used it, refers to our mestisaje, that is, we are a combination of Native American, European, Asian, and Arab influences. Even when incestuous marriage was the rule in patrimonial societies, it is difficult to speak of "purity" of races since conquest of peoples may be traced throughout recorded history.

It is understandable, even inevitable, that a people that has been subordinated by white supremacy would seek at some point retribution. It has been crucial for Chicano/as to reassert positive attitudes about our skin color, our indigenous background, our languages, and other aspects of our culture so reviled by WASP domination. However, the fundamental basis of nationalism is rooted in a divisive, aggressive, and destructive desire for material power. When we speak of machismo, we immediately refer to a division of power between male and female, between a world power and colonized nations.

It is of utmost importance to understand the damage that machismo has done and continues to do to humankind in the name of tradition and in the name of much that we hold sacred through institutionalized religion. We must recognize that certain behavior that has been accepted by our culture and sanctified by the church is not innate. Men are not born macho, they are made machos.

By the same token, while there are those of us who are critical of the way that machismo permeates our relations at all levels of society, there are as many among us who find feminism to have equally unappealing connotations. Those people, including women, regard feminism to be the same as machismo except acted out by females. That is, they believe to be feminist is to "want everything that a man has."

Machismo has divided society in half. It divides the world into the haves and the have-nots, those with material power and those who are rendered powerless. It has divided our behavior into oppositions, our spirituality regards Catholicism in dualistic terms of good and evil, and an economic world politic based on brute might. The feminine principle is not the opposite of machismo. "The feminine" may be generally termed as the *absence* of machismo—all the qualities that have been negated, denied, denigrated, and made to be essentially valueless by our society. Machismo has served to distort our perceptions of humanity, which includes the feminine.

Although the feminine has been so devalued by society it does not mean that the goal of feminism is to appropriate all "that a man has," on the basis that "everything a man has" is what has been given status, power, and value by our society. But the feminist struggle to restore value to the "feminine" could take as long as it has taken for us to believe that dualistic concepts are inherent in human nature and failing that, sacred. Thousands of years? No, there isn't time.

The starving populations of México and even in the United States, not to mention in the world, demand an urgent resistance to power and control of the majority of the population, and women, indeed, *are* the majority of the population. Among the labor force, women, particularly women of color, are among the majority. Among the poor, it is women again, and our children who have the greatest number living in poverty.

As a product of U.S. society, nevertheless with strong ties to my ethnic and mestiza identity, and as a woman of conscientización, I believe our views must expand to make world connections from which we will see that our particular culture has infinite affinities with other women, especially women who like ourselves, have for so long been denied a voice within our own societies.

I wonder if she recalls with my fondness when we were in the third grade after Catechism class after school, we had one hour of freedom during our long walk home. We were scabby-kneed little girls with long ribbon-entwined braids, brave with new English on our lips, chewing chunks of Mexican nun-baked bread given charitably to families like ours. Unconcerned with the scolding she'd get from her mother for getting home late (mine was at work), we stopped and played here and there as the sun went down over the city's horizon during our childhood long ago.

By voice, I don't mean one that echoes men's cry for social justice in the face of our racial conqueror, but one that truly articulates our particular experience in society. It is an invaluable step for our own personal transformation as Xicanistas as well as for our advancement in society as a people. It is important for us to understand our various histories so that we can better formulate our vision, but we need not look back for too long. There is nothing sacred about traditions that insist on the subjugation of vast populations on the basis of gender, class, sexuality, and race. Mexican/Chicano culture can survive critical challenges. Our world cannot survive without them.

1993 POSTSCRIPT

She came to see me at her mother's home, with only half her brood following behind like a row of ducklings. The oldest son, driven out of the home by his father when he turned eighteen, joined the Army and was stationed in Kuwait. The oldest daughter, too, was going into the Army as soon as she graduated high school. Ifigenia's husband has been on the wagon for the last two or three years now. She has taken a part-time job as a recreation counselor at the local park district.

We laugh, all the women, the mothers who are sisters, our sisters who are mothers, the men are strangely and visibly absent, in this reunion. There is plenty of food, arracheras, enchiladas, pastries. The vintage stereo plays scratched rancheras. She grabs me with old familiarity by the waist and pulls me in front of her when we take pictures, to cover her "fatness," she says. Her son, the one in Kuwait, has promised to send money so that she could get her own car. And he has, and she has. It is a brand-new recreation vehicle, big enough for everybody. When we leave, I watch her load up the little ones and drive off. Her license plate reads: Por Fin!

four
SAINTLY MOTHER AND
SOLDIER'S WHORE
THE LEFTIST/CATHOLIC PARADIGM

*In the nineteenth century, when the United States was leaping toward the
future with grand visions of expansionism, México was not ready for the
"future." Unlike the White, Anglo-Saxon Protestant, whose puritanism
shaped a democracy founded on capitalism, the Mexican comes from, in the
words of Octavio Paz: "a Catholic world of Mexican viceroyalty, a mosaic of
pre-columbian survivals and baroque forms."[1] Then, in the middle of the last
century, when certain Mexican intellectuals felt the very model of progress and
modernity lay just across the border—México was invaded and literally divided
in half by its model. In almost one fell swoop, the United States appropriated
territory greater than France and Germany together.*

But mestizas have had irreconcilable differences with WASP society that go much deeper than the issue of territorial invasion. In the
following pages I would like to discuss two doctrines that many
Chicano Movement activists in the seventies were motivated by—
consciously and unconsciously—in their struggle against WASP domination. These were a Marxist-oriented ideology (although it was not
as popular as the movement's nationalist overtones it was not necessarily separate) and Catholicism. I undertake this discussion because
many women still identify as Catholics and many feminists were first
exposed to socialist ideology as a way toward Chicana activism.

In the Watsonville chapter, I discussed the shortcomings of socialism for the mexicana turned activist. Although socialist feminists have
gone to great lengths to try to merge Marxist-oriented thought with
feminism, with the case of the mexicana/Chicana this is a highly
improbable course of action. First, the woman activista is not necessarily a feminist. Second, the communist stigma attached to socialism
causes most Latino/a activistas to shy away from even engaging in such
discussions.

On the other hand, she usually is Catholic. Here, we will see how
the male dominated Chicano Movement and the Chicana feminist

have been unavoidably influenced by the permeation of our culture by Catholicism, despite leftist and nationalist language and overtones. I don't mean to imply here that Marxist-oriented thought by any means at any point had a real measure of influence among Chicano/a activists. The number of individuals who participated actively in the Chicano/Latino Movement who also identified as Marxist-oriented were relatively few in number. Moreover, Marxist theory is only about 140 years old and has hardly had the chance to be fully realized in the few countries in which it was attempted, while Catholicism, centuries old, as an institution has been a world power. Consequently today, Catholicism is synonymous with Mexican society.

Nevertheless, the very fact that the Chicano/Latino Movement (just like the Black Power and the American Indian Movements) was engaged in the active struggle for our civil rights—denied to us for centuries through institutionalized racism—caused it to be seen by the federal government as a threat to *democracy* and to be identified as communistic. The late sixties and seventies are marked by murders, political imprisonments, and harassments of leading activists (men and women) from movements that challenge the United States to live up to its democratic promise.

The systematic quashing of the Chicano/Latino Movement that resounded throughout Latin America wherever Latino activists made alliances, resulted in the 1980s in a new generation bred on doublespeak. Many Latino/as who came of age during the 1980s not only did not believe in the premise of collective action but rejected it for the individuated free-enterprise one espoused by WASP ideology. Moreover, they disowned the Chicano/Latino Movement for being what they understood as unnecessary radicalism, engendered by unsophisticated grass-roots revolutionaries with huge chips on their shoulders. In the communities, activism also waned due to the severe cutbacks for community related programs, such as rehabilitation training, as well as because of the economic depression, and gang and drug-related violence that followed.

Conditions of people of color in the United States, Latin America, the Caribbean, and elsewhere throughout the world have increasingly grown worse since the successful dismantling of the Chicano/Latino, Black, and American Indian Movements by the United States government. Furthermore, at this writing, with the dissolution of the Soviet Union, the capitalist enterprising of China, and the strangling of Cuba, it may be said that the United States has successfully rid the world of any real "communist threat."

Although, as I stated above, most activists were not self-identified as communists, Marxism grants the right of the masses to rebel while indisputably the "free-enterprise democracy" of multinational interests does not desire, and will not tolerate, retaliation from its sea of underpaid human resources in this country and throughout the world. Although a response to the exploitation of human and natural resources by gross capitalism is needed, I will focus my arguments in the following pages on how the omission of the feminine principle in both Marxist-oriented ideology and Christianity prohibit woman's full participation in society. More precisely, omission of the feminine principle in society prohibits true social transformation, that is, one based on inclusion and not exclusion.

Inherent in both doctrines—Christian and socialist—that influenced Chicana conscientización is a male-dominated perspective. With examination and review Xicanistas may conclude that the merging of feminism and socialism may not be considered as the sole plan of action. By recalling the long forgotten ways of our Amerindian heritage, we will be led back to a view that all things created in the universe are sacred and equal.

The U.S born and national mexicana, in most cases, is very far removed from her Amerindian ancestors, although she may look very india, feel india, and be regarded as negatively as Native American women are regarded in dominant society. Unlike white feminists who freely borrow myths and rituals from the Eastern and Western traditions and investigate Native American traditions, especially in how they are connected with the feminine principle, we do not feel comfortable laying claims to Amerindian ways. As Christianized mestizas we have been conditioned for generations to reject our indigena blood, as well as invalidate folk medicine for Western medical practices and, above all, to put our faith in God the Father.

However, the feminine principle to which I refer is concerned with preservation, protection—especially of the young and less fortunate—and affiliations of communities for the common good. This positive feminine, which lies within both man and woman, is best recognized in our devotion to Tonantzin/la Virgen de Guadalupe. Our particular ancestors in Tenochtitlan worshipped Tonantzin. Jesus Christ the blameless, incarnated God and revolutionary, and God the Omnipotent Father, whom we fear, remind us to stand guard against men, against ourselves, so fallible and capable of betrayal. But only by calling forth the Virgen de Guadalupe/Tonantzin—the feminine principle within ourselves—do we truly receive courage. It comes from her unconditional compassion and acceptance, not from our fear of inadequacy. And as we receive from her, so denigrated and rendered powerless by the Church, state, and men's movements—except to serve their cause— we first give to ourselves, those around us, and to the world. It is a natural law and knows no doctrine.[2]

THE CHURCH HAS A VAST HISTORY OF DOMINATION throughout the world. Most women activistas were aware, at least to an extent, of the ruthlessness of the Spanish Inquisition and the persecution of countless Amerindians as a result of the Conquest. In fact, the Inquisition lasted approximately three and one-half centuries and with the conquest of the Americas, "new heretics" were seized upon: the indigenous populations. Although there seems to be no way of knowing just how many people were tortured and murdered as heretics throughout Europe and later in the Americas as a direct cause of the Inquisition, it is agreed by most historians that an overwhelming majority were women.

Conquest/ Conquista — dares

    The Roman Catholic Church once stood indisputably as a wealthy and political world power. It was no less intent on accumulating wealth in the Americas than it had been throughout Europe. Little, if any consideration was given to the native peoples who were at first regarded as less than human and used strictly for labor. "Central México, which had once had some 25 million inhabitants, was reduced, it is estimated, to a residual population of one million."[3]

    The marginalized Amerindian living a subsistence existence in present México is the descendent of the Amerindian slave of colonial México. The mestiza today, descendent of this heritage, has been shunned for being of mixed blood in México, the United States, and elsewhere. Such are the resounding effects of the imperialist world power that the Roman Catholic Church once was and that, with the Spanish monarchy, conquered indigenous México.

Yet, Chicana activists, fervent about their struggles against racism and sometimes sexism within and outside El Movimiento, have donned the white gown symbol of virginity, veiled their faces, and taken marriage vows at the Church's holy altar to sanctify their lives and to fulfill its doctrine. They attend its Mass, observe original sin by having their children cleansed of it during baptism, are soothed by its rituals. And because of their political consciousness they struggle with their worship of the indomitable Father and the overtones of female shamefulness that are imbedded in the Catholic Church's doctrine.

Since Mexican culture is also hierarchical, women are made answerable to figures of authority in their immediate world. With regard to the low status of mestizas in society, most women in El Movimiento may not have openly rebelled against the church's teachings, if for no other reason than because to oppose the Church would mean causing conflict within her own family and community.

IN THE 1970S a move from Catholicism to a socialist-communist idealogy for a Chicana activist in El Movimiento may not have seemed so contradictory to her inherent beliefs. The two ideologies have several qualities in common: the polarities of good and evil (U.S. imperialism representing evil or sin, the masses organized through socialism representing the good); a deference paid to a higher good (God for Catholicism and the needs of the pueblo as defined by the male leadership of the Chicano Movement); and the respect that both have for patriarchal order and hierarchy.

While radical groups publicly denounced the church for its institutionalized oppression of our people ("Although more than half of the Catholics in the Southwest are Chicanos, the Catholic Church hierarchy has continuously insulted its Chicano membership by its racist practices . . ."[4]), many activistas categorized religious traditions as part of Chicano culture in their urgent desire to induce immediate social change.

Some radical activistas in addition to ideologically rejecting the church, moved toward indigenismo and began to practice Native American and Mexic Amerindian ways. But most activistas went on

living their lives, which remain today affected by family and community and generations of Mexican customs. They worked in government-funded jobs in their barrios in Chicago and on Christmas Eve made tamales with mothers and tías and went to Midnight Mass. They started bilingual pre-schools in San Francisco and stood up as the Maid of Honor at their best friend's wedding. They painted socially relevant murals in San Diego and sponsored a niece for her quinceañera. And when a family member died in Texas or a new one was born in Michigan they went to church to have the appropriate ritual performed for their loved one. Roman Catholicism permeates Mexican culture and Mexican traditions exude Catholicism.

In the late sixties and in the seventies—as has been well established by many a feminista today—the leadership of the Chicano Movement was in the firm grip of the men, many of whom espoused a leftist ideology. In spite of the male leader's commitment to Marxist-oriented ideology, his immediate world was informed by Catholicism: A child who is cleansed of original sin through baptism, then receives the sacrament of the Holy Ghost when he is about seven years old (the age of reason), is then sent on to accept in full conscience the teachings of his faith through confirmation. The Catholic Chicano's godparents are often more meaningful than blood relatives because the relationship was sanctioned by *God the Father*. By the time he is a young adult his psyche is solidly influenced with the Christian principle of duality: life is divided into opposites. You are either good, doing good, represent the good, or you are bad.

The rituals of going to Mass every Sunday, Christmas celebrations, heterosexual marriages, and the children's baptisms that naturally follow are no less a part of his comprehension of life than the iconography that surrounds him in his environment. In his parents' home there may have been an altar, a crucifix above his headboard, the Virgin of Guadalupe everywhere (for it is said that all Mexicans are Guadalupanos), the whispers of rosary prayers over the sick, the constant exhortation to place one's trust in higher powers, not only in the Holy Trinity, but in the retinue of God the Father's heavenly saints who will guide and assist him through the rigors of life and on to paradise in the afterlife.

The idea of eternal life or the existence of the soul does not belong exclusively to Catholics. We know that church officials in México after the Conquest argued as to whether Amerindians indeed had souls, but indigenous philosophy also recognized life after death. These beliefs have been inherent in the mestizo/a's way since pre-Conquest times. The soul is a Mexican reality.

However, the materialist analysis of Marxism that addressed the economic exploitation of the working class (Chicanos adapted it with a specific focus on racism) did not acknowledge spirituality. The failing of Marxism lies in its inability to separate spirituality from the collusion of institutionalized religion with male-supremacist, profit-based society. When Marxist-oriented activists thought they had freed themselves from the church's strangle hold and surrendered to materialist theory, how many were actually convinced of their existentialism that denied all questions of non-material nature?

Leftist ideology did not resolve or reconcile this conflict for the activista. In terms of internal critical issues that contributed to the eventual dissolution of the early Chicano Movement, I believe that prominent among them was that most activistas could not fully assimilate socialist views that were exclusively based on materialism. Although there were pretensions on the part of politically conscious activists to reject Christianity, it remained an ongoing undercurrent of our Chicanismo because of its permeation of Mexican culture. In addition, for the Chicana, especially, both forms of thought meant a reinforcement of patriarchal oppression. As for those women activistas who did join the male calvary's call to socialism—how did they take to socialist-communist ideology? Imagine a Mexican Catholic mestiza in the United States replacing her religious beliefs with the convictions of non-Christian male thinkers, not simply the white Europeans Marx and Lenin, but also revolutionary leaders from Mao Tse Tung to Che Guevara. The fact is, most women who participated in the Chicano Movement could not.

In fact, most did not follow any specific political line. The early activista was usually pragmatic regarding her activism, moved by personal experiences and guided mostly by male hegemony. The most prominent figures of the Chicano Movement of that epoch were men, Cesar Chávez, Corky González, Reies Tijerina, and Luis Valdez, among others. Throughout all aspects of El Movimiento men set a revolutionary tone for what our roles as activists should be but, that tone was underwritten by the values and traditions of Catholicism; both were hierarchical and patriarchal.

A large number of women activistas subscribed to an equally animated sector of El Movimiento known for its cultural promotion of Chicano nationalism. In the late sixties to mid-seventies, we were asked to emulate the *past* in the role of the soldaderas of the Mexican Revolution, the young women who took up arms and followed their men, carrying a comal and molcajete in tow to feed the soldiers, as well as providing various other services—sex and picking up an escopeta to fight were not the least of them.[5]

In the spirit of cultural nationalism however, early activistas did in fact dress and behave appropriate to the role Chicano ideology assigned to them. Efforts to bring about egalitarian representation of women in that era were often patronizing at best. With the flamboyant defiance of Frida Kahlo (celebrated painter and wife of Diego Rivera, a "cultural nationalist" in her own time) women donned the rebozos of their Revolutionary grandmothers and the huipiles of their Amerindian heritage. Even though Frida Kahlo, most active in the thirties and forties, was notorious for her eccentric flair, it apparently was her husband who insisted that it would be an act of betrayal on her part to dress in North American gringo fashions.[6]

Poetry by men and women of that period called the pueblo to arms even as it urged women to stand by their men. Some women's poems, however, eventually surfaced to indicate that we were not all that satisfied with our new nationalist image. The poems were filled with ethnic pride but tinged with anger and frustration at the severe restrictions on our participation in El Movimiento. The following excerpt from Lorna Dee Cervantes' well known poem of that era, "You Cramp My Style, Baby", best highlights this point:

"You cramp my style, baby
when you roll on top of me
shouting, "Viva La Raza"
at the top of your prick.

. . . And then you tell me,
'Esa, I LOVE

this revolution!
Come on Malinche,
gimme some more!"[7]

In the Chicano Movement men's regard for women's activism went from dominance to condescending tolerance to finally, resigned confusion if not, outright resentment.

CULTURAL NATIONALISTS DID NOT HAVE A STRUCTURED IDEOLOGY

Like most poets and artists—of whom there were many—cultural nationalists found the black and white schema of social scientists constricting. As creative individuals, they did not articulate their criticisms (of broad society and of their own Movement) and their perceptions except through their often misunderstood and underestimated artistic endeavors. On the other hand, the Marxist-oriented activists suffered from the myopia of their nineteenth-century dogma.

Just as there were women actively working among the Marxist oriented activists yet getting little visible recognition, there were numerous women among the cultural nationalists who went ignored. It has not been until nearly two decades later that the public has become aware of the artistic and literary expressions of those women who have 1) remained steadfastly dedicated to their work as artists and writers and 2) turned to some strain of feminism to gain support as women for their perspectives. It is at this historical juncture that I define the activista as Xicanista, when her flesh, mind and soul serve as the lightning rod for the confluence of her consciousness. Xicanistas may also arrive at this consciousness from roads other than the ones discussed here, to be sure; and one generation later, young Xicanistas are contending with the polemics of the Bush-Reagan years that affected their generation. The regressive nature of the 1980s Republican era brought on a renewed macho vigor in that generation of males and many young women found themselves contending with the same sexist issues of their forerunners in El Movimiento. The resurgence of supermachismo lodged by the old Anglo leaders of the Republican Administration was equally conservative. This conservativism also influenced the thinking of the new generation. It was a return to the days of American glory when the Fords and Rockefellers were in the making. But that self-made millionaire potential was no more real for most U.S. Latinos in the 1980s than it was in the past. Nevertheless, this caused a major backlash against the Chicano tone of the seventies. While cultural pride remained, the Latino Movement's leftist collective fervor was subdued.

For the early activistas, remaining steadfastly dedicated to our own work has been no small feat. Oftentimes, we were married and had children. We had to work to help support our families; frequently, we were unable to get financial help from relatives. At the same time, we may have been attempting to get a college education on a government grant, loan, or academic scholarship. By and large, we did not identify with the white woman's movement and therefore received no intellectual verification of the injustice we felt as women. We experienced social and religious constraints with relation to our roles as daughters, lovers, and mothers. In addition, women sometimes had to live with alcoholism, drugs, physical and mental abuse: no resources and no recourse but to manage however we might.

The strength of our collective resistance to dominant society motivated us onward. In a similar nationalist spirit as that of the Black Power Movement, which also "returned" to its roots, we refused to cut our long braids, to conform to standard English for the sake of being tokenized in the job market. We gave our children pre-Conquest names like Xochitl and Cuauhtémoc, tirelessly volunteered in our barrios and started health clinics and daycare centers. To affirm our mexicanidad and to give us courage we resurrected every pre-Conquest and Catholic icon, ritual, symbol possible—from the Aztec calendar to the Virgen de Guadalupe banner.

All the while, we wrote poems, we painted, we told stories. Many women who showed great creative promise did not continue. Some were forced to stop. Some went mad. Others died. We know who they were; we remember their names. We know how well or how bad their children turned out. The fiery conviction that made women refuse to assimilate into the white dominant culture took its toll.

The new generation of women who followed suit have these obreras culturales as unprecedented models who served to validate their own perceptions. The young Xicanista (not just Chicana, not activista for La Raza, not only a feminist but Chicana feminist) now has documentation of her particular history and present condition in the United States in the form of books, plays, murals, art, and even films that the culturalists have produced.

WOMAN REMAINS DEFINED BY RELIGIOSITY

Above, I held forth the view that early Chicano activism was influenced by socialist ideology but remained Catholic. Most women were not as apt to follow any socialist line, however as they were inclined to assert a pride in their ethnicity, that at the extreme end became Chicano nationalism. Even among the minority who "returned" to indigenismo so as to more adamantly reject Western culture and white supremacy, it was difficult to eradicate Christianity from their lives because Christian symbols and beliefs have infiltrated many indigenous practices, family and community ties remained Catholic, and many Mexican customs are tied to Catholicism.

However, the point I would like to stress in this chapter is *not* that socialist doctrine as it has been practiced in other countries and within the Chicano Movement has not shown itself to truly liberate women. My point is also not the historical abuse of women and indigenous people by the church, nor that today, its most repressive mandates are in relation to women. What I would like to emphasize here (and throughout this book) is that beneath the definition established by the cultural fervor of Chicanismo was and remains a significant component of the mestiza's identity—her spirituality. For the most part, as stated above, this manifests in her life in the form of Catholicism because it is the religion she has been taught and that is sanctified by society. However, this undercurrent of spirituality—which has been with woman since pre-Conquest times and which precedes Christianity in Europe—is the unspoken key to her strength and endurance as a female throughout all the ages.

While we do not acknowledge other important influences so readily, our religious orientation is a combination of Christianity, Amerindian, and African influences, but primarily passed on to us through the filter of Mexican Catholicism. Although the Catholic Church as an institution cannot, for a number of reasons, guide us as Mexican

Amerindian women into the twenty-first century, we cannot make a blanket dismissal of Catholicism either. Rejecting the intolerant structure of the church does not automatically obliterate its entrenchment in our culture.

LIBERATION THEOLOGY

If some activistas have agreed that traditional Roman Catholicism is not a satisfying religious doctrine to serve the needs of their communities, alternative ways to apply their Christian beliefs have been considered, such as liberation theology.

This re-vision of the Catholic activists is mostly heard of today within the context of revolutionary work in Latin America. In the United States many Latinos, Amerindians, and Chicanos are also being forced to reflect on the role of the church in their lives and communities because it has not only added to their devalued social status, but also suppresses their intuitive spirituality.

In this section I would like to discuss the liberation theology movement as it affects us as Xicanistas. I use two sources here that speak directly to us about this subject and compare and contrast how men and women see this movement with regard to Latinos in the United States. Liberation theology in practice is a blend of Marxist and Christian beliefs. However, both ideologies are male-centered, have hierarchical structures, and significantly repress the feminine principle that is crucial to our spiritual and material aspirations as Xicanistas. I discuss these issues more fully in other chapters and prominently in chapter 7.

It has been noted by white feminists that women experience culture differently from men to the extent that some of them consider themselves "bicultural." Likewise, the women in the Chicano Movement experienced their struggle for social justice differently from the men. Likewise, we experience institutionalized religion differently.

According to the Chicano cosmic consciousness, woman was defined by the religiomythology of the Mexica pantheon; in everyday practice, the Mexican mestiza was defined by Catholicism. Because male and female activists used Mexican models they could not escape from defining woman in religious terms. By doing this they ignored the fact that both sixteenth century Aztec society and Spanish Catholic culture treated females as commodities. The role of mestizas in both societies was to serve the economy: with her labor and her children. Each religion perpetuated this role by divinely sanctioning it.

The Marxist oriented activist of the Chicano Movement may have claimed to address women solely from a materialist perspective but he was nevertheless still regarding woman in religious terms—and those religious terms subordinated woman in Chicano culture.

An example of how male activists differ in their view of women's experiences may be found in Andres Guerrero's book on Chicano liberation theology, *A Chicano Theology* published in 1987.[8] In contrast to the methodology employed by Isasi-Díaz and Tarango, in their book *Hispanic Women's Theology: A Prophetic Voice of the Church,*[9] who took great care to propose a theology that was relevant to those women whose lives are directed by their religiosity by surveying women who are actively changing Catholic thinking, Guerrero chose as his informants nine individuals whom *he* considered to be spokespersons for the varied communities to which our people belong throughout the United States: "The Chicano experience of oppression is best brought out, I believe, by Chicano leaders as they express their struggles, fears, and hopes for the Chicano community" (pp 33–34). It is important to note here a patronizing attitude in Guerrero's approach. First, he has *designated authorities* to represent millions of Catholic Chicano/as and second, he presumes that these designated authorities can speak for the needs of millions of Catholic Chicano/as by solely addressing the racist and economic inequities they experience in the United States. Guerrero's leaders are selected from among activists of the Chicano Movement of the 1960s and early 1970s. Their achievements notwithstanding, we now have an entirely new generation largely incognizant of the work many of Guerrero's respondents performed more than two decades ago. More significantly, we now have new voices emerging that are reassessing our vision as a people based on a current summation of the past twenty years.

Among those nine individuals whom Guerrero interviewed, some well recognized for their long-time commitments toward improving the living conditions of certain communities of ours, only two were women. Two of the men were Protestant. Two were officials of the Roman Catholic Church.

"BY UNDERSTANDING GUADALUPE, YOU UNDERSTAND CHICANOS" (pg. 117). Guerrero sees la Virgen de Guadalupe as the symbol of hope for liberation. We are told that our Mexican patron saint will not forsake us despite our suffering, and we are asked to take a "leap of faith" in her. However, la Virgen de Guadalupe again is manipulated by men to serve nationalism, and historically, this has ultimately implied violent action. In man's society, a "Protectress" always condones war and sanctions nationalism.[10] The Catholic Church—the entire history of Christianity, in fact—has condoned the violence and destruction of its Holy Wars. Two of Guerrero's respondents, José Angel Gutiérrez (founder of La Raza Unida Party) and Ricardo Sánchez (poet), both advocated violence as a potentially necessary form of action when questioned on racism and how we might best contend with it in white society. Most significantly, Guadalupe is reinstated here as man's "mother." She is a deity who blesses men's aggression against their enemies and provides her devotees alone with her nurture, comfort, and protection.

On the issue of "machismo y la mujer," we hear (predictably) from the two women, Dolores Huerta and Lupe Anguiano. Their answers reflect the previous generation of Chicano activism but neither defines herself as a feminist in the interview. Both women acknowledged machismo in the movement and female oppression in the church. "The church has been responsible for a lot of the machismo because it does not do anything to counteract it," replied Dolores Huerta (page 40). The only male respondent whose opinion on the subject of women within the context of liberation theology we are privy to is Monsignor Reyes.

In an unfortunate demonstration of conservative male-centered thinking, Monsignor Reyes believes that *women contribute to their subordinate roles by orienting male children into a privileged position over females.* Completely unaware of feminist analysis on this subject, neither Guerrero nor Monsignor Reyes, seem to recognize that woman has been conditioned and directed toward perpetuating male privilege. Moreover, for centuries sons have had birth-given privileges that override their mother's own authority in the home. Monsignor Reyes sees woman as mother therefore the "maker" of men. Women do not make men, women bear and raise their children. It is society that makes men and women. In a traditional Mexican household, for example, a father will order his children to obey their mother. (*¡Hazle caso a tu mamá!*) One is given the impression that the mother holds some authority in her home. Note however, that the children are not obeying the mother so much as following the father's order. More significant than this small example of the dynamics of traditional Mexican homelife are the countless ways in which sexism is enforced in society: by the media, various civil and private institutions, as well as the male-dominant hierarchical structure of the Church and government.

Although all nine individuals were asked the same questions, we do not hear from the others on the subject of male dominance. Likewise, we are not always privy to the responses of the two women on other themes. Recalling Gutiérrez's and Sánchez's advocacy of violence as a possibility in bringing about social reconstruction, we are left to wonder what their particular views were on the subject of "machismo y la mujer." Let's keep in mind that a large measure of the work force requiring social justice is composed of women who, if they protest their conditions, are ultimately terrorized by men recruited into police forces and armies. With what—or rather—how, are dispirited, underpaid people supposed to fight men trained, armed, and sent out to torture and kill on behalf of their government's interests? Haven't we witnessed such massacres of obreros in Latin America within our own lifetimes? Furthermore, governments have shown no tolerance for those liberation theologians who have attempted to defend the rights of the poor.[11] The outright assassinations among the Catholic clergy—Archbishop Romero gunned down while giving Mass is one shining example of this. What phallocentric ego could imagine this suicidal strategy as the basis of a religious ideology? Nevertheless, according to Guerrero, the opinions of these nine respondents are the "valid and viable groundwork for creating a new Christian theology."

A Chicano Theology serves as evidence of the paternal attitude inherent in our culture among those, including those on the left, who elect themselves as our representatives. Chicanos cited Engels's claim that half of the work force consisted of females and today, more than half of the world's work force, in fact, consists of women. Moreover,

half of the world's Roman Catholics are Latin American, and I would
venture to state that at least half of that membership is female. Therefore addressing women directly on the subject of social injustice is
crucial. Women do not want to take up arms against soldiers and
police. Women do not want to be subject to non-consenting sterilizations by government and private industry officials. Women do not
want to have infants with no medical care. Women do not want to
give up their faith in a higher being despite their dismal circumstances
because it is that very faith that often keeps them from despair.

Guerreto sees feminists as a "special interest group" marginalized
by dominant society along with ethnics of color. Whereas in the early
days of the Chicano Movement, feminists were still associated with
white dominant culture, there is substantial documentation now by
women of our culture who are also feminists and could have lent this
text the benefit of new insights.

While the book as a whole espouses a theology that demands
some restitution on the part of the United States government for the
poverty and the racism to which our people are subjected, its approach
is clearly reminiscent in language, tone, and attitude of the rhetoric
widely used in El Movimiento's heyday. It is difficult to imagine that it
realistically aims to communicate with the present generation, with
women-identified activistas, or with the majority of today's low skilled
work force who are poorly educated, impoverished women.

In Guerrero's book, women are misread and underestimated—
again—by male activism; he seems hardly aware of the male dominance embedded in his proposed Chicano liberation theology. The
"leadership" that he identifies in his book, for the most part suffers
from a reluctance to rethink anachronistic Marxist-oriented convictions. When Guerrero requests a discussion on the theme of theology
as a mechanism that has historically served the needs of the "oppressor," his respondent, Tomás Atencio, a Protestant, replies, "The
best way to look at it is from a Marxist perspective . . ."

For the sake of holding on to their political beliefs at all costs (with
the same relentless devotion they have had for their Christianity), some
male leaders have caused their marriages and families to become dysfunctional. And again, women were left with children to raise with
little assistance from men or their professed beliefs.

"HISPANIC WOMEN'S LIBERATION THEOLOGY"

Ada María Isasi-Díaz and Yolanda Tarango state that "the self-definition of a vast number of persons is an intrinsic element of reality. The overwhelming majority of Latinas see themselves, understand themselves as, and claim to be Christians. The majority consider themselves Catholics even if they go to other churches."[12]

According to Isasi-Díaz and Tarango, women see their culture through "Christian" eyes on the one hand, and understand their Christianity through "culture," on the other hand. Religion, over the millennia, has remained the most significant structure in women's lives. It is not difficult to deduce that one who aspires to adhere to her Mexican identity will find it nearly impossible to do so if she dismisses the influence of the church

Isasi-Díaz and Tarango claim that Hispanic women's liberation theology *is* "Hispanic Women's experience." As such, it is a synthesis of all that informs her reality, including popular religiosity in the form of Native American and African religious practices. Women who do not want to give up their religion because it is too tied up with their identity are turning to their own experiences to understand their spirituality and the Christian form it takes for them. For example, a Xicanista may still believe in the Holy Trinity of the Catholic Church, yet, her feminism may lead her to give the Virgen de Guadalupe greater importance than God and his son, with regard to her personal faith. The Virgen de Guadalupe, again, while being relegated by the Church to a secondary role as the mother of Christ, is regarded by Xicanistas as spiritual mother and the successor of the Nahua goddess, Tonantzin. Therefore, the Xicanista combines the traditional view of the Christian god with goddess worship to give her a source of inner strength.

With the radical feminist notion that the personal is political, women throughout the world are developing a theology appropriate for them. Examination of concepts and attitudes in unprecedented ways is the kind of serious work that social change requires. For example, in *Hispanic Women's Theology,* the authors suggest that the passivity prevalent in women's culture no longer can be viewed as a weakness, but as a mode of survival. While strength has often been associated with aggression in our competitive world, cooperation and conciliation may actually prove more beneficial to society.

Women's liberation theology is also women's struggle against anything in society that prohibits her full participation and contributions as a human being—imago dei. Women who see man *and* woman created in the image of God and who believe that God is the perfect guide and example for how we should all lead our lives on this earth, would out of necessity question why they are not treated as humans who also can strive for perfection. Traditionally, only men could hope for perfection because they image God. Women could only aspire to salvation by negation of self, that is to deny femaleness.

Hispanic women's theology is valuable insofar as it attempts to reflect woman's reality to enable her to overcome material obstacles and to participate in a communal process with other women, her family, and community toward economic betterment within the ascriptions of her faith. However, I see women's liberation theology as problematic in the process toward human liberation, both of spirit and body. Philosophically, Christianity is based on the belief in a remote god (generally still accepted as a male: father), far removed from our mortal, material selves. He is an inimitable model since he is spirit and we are flesh; and yet, Christianity is based on the struggle that requires man to imitate God. Because of our "crime" of disobedience to this Father God we must strive for redemption. *To be born is a sin in itself.* The only time that God became flesh was through his son, Jesus Christ; and the New Testament and Catholic doctrine have taken great pains to teach us that woman had nothing to do with this birth.

Christianity is based on the dualistic principle and polarization of good and evil. Christianity *depends* on our desire to *disobey*: to rebel against the repression of the human spirit and the desire to create a balance out of the celebration of flesh and spirit—to experience a life of ecstasy. The word ecstasy itself, if not related to the passion and suffering of Christ, implies sin.

Marxism and Catholicism alienated humanity from its spirituality. While Marxism focused too narrowly on class and economic inequities and denied the existence of the soul, Catholicism has a history of implementing an attack on humanity in the name of God the Father. In 1993 the Pope has reiterated his position against contraceptives and homosexuality. The church only permits sex between husband and wife for the sole purpose of reproduction. The wildfire spread of AIDS demands, at the very least, that sexually active individuals *may* prevent its spread by using contraceptives. However, condoms are no guarantee against contracting HIV. According to Howard's International AIDS Index (as reported in *Elle* magazine) in 1994 70 percent of HIV cases are heterosexually transmitted and more than half of the victims are women. The church grants males sole authority, and these men to be worthy and holy must be kept from women.

The highest percentage of the Catholic faithful are women. Women are made responsible by government and church for the children they bear, who suffer all manner of disease and maladies from industrial poisonous exposure and poverty. Women are the lowest paid in the labor work force. The "proletariat masses" of whom socialists speak are mostly women. Women are spoken of and to by Church authorities, government officials, and male community leaders, but to date have had little voice themselves.

Socialist-communist doctrine as we have understood it in recent history and Christianity both fall far short as realistic responses to the urgent needs of most mexicano/as on both sides of the border. A sense of urgency may be gained from the example of México City, which is home to twenty one million inhabitants today, all of whom suffer from dangerous exposure to air pollution (the effects are equivalent to smoking a pack of cigarettes a day) and other polluted natural resources, and many, many, many people live there demoralized and in appalling poverty. México, D.F. is the most populated city in the world. People on both sides of the border suffer from similar dangerous and deplorable conditions, not to mention all the rest of us—from large cities like Los Angeles to small towns like Sunland Park, New Mexico.

COMMUNAL SOCIETIES EXISTED AGES BEFORE the rigid control of patriarchal Christianity and later, communist doctrine. A conservative viewpoint on behalf of some scholars and thinkers resists drawing conclusions about the possibility of matriarchal practices in pre-recorded history because of lack of conclusive evidence and because it is too controversial, or rather too threatening to what we have for so long accepted to be absolute truth in Western Civilization.

However, there is much worldwide archaeological evidence that proves the book of Genesis is a testimony of retaliation against the previous mythologies that associated woman with the power of creation. In fact, woman *did* create.[13] Aside from injecting his sperm into her womb, man's participation in the creative process is that of *observer.* With this in mind, we can understand why as male society took control—a long, long time ago—it felt it necessary to appropriate woman's "mysteries," along with her labor and her children. The Bible is composed of texts that could be used to argue any ethical or political point. But despite this fact, the Old and the New Testaments have shown indisputable contempt for women. Enrique "Hank" López writes, "Everyday throughout the world, millions of Jewish men utter a prayer thanking God for not creating them as women. There are, of course, millions of non-Jewish men who feel the same way, but their gratitude is not formalized in prayer."[14]

On the other hand, some progressive thinkers look to contemporary examples of indigenous matriarchal societies to prove that such cultures have existed and argue in favor of them because matriarchies are founded on preservation rather than on destruction and our planet and its inhabitants are in dire need of emergency conservation.

For too long we have been told what we are and why we are as women: mujeres mestizas (sino descendientes de sangre Europea, somos indias sin razón), católicas (sino ahora protestantes o pecadoras), social definitions embedded in a history that has subordinated the female gender.

Five hundred years ago the militant Mexicas knew they had lost their way and called to their/our Toltec ancestors as in the following ancient Nahuatl canto from mother to daughter: ". . . You will spin/ you will weave/you will learn what is Toltec/the art of feathers/how to embroider in colors/how to dye the threads . . ."[15] We must undo our anachronistic weave. Ultimately it may be a question of starting from scratch, gathering our own raw materials, applying our own dyes. Men (and the women who have been convinced of phallic worship) *will* learn to become humble participants in this process, to trust our millennia-old experience of cooperation and communion with every living organism. We will teach each other that submission need not be humiliating and that strength need not be synonymous with aggression.

five
"IN THE BEGINNING
THERE WAS EVA"

Even jade is shattered,
Even gold is crushed,
Even quetzal plumes are torn . . .
One does not live forever on this earth:
We endure only for an instant!

Perhaps we will live a second time?
Thy heart knows
Just once do we live!
—Nezahualcoyotl

AT THE TIME OF THE CONQUEST, in Tenochtitlan's neighboring Mexica city-state of Texcoco, the intellectual center of the Aztec Empire, a school of philosophy held the origin of all things was a single dual-based principle, which was both masculine and feminine. This god was called, Tloque Nahuaque, or Ipalnemohuani, "the god of the immediate vicinity," "that one through whom all lives."[1] Nezahualcoytl, king of Texcoco, philosopher, astronomer, scientist and poet, is credited for acknowledging the concept of a single creator. To be sure, this belief was not widely held by the populace; and I would like us to keep in mind that in our own times popular credences remain rooted in ideas many centuries old and not in the notions of contemporary poets and physicists. Be that as it may, the idea of duality at this point in Mexica history shows the tendency of the male mind to *split* his consciousness into opposing dichotomies, implying that we are divinely created with a dual nature.

It has been noted by some anthropologists that traces of Mexican matriarchy existed as recently as in the eleventh century during the Toltec civilization. But by the sixteenth century, the imperialism of the Mexica Empire had evolved to the point where the primary role for woman was to serve male-ruled society. Unlike certain egalitarian traditions still traceable in North American indigenous cultures,[2] the

Mexicas, while sophisticated with regard to the arts and sciences, were systematically subordinating the female gender—along with supporting their economy with slave labor. As in similar cases throughout recorded history, with the increase of nationalism woman's image became increasingly polarized along two juxtaposed positions of femaleness, which will be discussed in this essay.

THE MEXICA EARTH GODDESS, COATLICUE, SERVES AS A PRIME EXAMPLE[3] of comparison to the mythology of the Near East from which Judeo-Christianity descends. First, she is the earth goddess, goddess of fertility. She also represents death. With the rise of patriarchy, the gruesome side of death becomes more prevalent in her description. Her icon depicts her dressed with serpents; in the place where her head might be are two serpents that meet face to face. The serpent in global prepatriarchal religious practices was thought to control wisdom (magic), immortality, and fertility. As such, it was the special companion of woman, the creatrix of humanity, and it often guarded "earthly or celestial gardens of delight."[4] We see the parallel of Coatlicue not only to that of the pre-Judeo-Christian concept of the Mother of All Living Things and as Mary for Christians, but also in the idea of Woman upheld by Christianity in the myth of Eva.

In this discussion of Eve, the first model of a "real" woman that we have been provided by Catholicism, I would like to propose that three basic premises regarding mythology and religion be kept in mind: First, the mythology that has affected civilization in the last four to five thousand years was created out of the imaginations of men; second, its creation was dependent upon the needs of those men in power; and third, patriarchal mythology can be argued to have been based on a direct attack against woman as creatrix.

Before the writing of the scriptures, *real* women had for some time been subject to male authority. Woman was almost unexceptionally viewed as man's property, a tool by which to produce an heir, to provide him with her servitude, and to give sexual pleasure. Her representation, therefore, in his doctrines, literature, and art was by and large depicted to illustrate his ideas and to promote his continued power.

Throughout the world—from the Bronze Age in Crete to just

five hundred years ago in México (not to mention the present West)—
the tendency of patriarchy is an eventual phallocentric *rising* up of
structures, pyramids and high rises, unholy stones piled up, as men
separate themselves from other men to strive toward *higher* levels of
stature, always sanctioned by a Sun God *elevated* to the remote eternal
sanctity of the astros. Women, on the other hand, in their reproductive
role are methodically *lowered* in social status, *down* to the earth, *below*
the depths of the murky ocean. Their creations can mean nothing
because they are always tangible and transient, never lasting, they
eventually *die,* and are sent back *down* to the ground, where they do
not last but decompose.

THE SUBORDINATION OF WOMAN'S SEXUALITY was cru-
cial for the survival of patriarchal religious practices. Female sexuality
was viewed as perverse. A Hebrew myth illustrates this point as it
attempted, perhaps, to explain the ambiguity of the creation of two
women in the book of Genesis.[5] It refers to a woman by the name of
Lilith who was created before Eve and who became Adam's first wife.
Having been created at the same time as her husband she was not
prepared to be subordinate to him, specifically in the realm of their
sexual activity. She fled to the Red Sea where she fulfilled her sexual
desire with demons. It seems that Lilith desired oral sex; this, among
more significant aspects of her myth, has led some feminists to think
that perhaps Lilith was punished for being lesbian. According to
Jungian analyst, Karin Lofthus Carrington, in her anthology on gay
and lesbian unions, *Same Sex Love and the Path to Wholeness,* Lilith and
Eve represent an incestuous sister bond that precedes the patriarchal
split of woman as virgin/whore. For lesbian partners who see themselves retrieving the lost sister from whom they have been separated,
this myth may present the opportunity for healing that irreconcilable
separation.[6]

What is evident in the Lilith account, however is the obvious
repulsion the early patriarchs showed for the female body. According
to the story, her regret over her behavior prevented her from returning
to Adam. As she was not present in the Garden of Eden during the
Fall, she did not die. Instead, "She lives forever as a demonic, highly
erotic night spirit who snatches newborn children (particularly males)

and assaults the bodies and senses of men who sleep alone (presumably an explanation for erotic dreams)."[7]

Lilith was portrayed as a winged serpent. As late as medieval Europe, the serpent in paradise is pictured with a woman's head and breasts. Lilith portrayed as a snake, as in various other pre-Christian sources, represents goddess worship. In patriarchy, the snake goddess begins to connote death and destruction rather than the regeneration of life.

As Xicanistas and heiresses of a Christian based culture, the book of Genesis is *the* document where we may witness the male takeover of woman's autonomy. Tied to her economic autonomy was her reproductive ability; her children had belonged to her. The products of her labor in the fields belonged to her and were passed on to her children. In the Bible, woman's bloods, associated with birth (and death), were deemed contemptible taboos and replaced with the letting of male blood through circumcision, a false menses, an imitation of woman's association with all creation.[8] The Maya, who were once thought to be peace loving are now known to have been no less war prone than the Mexica who succeeded that civilization and Mayan priests also performed blood letting rituals. Blood from the penis was thought to reveal sacred messages. This genital blood letting I interpret as an imitation of women's menses, symbol of fertility and divine power for indigenous peoples.

Along these lines, there is comparable testimony in the "Council Book," or the *Popol Vuh* that in the mythistory of the Quiche-Maya (Guatemala)—at least after the Conquest when the version that we have was written—women were given secondary roles as goddesses and in the flesh, despite the "unified dual principle" of Quiche-Mayan philosophy. The first four humans were male, created without mother or father but the male god Quetzalcoatl (Toltec) appears to have played a big part in the successful creation of the first humans. Their four wives came later.[9] This is a simplistic interpretation of their creation myth, of course, but my point here is that at the time of the Spanish Conquest the Mayan civilization was militaristic and following similar patriarchal progression by diminishing female power.

Among the Mexica, the universal concept of the Mother Goddess who, by tasting of the fruit of knowledge forbidden to her,[10] has lost innocence for humankind, is represented by Xochiquetzal. According to the myth, the world tree of the Mexica grew in Tamoanchan. Xochiquetzal—the goddess of love— was the first female to sin, "a reference to the fact that her patronage extended to illicit as well as to socially acceptable love."[11]

Xochitqueztal as the willful goddess who lost paradise then is transfigured into Ixtextli (Ashes in Eyes). She is blinded by her weeping and can never again look out into the open skies of day or at the sun. The sun, we can recall, is represented by the formidable Aztec god, Huitzilopochtli. Even the Dionysian-like Tezcatlipoca, who in various myths is also known for partaking in sex and alcohol, is not responsible for losing paradise and his outright sexuality is not the cause of disasters that fall on humankind as a result. Instead, it is the goddesses in their changeable roles who are given this emphasis.

Popular Mexican culture, as every child knows, has its own variation of Lilith in the legendary figure of La Llorona, The Weeping Woman.[12] Folklore has it that she drowned her own children to go off with a lover and then was cursed by God to search for them throughout eternity. She is almost always sighted near water; and men, above all, fear the vision. A nationalist version prefers to see her as an Indian woman who is lamenting over her lost race after the Conquest. In fact, as the snake goddess, Cihuacoatl, she appeared as the sixth omen predicting the fall of the Empire of Tenochtitlan when she was heard wailing in the night, "O my children, you are lost; where shall I hide you?"[13] This same concept became personified in Mexican history by Malintzin (La Malinche and more vulgarly, "la Chingada," the fucked woman), an actual historical figure who was stigmatized by the Eve theme.[14] The insinuation here also is that female sexuality is at fault again, since it is woman who conceives and who therefore gave birth to the new race.

This notion predated the Conquest, however, as we see Coatlicue emerging in the pantheon as Cihuacoatl. Cihuacoatl, who wailed and moaned in the night air, was, among other things, the patroness of women who died in childbirth. In the past people believed that she had passed by when they found the empty cradle in the market place with a sacrificial knife laid beside it.[15]

The gods and goddesses of the Mexica pantheon may seem at first reminiscent of some found in Greek mythology, such as Xochiquetzal with Aphrodite, but with closer examination they have serious differences. Xochiquetzal, for example, is nearer in description to the Earth Mother in her role as matron fertility goddess. "Unlike Greco-Roman and Western European cities which grew from a political and commercial base the isolated Meso-American were founded on religious mysticism much like the first communities of the Middle East." This reliance on mysticism continued to be fundamental to Amerindian philosophy beyond the Conquest and accommodated such things as the absorption of new gods, gods continuously changing roles and having numerous titles. Furthermore, as mentioned at the beginning of this essay, there were those in Texcoco devoted to Tloque Nahuaque, called the tlamatinimi, and who did not believe in multiple deities. "The tlamatinimi conceived of monotheism, with a strong feeling toward yin and yang, to explain the workings of the universe."[16] Therefore, while I occasionally suggest such comparisons here to better understand our contemporary interpretations of sexuality in Western civilization I cannot rely fully on them. Again, this leads me to reiterate the point that as conscienticized mestizas, our world view is markedly different from the Eurocentric one accepted by white Americans.

The Aztecs, as did the Maya to some extent, traced their actual and mythological history to the famous Toltecs. Likewise, the sex goddesses of the Aztecs were said to have originated in Tula. They are represented in quadruplicate, in all probability the moon's phases. According to Brundage, the Ixcuiname, as the four together were called, stood for more than sexuality and desire, " . . . for their mythology states that they were present as a sisterhood in the darkness which preceded the first rising of the fifth sun [age of the Aztecs and their attending Sun God] and that they, along with the Mimixcoa, represent the stars."[17] Again, we see the parallel of myths with others throughout the globe, with the rise of the sun god comes the fall and eventual subordination of the variable moon goddess/fertility goddess/goddess of carnal knowledge and all wisdom.

THE TRANSCONTINENTAL EARTH MOTHER

Once again our multi-deified Coatlicue enters Mexica society in her role as Tonantzin, "Our Holy Mother," Tonan simply "Mother," as well as Teteoinan, "the mother of the gods" (note one of Mary's titles is that of "Mother of God"). Tonan in Nahuatl is the name given to several mountains where the Earth Mother was worshipped. Tonan was the earth and the Mexica worshipped her as the Great Mother present at the inception of humans. As Teteoinan she was lifted to the highest level of divinity and "played an almost gynarchic role."[18] Because of the destruction of Indian religion and codices, we must rely considerably on the interpretations by early Spaniards of the Aztec pantheon and beliefs that don't distinguish the Mother's titles and the conceptualizations of her. Therefore, there remains much in archeology about the Mexica goddess left open to interpretation. Again, as women and as Native people, we must reconstruct our history with what is left unsaid and not what has been recorded by those who have imposed their authority on us.

On the very hill of Tepeyac where Tonantzin was said to have been worshipped, Juan Diego, a recently converted Catholic Nahua, witnessed the visitation of the brown virgin who was eventually named the Virgin of Guadalupe by the Church. Speculation may be that converting the mother goddess, Tonantzin, into the Virgin Mary as Guadalupe, the brown virgin, was the Mexic Amerindian people's way of attempting to hold on to their own beliefs.[19] As a spiritual attempt at grappling with the trauma of social and political upheaval, Juan Diego's personal experience was subsequently encompassed by all Mexicans, Amerindians, and mestizos alike. Guadalupe's appearance is seen as a divine blessing on la Raza and thus, her banner has led revolutions for freedom and justice. Her association with nationalism is indisputable as is Tonantzin's surrender of all creative power to men in the form of the sublime Virgin Mary.

In Christianity, the Mother Goddess is introduced in the Old Testament in the form of Eve, but she is finally rendered without power. Adam's second wife, Eve, is sentenced to total subordination to man as a direct consequence of her "will" to *maintain* her consciousness, through her metaphorical association with the serpent. She is punished by having to suffer the labor of childbirth; and she must deliver her children up to man/God.

If certain curanderas are as knowledgeable or more savvy about the medicinal properties of plants than some university trained botanists, should we not accept that early women had found natural ways to ease their labor and when necessary, even to expel a fetus as natural birth control? According to Barbara Mor and Monica Sjöö "[T]he earliest recorded abortion recipes yet found date from circa 2700 B.C. They were inscribed on Egyptian papyrus scrolls" and "[I]n Ancient Rome and Greece vinegar or lemon juice were used as acid spermicides, and one-half of a squeezed-out lemon is a pretty good 'cap'." In the times of Tenochtitlan, women among the populace resorted to abortion[20] and infanticide when unable to provide sustenance.

In terms of fertility and contraception there is plenty of documentation that shows herbal use in Mesoamerica in Pre-Conquest times. Many of these remedies are still in use. For example, in Coban the leaves of Mexican giant hyssop were cooked with other plants and the liquid drunk for the purpose of inducing abortion. There were several herbal concoctions known to alleviate the pain of childbirth. A species of greenbrier was used in seventeenth-century Guatemala to make sterile women fertile.[21] Native American women in North America used ragwort to speed childbirth and induce abortion, and wild raspberry tea is still widely used by women for prevention of miscarriage, increasing milk, and reducing labor pains (as well as cramps).

Both the Catholic and Protestant churches have been known to condemn women for using ancient methods of contraception. Examples are the well-documented witch hunts of New England in the 1600s that burned midwives and the Catholic Church's ongoing position against contraceptives and abortion. Not much more than a decade ago a woman in Catholic-dominated Spain could be jailed for having an abortion. Therefore, the punishment meted out to woman in the scriptures was much more than symbolic. If we dig into our primordial memories or just use common sense, we know that the authors of the scriptures were about the business of female control.

Woman of the scriptures goes on "as ordered" to be fertile and to populate the world as women had always done, but her creatrix ability was extracted from her identity and appropriated by the male god and his motherless child, Adam. In the New Testament, Jesus, too, ultimately disowns his mother, whom it is understood was nothing more than a vessel that delivered the Christ child to the world.

Henceforth, the crucial point to keep in mind here is that without the assistance of a female, the male god has created man. From *man* alone humanity is created. In reality, of course, it *is* woman who brings forth men and women. Only as recently as 1827 the female ovum was discovered. Until then, for thousands of years, the male was seen as the sole generative physical force and the female as little more than receptacle. Today, through research in the area of parthenogenesis, it is believed to be possible to produce a fetus with two female eggs—that is, without the male sperm.

Man was so afraid of mortality that he cursed woman—a reminder of his birth—for being the one who has the ability to "create" him. "Unto the woman he said, I will greatly multiply thy sorrow and thy conception, in sorrow thou shalt bring forth children and thy desire shall be to thy husband, and he shall rule over thee" (Gen. 3:16). Woman today is still being punished for her femaleness by the male-run medical field, the public deliberation of the personal issue of abortion, the social persecution of being a rape victim, and religious control of her reproductive rights, among other things.

In an attempt to reconcile this misogynist effort to put the blame for the Fall solely on woman, theologians recently have been saying it was the fault of both. In 1990, I attended a Mass where the priest happened to be giving a sermon that Sunday on this very theme. He said the story of the downfall of man was not intended to denigrate woman. The point of the story was not to blame woman nor the serpent, he said, but to state that sin had entered the world. Nevertheless, woman as perpetrator of the Fall is ingrained in popular culture. The damage that this belief has caused to women throughout Christianity's history can hardly be recompensed by a recent, and not widely recognized, change of heart in theological doctrine.

SINCE ADAM FAILED HIS TEST IN PROVING HIS LOYALTY TO THE FATHER GOD, man gets a second chance for redemption and eternal life in the New Testament. Jesus is said to recapitulate the story of Adam but this time when tempted, he remains faithful to the Father God and thereby overcomes the transgression of Adam that resulted in man's separation from the Divinity.[22] The Virgin Mary appears in the New Testament as the redeemed version of the first woman, Eve. Catholic theologians have relentlessly set out to prove her worthiness as Mother of All Living Things by rendering her less human. Completely obsequious, she accepts the Annunciation for the virginal birth. The mother goddess is restored to heaven but her image is rendered powerless. Although it was long considered dogma, it was only in 1854, that the Roman Catholic Church actually made official the doctrine of the Immaculate Conception.

Another example of this relentless desire to prove Mary's ideal state came even more recently. In 1950 the Pope declared Mary's deathless ascension into heaven as doctrine—death as the inevitable result of sex was unacceptable in the case of the Mother of God. The ancient association of sex with death is still prevalent in Christian belief. The soul and the body are paralleled: the dead body reflects the corruption of the (lustful) soul. Also, copulation associated with birth inevitably leads to death, which man has feared most of all.

While this fervent process of redeeming Mary had its beginnings in the fourth century, as recently as 1968, the Credo of Pope Paul VI reconfirmed the dogma of the Assumption. During an age when the vastness of space is being comprehended, Mary's body is being risen to the sky. "Even assuming that Mary's body could travel at the speed of light—an impossible idea to begin with—it would be only two thousand light years away at the present time, about one-fiftieth of the distance across our own galaxy, let alone plunged into the unthinkable immensity of intergalactic space."[23] As redeemer of mankind, symbolic promise of eternal life, the Divinity Himself made into flesh, Jesus could not be born of human copulation or of an ordinary woman.

THE CHRISTIAN GOD WAS NOT THE FIRST DEITY TO CONSORT WITH A MORTAL WOMAN to produce a divine prodigy. Marina Warner argues that "Pythagoras, Plato, Alexander were all believed to have been born of woman by the power of a holy spirit. It became the commonplace claim of a spiritual leader . . ."[24] However, in the Hebrew myth, unlike previous creation stories, Yaweh (Hebrew God) does not have any physical contact with woman, an indication of both the contemptibility of woman and the fear of her by her creators.

In his book *God of Ecstasy,* Arthur Evans has done extensive research to argue that the authors of the New Testament did not only not know Jesus but borrowed their writings from a play written by Euripides, based on the myth of Dionysus, which was to have a great impact on Greek religion. In Euripides' play, "Bakkhai," written five hundred years before the birth of Jesus, the god Zeus has sexual intercourse with a mortal woman. The prodigy, Dionysus, born of this union is human and divine.

A religious sect of that period known as the Orphics, emphasized spirituality in the Dionysian cult, which was based on a belief in an afterlife. At the time of Jesus' birth the following theme according to Evans, was already part of contemporary religious belief:

> The Son of God has been born from the union of the Father
> God and a mortal woman; wine is his sacrament and shepherds
> are his heralds; he has come as a liberator of the human race;
> he has died and risen from the dead; the purpose of religion
> is to cleanse oneself from the moral imperfection, inherent
> and otherwise, of being human; the mechanism for this moral
> cleansing is participation in certain sacraments; the effect of this
> cleansing is a continued life after physical death.[25]

While in the cult of Dionysus there is a celebration of physical life, we see a deliberate move in Christianity to separate physicality and spirituality, thereby immobilizing the human spirit by making expressions of ecstasy taboo. Humanity relies on copulation for its perpetuation and this became the only form of sex sanctioned. But we all know a woman's orgasmic ability is not confined to any estrus (the female mammal's "heat" cycle). The human female is receptive to sexual overtures at any time and for reasons other than the purpose of reproduction. To insist that sex only exists for the purpose of reproduction is to go against human evolution. To enforce this regulation through religious doctrine goes against our sensual and psychic affinities with our bodies and life energy; it goes against our spirituality.

Remnants of Greek mythology surface continuously in Catholic symbolism. For example, the black Catalan Virgin, La Moreneta, is portrayed with the Christ child and she holds a pinecone on her knees. The pinecone, a symbol of fertility because of its many concealed nuts, was also used as the crown on the staff of Dionysus. The Virgin Mary and her symbols are a well of hope for her followers. As the heavenly representative of fertility (a primary role for the earth goddess), her sash symbolizes fecundity. In Spanish, the word *cinta* refers to a sash and the word *encinta* means to be pregnant.

Chanting over beads sees its origins in the worship of Vishnu and Shiva in Brahmanic India. It spread to Buddhism and to Islam. Men throughout Greece, Asia Minor, and North Africa have a secular form of this in their use of worry beads. The use of the rosary was adapted out of a need for a private experience with God. The Hail Mary is recited over and over like a hypnotic chant. Above all, the Virgin Mary, Mother of All Living Things, presides over her children when they are dying, as the compassionate mediator between them and their Lord. As Warner points out, "That is why the best-loved prayer of the Catholic world—the Hail Mary—ends with the plea that the Virgin should 'pray for us sinners, now and at the hour of our death,'" Amen.[26]

IN MODERN MAN'S SCHEMA WOMAN MUST CHOOSE between one of two polarized roles, that of mother as portrayed by the Virgin Mary vs. that of whore/traitor as Eve. These two roles were revisited upon Mexicans in the figures of La Virgen de Guadalupe and Malintzin. Man's fear of his own death, which invariably will be linked to woman caused the perpetuation of contemptible female figures such as Lilith, Eve, "La Malinche," as well as Mary Magdalene, whom I have not discussed here, but who also is associated with sex and death. The unreal model of the "Virgin Mother" is no less cruel to women because it is an inimitable role for women.

But if men appear to have no advantage in creating any "positive" female model (assuming that the Virgin is a positive one) one might ask herself, why then, create the benevolent archetype of Virgin Mary at all? What purpose does she serve men, even as a modified or domestic version of the ancient creator-goddess? Throughout history, humanity has called forth the mother-archetype. Jungian psychology, which is not directly associated with Catholicism, proposes that all men want a virgin mother. We must remind ourselves, however, that the "Virgin Mary is not the innate archetype of female nature, the dream incarnate; she is the instrument of a dynamic argument from the

Catholic Church about the structure of society, presented as a God-given code."[27]

While we have been given the male god image in all its stages of life, from infant to eternal patriarch, we have no record of female infant goddesses. Therefore, we perceive the need to nurture the male infant (who will one day grow up to be a god) but not the female. We accept the idea that men must be nurtured. But there are no baby goddesses; no female child image worthy of our protection because she will grow up to be our all encompassing protectress. She simply manifests in mythology as a woman, full breasted and wide hipped.

Most women who consider themselves self-sufficient and who have successful careers, are nonetheless shadowed by society's notion that "good woman" means "mother." Good woman equals mother equals the Virgin Mary but not Eve, whose behavior is forever questioned. Not the earth goddess who has the ability to create and to destroy, but the docile, submissive, devout image that has received Father God's grace. Women are to be fulfilled by fulfilling the needs of men.

Even the woman who, for any number of reasons, chooses not to involve herself in an ongoing relationship with a man, is made to believe that motherhood is not an option but rather her duty as a female member of her family, community, and society. She can not reach maturity, truly become a woman, or earn good standing if she refuses to procreate. As Warner says, "Nothing it seems, even to non-Catholics, could be more natural than this icon of feminine perfect, built on the equivalence between goodness, motherhood, purity, gentleness and submission."[28]

By refusing to submit to a man/god, the way Lilith/Eve/La Llorona did, woman, according to myth, is to be punished forever. Such a woman may not only lose the very right to live, the stories tell us her "spirit" may end up suffering for eternity on earth/hell. Try as she might, even modern woman never completely escapes a combination of these archetypes.

RETREAT FROM SOCIETY WAS THE ONLY OTHER AL-TERNATIVE women had in Christian Europe around the fourth century. Many chose to remain chaste by devoting themselves to the service of God directly bypassing man, his mediator on earth. To renounce her womanhood, these women became like men: "As long as a woman is for birth and children, she is different from men as body is from soul. But when she wishes to serve Christ more than the world, then she will cease to be a woman, and she will be called man."[29]

We are reminded of the illustrious seventeenth-century Mexican genius, Sor Juana Inez de la Cruz, who took refuge in the cloister to pursue academic knowledge. But even in the case of a brilliant scholar, we see woman forced to succumb to the authority of male superiors when Sor Juana was ultimately ordered to give up her books for challenging male arrogance and authority over woman through her writings.[30]

By abstaining from sex, a nun shows a variation on her role as concubine of man and mother of his heirs. But the nun's pursuit of intellectual interests and spiritual fulfillment comes at the cost of her sexuality. She must equate her flesh with sin and sin with woman.

Today, one might say that the career-oriented lesbian is free to pursue her interests without the constrictions that come of heterosexual marriage and family obligations, and she doesn't have to forfeit her sexuality. Again, however, the lesbian does not do this without being forced from mainstream heterosexist society, which is still based on the religious patriarchs's law that forbids any sexual contact beyond reproduction. Therefore her personal life may be marginalized; and since she still lives in heterosexist society, she remains susceptible to its scrutiny and potential rejection, socially and professionally.

One might argue that a careerist need not be lesbian to choose her work over marriage. But if a heterosexual woman affirms her sexuality, her need for human affection and comfort, she will in some way find herself compromised in a relationship. While all partnerships demand some compromise, a relationship between a woman and a man would introduce many of the complexities under discussion here. A woman's relations with a man will always integrate her to some degree into heterosexist society. While she may not feel the same pressures as the lesbian to protect her personal life from heterosexual society's scrutiny, she is still vulnerable to potential sexism, socially and professionally. For both the lesbian and heterosexual woman, female sexuality is infused with social restrictions and heterosexual morality. Of course, there are always individual cases who work at being the exception.

The comments made here are intended as general observations of present-day dynamics.

Yet no woman is completely free of traditional doctrine to pursue all the possibilities of her own imagination. The dual ideal of the Virgin/mother archetype has set up a defeating model for women. Not seeing that the Virgin Mary is not an example of inherent femaleness or womanhood but an invented concept of the Church leaders to dictate social and political policies, a woman suffers great personal anguish believing she not only should aspire to, but *can* attain the qualities of the Virgin/mother.

Whether one chooses to accept the feminist notion that the earth once was organized by a matriarchy, one thing is clear: male gynephobia—fear of his mortality—his tyrannous arrogance, have built a world on the gross maltreatment of the hearts, minds, and bodies of females.

Even in the recesses of our psyches we find traces of the male definition of our very beings; it seems an insurmountable task to begin our own myth making from which to establish role models to guide us out of historical convolution and de-evolution. But Adam, after all, means "son of the red Mother Earth," and Eve means "Life."[31] With this in mind, we can begin to write our own story: *In the beginning, there was Eva.*

Six

LA MACHA

TOWARD AN EROTIC WHOLE SELF
t, desire

IN 1980 AT A WRITERS' CONFERENCE, a noted Latino poet who was having trouble with his hotel accommodations asked to use the shower in my room. I waited for him in the room since we were both expected soon at a dinner in our honor. When he came out of the bathroom, dripping, he dropped his towel and dressed in front of me. Afterward, he asked me for a cigarette and proceeded to smoke it stretched languidly in an odalisque pose on one of the beds.

"Talk to me about erotica," he said. "And what would you have me say?" I asked, disinterested, and not at all pleased by the wet towel left on the carpet. He had used up all the towels; moreover, the woman poet with whom I was sharing the room had not yet arrived. "And what gives you the impression that I know anything about erotica?" I added.

"Anyone who has written ten pieces on any subject *must* be an expert on it," he responded. I had recently published a chapbook, *The Invitation,* which I had taken great pains to have printed. I wrote the poetry and prose in that chapbook during my mid twenties and had relentlessly pursued its publication. The chapbook was created out of my sobering experiences as a Movimiento Latina. Sobering because I felt my physiology was demeaned, misunderstood, objectified, and excluded by the politic of those men with whom I had aligned myself on the basis of our mutual subjugation as Latinos in the United States.

With a poet's trust in her intuition, I addressed this anguish from the great compassion I have for myself as a woman. But even as I moved toward this untraced terrain, as a Latina and former Catholic I anticipated that the men within el Movimiento Latino, as conscienticized and as "liberal-minded" as they believed themselves to be, would look upon my invitation to discuss sexuality with all the inhibitions set upon society centuries ago. They would do as men have done to women throughout the ages whenever we embark on the subject of our sexual desire: they would not take my endeavor as serious intellectual discourse. They would not separate my work, my body from the woman I am, nor see me as speaking from the universal experience of "woman," just as they might write of their own desire as "man." Furthermore, being that as politicized Latinos we were already up against the block of the "white literary junta" it would appear to them as frivolous if I "simply" engaged in poetry about *sex*. My lot, according to them, was to remain true to the collective goals of the pueblo, which of course, were male defined.

There would be those, I predicted, who would dismiss me—as a result of the book—as a nymphomaniac, a lesbian (read: man hater), or a non-brain-tits-and-ass, young, hot-to-trot easy lay. Of course, my chapbook was not a personal "invitation" from me to come—to me—but a tragically overdue invitation to discuss within our various communities our spiritual, political, and erotic needs as a people.

I was so conscious of this inevitable reaction that I insisted my talented friend who agreed to illustrate the book not design an overtly suggestive cover.

My world in Chicago at that time was primarily Mexican, Latino, Christian, mostly Catholic and overlaid with the amorphous leftist politics of the mid 1970s. I had no idea what white feminists were thinking of in spheres far from my life in those asphalt, slush-covered streets of working class Chicago. My few African American friends were not feminists, although, they could always be called woman-identified and specifically united against racism. They knew who they were as women within their own culture and within white society. *My* women, likewise survivalists, also were gathering up our own particular strength in the face of Anglo dominance, while still being held tight by the reins of Mexican traditions. We maintained the business of our bodies behind closed doors. Efforts to discuss with other Latinas our sexual desire often left me frustrated. We had been taught not to name those feelings and fantasies, much less affirm their meanings. I am not saying we were not in touch with our sexuality—far from it! Otherwise, how could we entice with it, manipulate with it, have bed sheets to hide from our mothers, from our husbands . . . ?

But delivered as children into the grips of medieval nuns and priests who warned us against auto-stimulation and its many horrendous punishments and who regularly reminded us of our relation to Evil Eve, how could we acknowledge sexual desire to each other? A sexual woman was a woman begging rape, begging vulnerability to society, begging to be treated as nothing more than as what she was born: a female who merits no respect for her emotions, her mind, her person. No, if one admitted sexuality, she was discarding the disguise she alone had worn as the "decent" woman, the "good girl," and was revealing that underneath she was nothing more than a bitch in heat. Everyone knew that.

And how I wanted, needed to talk. I still need to talk. This is the reason for my invitation.

TRADITIONAL MEXICANS DO TALK ABOUT SEX and it is a misconception of people who have not really lived among Mexican people to think that they are so sexually repressed that they forbid women to do so in mixed company. There are sexually explicit jokes and there is sexually implicit teasing in mixed company, at times in the presence of young children. This kind of talk, of course, is superficial and not intended as serious discussion about people's actual needs and desires.

At the very moment when an adolescent's sexual consciousness emerges the censorship of adults begins. This is a major tragedy for young women, who especially begin to view their physical desire as something that should be occulted, that is sinful. Likewise, menstruation is directly associated with their sexuality and usually is not open to discussion between mother and daughter and sometimes not even between older and younger sister.

The taboo against woman's blood is inherently Judeo-Christian. In pre-patriarchal times, menses was the birth connection, a sacred element associated with agricultural fertility rituals. It is symbolic of woman's creatrix ability, once revered as magical. In Native American cultures, menses is still understood as an indication of woman's inherent power. But in the Bible, the patriarchs, loathing their mortality, and therefore desirous of taking material and spiritual control of woman's autonomy, her rights to her land, her children, made woman's blood forbidden, shameful and contemptible. Catholic women of Mexican background know the *shame* of menstruation.

The Bible is our documented evidence of the patriarchs' conspiracy against woman's reproductive and productive rights. The Bible

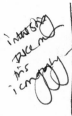

made woman's blood, the blood of creation, a cause for female ostracism and an indication of her potential betrayal of man/God, who symbolically appropriated the spiritual meaning of her bleeding in the circumcision rites reserved for Hebrew males. The wound on Jesus' side as he hangs on the cross is nothing less than an imitation of the vagina bleeding—symbolic of fertility—and once considered necessary for any male who professes magical powers, that is an imitation of the creatrix who gives birth.[1]

After centuries of being nullified as mestizas/indias by dominant, invading cultures and the teachings of the Catholic Church, we don't question *why* we are so ashamed of our menstruation. We don't ask why our lives change so radically at the age when we first begin to bleed—why we are put under immediate suspicion by mothers and fathers. We never wonder why work places are not conducive to women's cycles, why we aren't granted a day off for rest once a month, why we are so separated from other women on the subject, why we whisper to an office mate, "Do you have a tampon handy? I just got the curse." What civilized society would call the blood that creates life a *curse*? Because man has created a mythological, asexual male God who had nothing to do with women, in order to sanctify his abuse upon woman and by extension, upon the resources of sustenance-giving earth. Man gave us a male amaterial god and relegated sexuality to reproduction.

With such punitive taboos surrounding the female, a young woman's best strategy is to *deny* her sexuality. Of course, a parent's denial of her daughter's sexual development has not by any means ensured the young woman's abstinence. The high teenage pregnancy rate, especially among young women of color from the lower social strata in the United States, attests to this fact.

A humorous, but nevertheless telling account of the degree to which women are stigmatized when revealing any amount of sexual desire is in Carmen Tafolla's story, "Federico y Elfiria."[2] Tafolla's Tex-Mex narrative voice adds a special authenticity to this account of a young married couple and the husband's dilemma at discovering his wife's sexual passion, which to his mind, implies that she may be one of "those" girls, even when her passion has been solely directed at him. The story begins, "Pos, he liked her jus cause of that . . . She was a good girl, which is like saying that she wasn't a bad girl, nor not even a little bad, y'know?"

After viewing a movie with love scenes, Federico comes home to his wife (who is on her knees washing the floor) and proceeds to make abandoned love to her. She responds, and at the moment of his climax, he gives her a hicky. When he sees the hicky the next morning—which he knows he gave her—he begins to suspect her status of "good girl." His suspicions drive him to spy on her to see if she is having an affair. When she tells him she's pregnant, he's further upset "que la ingrata had gone and gotten herself that way right now."

Although this is a contemporary story, and Federico is a young man, he fully demonstrates the archaic notions held by our culture: woman is a possession to be vigilantly guarded, since, given any leeway, she will betray her master and get herself pregnant by another man. Olivia Espín argues "To shun sexual pleasure and to regard sexual pleasure as an unwelcome obligation toward her husband and a necessary evil in order to have children may be seen as a manifestation of virtue. In fact, some women even express pride at their own lack of sexual pleasure or desire."[3] It is only after the birth of their son that Elfiria convinces Federico that she is still a good girl, as a result of being not solely a wife but now also *mother*. Federico isn't quite convinced that marriage sanctions her sexual desire, but at the end of the story it appears that he will eventually relent: "Maybe eso de ser mother and wife let her do these kinds of things *plus* be a good girl."

The key here is woman's desire and her right to it. In Christian doctrine, we have been told that to have sex for any reason other than procreation would reduce us to the lowly status of beasts. The irony of this comparison is that *only* beasts copulate for the sake of reproduction. The human female alone has evolved away from estrus (heat), a state where she would only copulate when she was able to conceive. Instead of being restricted to "heat cycles," the human female is able to have orgasms at any time.

There is much talk these days on the subject of clitorectomies, which traditionally have been performed on young girls in Arab and African countries. This ritual is understood to be an effort at controlling women's desire for sex; she is only to have marital sex and only for the purpose of reproduction. These clitorectomies were designed to dehumanize the female, to eradicate *any* sexual pleasure at all, either by herself, or with the other women that she spends so much time with because of her enforced seclusion from the outside world.

Indeed, the Bible teaches us that menstruation is a taboo, worthy of castigating rituals; woman is under suspicion when she expresses sexual desire, and under no circumstances, either in marriage or motherhood, should a woman be free to have an orgasm, because the Bible is anti-evolutionary. A society based on an ideology that denies its own evolution as a species is bound for self-destruction.

Incest, a subject often censored within the home, its existence denied even as we are experiencing it, also victimizes young women, thereby adding further guilt to our erotic desires. The following excerpt from a testimonial by a young woman who was raped by her father at the age of eleven clearly exemplifies this:

> In spite of my feelings I still did not understand why I hated him so much. Why was the thing he had done to me so bad? After all, he had said he was only doing it to warn me of what was going to happen when I got married. What was so wrong about him wanting to warn me? I did not know why but I hated him. I hated, hated, hated him.[4]

Human sexuality has been regulated and shaped by men to serve man's needs. To this day, women's sexuality has not been "liberated" from these constraints. Our bodies do not belong to us. Modern technology has not yet given women a contraceptive that is both absolutely safe and effective. The majority of men from all backgrounds have not on their own taken responsibility for contraception. Furthermore, with the specter of sexually transmitted diseases and the AIDS epidemic hovering over all of us, we are told that sex should not only be limited to reproductive purposes alone, but even abstained from for the benefit of humanity, an attitude certainly validated by the values of Western culture as maintained for the last two thousand years.

"PORNOGRAPHY TELLS LIES ABOUT WOMEN, BUT IT TELLS THE TRUTH ABOUT MEN."[5] An example of a short-sighted attempt at female sexual liberation is the current belief that men can be objectified. For instance, in the 1980s there was a cropping up of "straight" women's bars that featured male strippers. Supposedly, women were titillated by this voyeurism, catcalling and slipping money into the jock straps of male dancers.

It is an absolute impossibility in this society to reversely sexually objectify heterosexual men, just as it is impossible for a poor person of color to be a racist. Such extreme prejudice must be accompanied by the power of society's approval and legislation. While women and poor people of color may become intolerant, personally abusive, even hateful, they do not have enough power to be racist or sexist.

By the same token, the objectification of body parts as erotic stimulants for the opposite sex is not inherently part of woman's perception. For example, women's breasts *are* erogenous (for the woman and her partner), but for men their size becomes of exaggerated importance. The degree to which men are afraid of this world they have created has led to the need to suckle for comfort and security. The bigger the breasts, the more comfort derived.

Those women who have bought into the false possibility of objectifying males, actively promoted by commercial enterprises, focus on the most obvious comparison to women's breasts: men's buttocks. Like women's breasts, buttocks protrude and can be perceived through clothing, unlike the concealed penis. But men's buttocks do not stimulate a woman sexually the way a person is stimulated when her breasts are fondled and suckled; nor can a man experience the comparable sensation from fondling of the buttocks that a woman feels through the stimulation of her nipples during heterosexual sex. The attempt at objectifying men's bodies, seems only a mocking simulation of what has been done to women through the ages, primarily through voyeurism. That is, through fantasy one can be aroused. Part of the arousal of objectification through voyeurism is a sense of control (power). For women, in heterosexual society, this sense of power is ultimately little more than part of the fantasy.

Technique and erogenous-zone polemics aside, the objectification of females in society has been the result of man's enforced economic dominance and spiritual repression over humankind. At no time, when women attempt to objectify a man and to derive pleasure from his sexual exploitation—all in the name of liberated women's good fun—is a man made into a possession, reduced in social status, humiliated, or otherwise abused, as has been the case with women. On the contrary, men—who have not been systematically punished for their heterosexual sexuality—are sexually accessible and their own aggressive sense of desire would not on its own cause a woman to "need" to commodify male sexuality. On the contrary, this new trend appears to be financially profitable for entrepreneurs through male dancer clubs, male strippers, major advertisements that eroticize heterosexual males and so on.

Objectification, which we now understand philosophically as the "other" of man (Octavio Paz also considers Mexicans as the "other" of North American Anglos—I would say, because we are indigenous people, dark and full of mysteries, just as woman is perceived by man) causes woman to feel alienated from herself when making love with men. Romance, an archaic carryover from the time when woman was even further reduced to "object of desire," is still an important part of sex for heterosexual women. Through the rituals of courtship, woman at least, aspires to be the "special" object of his desire and devotion. Without courtship, she may feel that the "services" she provides to a man (and which amount to much more than sex) are being taken for granted.

Our eroticism cannot be short changed by a pretention of pleasure through pornographic materials or male strippers. By pretending to commodify men sexually, people perpetuate the male fantasy that women desire men in the same way that men desire women: through the objectification of the body, the intense importance placed on youth, and the proportion and size of physical endowment. While young men may take steroids to pump up their muscles, will they also submit to having their penises injected with silicone for the sake of satisfying women's desire for large size and to get women's approval, just as some women have done to their breasts for men?

Hypothesizing such gross possibilities also suggests a heterosexist, ultimately misogynist, mentality, implying that women would want to enforce the same distorted aesthetic values of objectification that they have suffered under patriarchal capitalism. Finally, we must not overlook the extent of violence that accompanies woman's reduction to a "sexual play thing." Historically, women have not, as a rule, reduced men to sexual property or otherwise physically abused men.

The Catholic Church has enforced female sexual repression within our culture with a vengeance. Woman is not only man's property,

through the sanctification of the church, but her children also belong
to him and the church. The violence of European colonization and
enslavement of primal peoples, always had the blessing of the church,
which was and remains a wealthy institution. When the church dominated Europe, it was considered a crime against God for a woman
to miscarry. In the Americas, Indian women who miscarried were
whipped in front of the church, as they were suspected of having
intentionally aborted, robbing the Church of its human labor property.[6] While it is possible that the conditions these women were forced
to live under would be cause enough to miscarry, it is also likely that
they did, in fact, abort intentionally. The raped conquered Indian
women of Puerto Rico ate dirt to abort. Indian women, throughout
the Americas, using their own wisdom, preferred abortion to bearing
children who would suffer inhuman conditions and slavery.

Most of our female saints, maintained as models, established their
beatitude by repudiating sex. Today a rape occurs somewhere in the
United States every three or four minutes. Struggle to the death, as
with the women martyrs of medieval Christianity, is hardly an ade-
quate response for so many women whose lives are under constant
threat. Furthermore, female saints and martyrs are upheld as models
because of their ability to forgive their attacker, an act that permits
repetition of such violations. Rape has nothing to do with sex, but the
violence is evidence of the misogyny integral to our society. What
kind of convoluted message do we give young Catholic women when
we teach them to be obedient and submissive and yet to protect their
virtue even on the pain of death?

Federico sends his wife to Mass while he stays home to try to
figure out why he considers his wife one of "those" girls. Along with
the rest of humanity, he suffers from a deliberate repression of his
primordial instincts, if not a resistance to developing his higher orders
of thinking. Although he is unduly jealous, it isn't in his imagination
to sense that his wife must be indoctrinated—spiritually and legally
coerced—into denying her sexuality because her sexuality *is* real. When
she has a moment, such as that one night of lovemaking when she first
becomes aware that indeed, she does have the capacity for experiencing
ecstasy, she is ready to go with it. Why not? She has been an obedient
daughter, agreed to marriage, and allowed herself to remain property

from father to husband. She has further obliged her prescribed role as mother. She discovers through her husband the joy of her orgasmic capabilities, her evolution, freedom from estrus, her humanity. Good for her! In the good/evil dichotomy of female sexual repression she must struggle against her sexual partner's ignorance of her right to joy, but the story leaves the reader with a sense of victory, because she has rediscovered it and we know she will not continue to live in a state of numb bestiality—succumbing to sex only for the sake of reproduction and as an instrument of her husband's pleasures and fantasies.

The young woman mentioned above whose father raped her, doesn't understand why she hates him, because she had learned that woman's status as possession allows men to violate females. And she knows her father owns her. Yet she also believes that sex is bad and that she as a female is synonymous with sex and therefore born bad. All the violence that she is subjected to must be her fault. Let us not forget that until the 1970s, a raped woman was seen by the courts as merely a witness to the crime, which was against the state, not the victim. En masse, woman has been violated because of her role as man's property in the economic system in which we live. Throughout men's wars women have been seen as part of the spoils. It has been said that the Conquest of México was the conquest of women. June Nash clarifies this point from an economist's perspective: "the conquest was not one of women, but of Indian male control over the productive power of women . . ."[7] As descendants of Mexican customs, we live in a society that long ago made woman into a dispensable acquisition.

But the conquest of woman is not based on economic takeover alone. It has been intrinsically tied to men's fear of her creatrix ability. It was a conquest of her wisdom, her cultivated knowledge of propagation, her knowledge of organically regulating the population on the basis of the needs of her particular social groupings. This knowledge was antithetical to greed on which patriarchy is based.

An attempt at a survey of Chicanas for this essay did not yield sufficient response for me to draw any specific conclusions on our attitudes about our sexuality.[8] Nevertheless, I have had the opportunity to informally interview women about the process they have undergone coming out as lesbians. "E," while working as a family counselor in the late 1970s, had to struggle with a disastrous marriage to a white, philandering husband and the severe racism in the part of the country where they had relocated together; these struggles were further compounded by her own alcohol problem. In addition to the social and familial constraints that caused her to deny her lesbianism— even to herself—she was further disturbed by the fact that homosexuality was "scientifically" classified as a mental disorder according to the psychological diagnostic manual (until 1985), an indispensable source for the mental health profession.

"E," not unlike other women whose mothers are Mexican Catholic, struggled through early adulthood with her own sense of what might constitute personal fulfillment for her and the constant pressure to please her mother, her family, and her community. Our identification with our mothers is often so acute, or at least the identification with the role of "obedient daughter" is, that regardless of the new terrain we are able to tread upon on North American soil, in white, male, English-speaking institutions, we still are determined to accommodate the expectations our mothers have of us. This pressure pushed "E" toward self-deprecation until, through therapy with a sensitive counselor, she came to the realization that, in her words, "My mother will never be happy with me. I'll never be able to give people what they want." From then on, she pursued her own goals, which have included a profession as a therapist who works with other lesbians and Latinas.

Witnessing our mothers endurance of husbands' physical abuse, alcoholism, and extramarital affairs, *sometimes* serves some women, (particularly women who pursue higher education) as an example of what *not* to tolerate in their lives. But it would be a mistake to assume that being witness to these abuses (as well as victimized by them) would necessarily direct a young woman toward not repeating them. There have certainly been ample studies documenting that wife battering, child abuse, and alcoholism are often passed through generations. It is also a mistake to assume that lesbianism is the end result of sexual and/or physical abuse. For if lesbianism were solely a reaction to male dominance or "machismo," the vast majority of women in this world would be lesbians. In *Compañeras: Latina Lesbians* in "Marta's" [a pseudonym] testimony regarding her father's physical abuse of her sister and her, she says this: "No, daddy, your actions didn't 'turn' me gay. My lesbianism is a recognition of what I've always been. Luckily, you couldn't alter that. But you . . . have filled me with a . . . suspicion that you and others like you have never, and will never, regard me as your equal."[9]

A LOVER OF WOMEN had no role models in the past. That is, women were forced to emulate those roles played out through hetero-sexist relations, which are antithetical to human evolution. Ultimately, the butch/fem dichotomy has more to do with woman's social and political immobilization, than how women really love and love each other in their intimate relationships, or rather, would, if society was not defined in patriarchal terms. A woman named María, whom I interviewed for the publication *Esta Puente, Mi Espalda*[10] eloquently summarized why there is sometimes abuse within a lesbian relationship:

> Muchas veces las compañeras lesbianas no tenemos una iden-
> tidad clara, y no tenemos clarificación y entonces hay opresión,
> hay cierto tipo de abuso, dado que no tenemos un patrón. Por
> ejemplo, es bien comodo ese es el rol que tienes que jugar
> como mujer, okay? — y ese, el rol que tienes que jugar como
> hombre. Pero cuando tu te enfrentas a una onda de que no
> sabes ni quien eres y lo que eres, es malo—entonces es terrible,
> ¿no? Dices, ¿A quién tengo qué copiar? ¿A Cristo? ¿A Safo? ¿A
> Alfonsina Storni? ¿A Miguel Angel o ¿a quién fregados tengo
> qué imitar? Entonces no hay patrón. No existe un rol a jugar, y
> tienes que crear un nuevo rol. Y esa es la razón por la que digo
> yo ahora cual es mi meta.
>
> Very often the lesbian sisters don't have a clear identity,
> and we don't have clarification and then there is oppression,
> certain types of abuse, given that we don't have a model. For
> example, it is quite convenient to be told, "This is how you
> must behave because this is the role you play as a woman, okay?
> And that one, the role that you must play as a man." But when
> you face up to a situation where you don't know who you are
> and what you are is bad—then it's terrible, no? You say, whom
> do I have to copy? Christ? Sappho? Alfonsina Storni? Michel-
> angelo or who the heck do I have to imitate? So there is no
> model. There doesn't exist a role to play, and you have to create a
> new role. And that is why I now say I know what my goal is.[11]

What María has accurately analyzed here is that heterosexuality, the only sexuality legitimized in profit-oriented society, is sexist. Lesbians are forced to emulate, often only superficially, this dominant standard. *well said*

A friend of mine shared with me the story of her youth when she was anxious to find out something about the lives of women who loved women, which she knew since age seven she would do. She knew of a woman's bar somewhere in the barrio of East Los Angeles She was eleven years old when she peeked through the window one night, eager to know more. She saw women who were dressed and acted like "women" as well as women who dressed and acted like "men." Since she had no doubt that she was a lover of women, she was left with the dilemma of which kind of lover she would be. She quickly and enthusiastically resolved that she could be *both*. Why not? she thought.

Years later, as a young adult and having assumed her life as a lesbian, she found herself in a bar one night enjoying a game of pool. That is, until a large, tough-looking Latina asked her to dance. When my friend refused, the woman (obviously taking rejection hard) interpreted my friend's lack of interest as her declaration as a marimacha (butch). She dragged my friend out to the parking lot and gave her a deep gash in the arm with a broken bottle. Thus have been the trials and tribulations of loving in a world governed by strict roles and where sex is more associated with dominance and submission than with giving and receiving pleasure.

In our culture, not so unlike Anglo society in this respect, sex roles are rigidly defined. Cross-dressing and cross-gender behavior, therefore, are not a surprising phenomena among women who love women. Clothes, which in the past were much more rigidly designed in terms of the sexes, serve as a "costume" for enabling such behavior. In recent years, the fashion trend has become "androgynous," which to me implies, more masculine. I use the words masculine and feminine here in the manner in which they are commonly considered within our social construct. However, there also are new styles for men that a generation or two ago would have been considered effeminate and therefore unfit for "real" men.

Because of the strict social attitudes toward open sexual expression, most lesbians of our culture have not politicized their desires nor openly declared them as a way of life. The traditions of our heritage, the rules of the Church, and importantly, economic dependency, still make most women who feel themselves to be lesbian or bisexual opt for a heterosexual lifestyle. This does not mean that there are never "out" lesbians or "marimacha" types in traditional, poor or working-class communities. Any of us who were brought up in a Mexican environment regardless of which side of the border, can attest to the existence of women of the butch type (manflores, machonas, mari-machas). My point is that our culture, adhering to so many antiquated attitudes, will provoke most women who feel themselves inclined toward women to negate this awareness or to hide it so as not to lose social status and financial security. Many lesbian or bisexual women may be mothers; the added risk of losing their children terrorizes them. Above all, they do not want to lose the love and sense of place they feel within their families and immediate communities. In light of intense alienation from Anglo society, their community is crucial to their sense of identity.

It has been observed by white feminists that the economic privilege of white women (compared to people of color in general) in the United States has probably enabled white lesbians to politicize their lifestyles or at the very least, to instate them. Financial autonomy, higher education, and a sense of belonging to mainstream society contribute to this possibility.

Presently in the United States (I think it is still much more difficult for women in México), young Latina lesbians who are not finding it as difficult as it was in the past to pursue higher education, to establish professions that will enable them to be self-sufficient, who are postponing motherhood or canceling it altogether, are working their way out of the strict gender roles and dress codes of their backgrounds. This is also leading them to break down the male-female roles in their personal relationships and interactions with other lesbians.

Costumes and cross-gender postulations aside, the emulation of cross-gender behavior for women seems superficial. In a heterosexual relationship, the same woman who is aggressive, demanding of her male partner, and otherwise behaving in a way frowned upon by her culture and even approximating masculine, might, in a lesbian relationship be the more "feminine" member of the partnership. On the face of things, she is through costume and gender-defined behavior the "woman." By the same token, the "butch," the woman who chose male costume, postulation, and perhaps a cross-gender livelihood, does not necessarily dominate the relationship, certainly not the way society permits a man. We must keep in mind María's words regarding our oppressive culture, as well as the subjugation we experience due to our poverty, race, and ethnicity, especially in the United States. Whereas a man may or may not exercise abusive dominance over "his" woman, he is always aware that society has traditionally condoned such behavior in varying degrees. Regardless of how much a lesbian couple may role play, its reality is entirely subordinated by society. This awareness may lead to a form of self-contempt heaped upon the partner, which is very similar to the social political definition of machismo, with the main exception that in the case of lesbians, no one and nothing endorses the dominance exerted in the relationship. Instead, regardless of the dynamic of the abuse, both women play the "female" role in the ethnosociological definition of machismo. Both see themselves and each other as equally denigrated entities who are even further denigrated than the heterosexual woman. A further note regarding the dynamics of butch/fem role playing. The butch is intent on satisfying the fem. This is not *always* the case with macho men, who at times are not interested in satisfying their female partner and do not.

On the positive side of lesbian and homosexual relationships, we may observe a less resistance to break away from the racist, classist, and heterosexist ties permitted by society. Within lesbian and gay relationships, there is a prevalent transgression of the restrictions upheld by hierarchical society. Not only do we see more mixed-race relationships and relationships composed of members from "both side of the tracks," but the aesthetics assigned in this misogynist and racist society quite frequently are dismissed. There are also not a few cross-generational relationships. The standard for beauty upheld by heterosexual, racist society is often disregarded in lesbian relationships and in particular, in those that are feminist. The older woman is valued for her life experience. She is perceived as physically beautiful because her years represent to the young lover infinite dimensions of pragmatic knowledge. The true feminist, white lover may see the dark woman lover as ra-

diating her inner strengths cultivated from surviving racism and poverty, instead of objectifying her into an exotic creature or the mysterious "other" of herself. By the same token, the lesbian of color may
choose to be with a white lover because of genuine compatibility and
attraction rather than because of the status and privilege white people
have in society.[12]

I state these opinions after a lifetime of observation and interac-
tion with Mexicans, Tex-Mex fieldworkers, Mexican City urbanites,
the young women with whom I grew up and with whom I went to
school, and from my professional and personal associations as an
adult. Sexuality remains a difficult subject for discussion, even among
progressive, formally educated women. Many activists do not see it
as a priority issue in light of our ethnic and gender conflicts with
society; while some scholars are converting the subject into academese to advance their careers. In the public sphere, sexuality (just
like our spiritual beliefs) remains an impolite and inappropriate subject. Failing to accept sexuality as a topic of discussion that affects our
personal and professional lives is a reflection of the hierarchical frag-
mentation of the self in society. All of our conflicts with dominant
society, all of the backlashes we suffer when attempting to seek some
kind of justice from society, are ultimately traceable to the repression
of our sexuality and our spiritual energies as human beings—which
are at no time during our breathing existence on Earth apart from
the rest of who we are. They are, in fact, who we are: spiritual and
sexual beings.

IF THE INTENT OF THE SOCIALIZATION PROCESS has been
to mold each woman and each man into an appropriate role, not only
according to her or his gender but color, ethnicity, and class as well,
then of course, our sexual behavior has also been predisposed. Sexuality for the Catholic woman of Latin American background has, at
best, been associated with her reproductive ability (or lack of it),
repressed, or otherwise, misunderstood.

In the case of lesbians who assimilated into Anglo society, but who
later return to their "roots," reclaiming a Spanish-tongue heritage, and
learning to embrace their "foreign" mothers, the need to affirm their
ethnic identity accompanies or occurs soon before or after the affirma-

tion of a sexual identity. I believe this occurs because it is part of the process of self-acceptance that the lesbian Chicana/Latina undergoes with conscientización.[13] In the case of heterosexual woman who become ethnically conscienticized after a life of attempting to be white-identified, the sexual investigation may not necessarily occur. Again, speaking only from observation, what seems to transpire in the case of "straight" women is a tendency toward nationalism rather than a celebration of femaleness free from traditional views of "la mujer," the role of mother sometimes becoming paramount to self-identification.

On the other hand, for those women who, because of their dark skin color, poverty, and conscientización could not assimilate, race and class are the first determinants in their lives. Sexuality adds a dimension to their lives (especially as lesbians) but is not separated from nor more significant than their ethnic and class identity. In their case, sexual identity seems to follow ethnic, class, and gender identity.

In the face of white dominant culture, consumer fever, and race and class privilege, girls are strongly affected at a very early age by the ostracism of those compounded forms of prejudice. A young woman who is light-skinned, or of mixed-background, and/or is born to parents who are professionals or are upwardly mobile, will in all likelihood attempt to assimilate into dominant society. On the other hand, a young woman who is poor and/or dark skinned and who must depend on her own resources to deal with the horrendous rejection by society, usually identifies strongly with her difference. This sense of being different is not always felt as positive.

In Compañeras, conscienticized women from poor backgrounds display strong loyalty to their people, a loyalty that they have felt from earliest memory. Aleticia Tijerina, mixed Native American and Chicana begins her testimony: "Because I am brown I am oppressed." She also says, "Poverty is violence. Calculated and directed, North America means to keep hidden the legislated fates of the Mexican farm workers. My mama's and my life as only two of the many whose stories have remained untold." It is important to note in the testimony of Aleticia Tijerina that she does not discuss her lesbianism (in a text about lesbians) at all. It is also important to note at this point, that her analysis seems based on Marxist orientation that focuses on economic and class struggle and excludes an understanding of "sisterhood" in the white feminist use of the term. For example, when she tells of an occasion when she was in prison and encountered a white woman, she does not empathize with the woman as another woman, nor as a lesbian does she see the woman as someone she might potentially love. Instead, at the moment of their encounter, her hatred for white people wells up. Unable to contain such repressed anger any longer, she later resolves to "cease hating."

Those of us who have experienced hunger and the hardship of economic deprivation, as activists take up these issues. If we are not activists, these early experiences nevertheless make an indelible imprint on our psyche. However, the analysis on this subject until now has been given to us by men or more specifically, by male-defined terms. It is the responsibility of women and of those who truly consider themselves desirous of a more humane world to examine the complexities of oppression that have affected us for thousands of years.

"Belinda" (a pseudonym, in the same anthology) also does not discuss her sexuality as much as her struggles with racism and the drug and alcohol dependency she assumed as a way of dealing with misdirected anger. Her only comment about her sexual desire for women is in a remark regarding the tricks who "go down" on her, an act which, with men, makes her emotionally uncomfortable. "Belinda" begins: "My parents' goal in life was the 'Great White Way.' and they just gave everything for it." While she does not indicate at any point, any political concientización, nor does she ever seem to politicize her lesbianism into a feminist act, she does see herself as a "Chicana." Along the course of her narrative, she has a black male pimp and later on, she is pimped by a white lesbian. She says of her white woman pimp: "She was from a middle-class background and very much of a business woman." In comparing her woman pimp to the earlier male one, she says the woman was quite self-assured: "She was always telling me that I need to talk differently and she always checked out the clothes I wore before I went out . . . She was also a lot more demanding and arrogant. Like she just assumed a lot more rights over me and over the men." "Belinda" considers turning tricks no different than what men do to her in straight jobs.

Quite unlike white women, Latina activists and academics, as is evident by the *Third Woman* issue and *Compañeras,* don't analyze the sexual politic as much as they expound on our struggle against racist and classist North American society along with the sexism found within and outside the home.

Yvonne Yarbro-Bejarano, a feminist-lesbian scholar, who attended the "Primer encuentro de lesbianas feministas latinoamericanas y caribeñas," held in Cuernavaca, Mexico, in fall 1987 documents attempts at the conference to grapple with lesbian sexuality and its dynamics within relationships, as well as social political obstacles that confront all Latinas throughout the Americas. According to Yarbro-Bejarano's report, latinoamericanas reacted angrily to the U.S. Latinas because they were perceived as privileged citizens of the "First World." Again, we are witness to the tendency of conscienticized Latina feminists to give their sociopolitical concerns greater weight as a focus of their activism. The long struggle for identification as Latinas unexpectedly struck the U.S. lesbians, who, ironically and obviously unbeknownst to people abroad, live or have lived in Third World conditions in the United States.

The search for identity and the politics of our sexuality, of course, are not relegated to lesbianism alone. Because lesbianism is first of all a declaration of one's sexuality, indeed, of being sexual at all, it is somewhat easier to make certain observations concerning this aspect of our lives.

Lesbians and heterosexual women alike grappled for many years with their Catholic indoctrination, which has adamantly repressed female desire. While heterosexual women may not feel the Catholic Church controlling their sexual behavior as much as in the past, they are still conscious of a restrictive stance against the use of contraceptives and abortion, issues that directly affect their sexuality. The Mexican-Catholic lesbian, rejected by family and ostracized by her immediate community, may find it painful and even impossible to acknowledge a direct connection between her faith and the rejection she suffers as a woman who loves women because Catholicism is so much a part of her sense of self.

Many women come from homes where they witness blatant privilege accorded fathers and brothers. Furthermore, they are subject to their maltreatment, demands, subjugation, sometimes physical abuse and sexual violations. For many women (including activists from el

Movimiento) a confrontation with their sexuality seems to be the last frontier of their Xicanisma activism. We may witness this in the testimonial of Victoria Alegria Rosales:

> There are many things that irritate me in life now that I'm forty-eight, an age when I should be mellow and at peace with myself. Two of the things that irritate me are to hear about sexual abuse and to be told that I don't look Mexican.[14]

In the course of her story, she describes her struggle to escape an abusive marriage, one in which her white husband would spit on her face as he was raping her. He would ask her if she loved him, if she said no, he would spit on her; if she said yes, he would call her a whore or a puta while "sticking his swollen penis" into her. Her determination to start a new life ultimately enabled her to do so, but not without much difficulty and courage. "I wanted to have a goal instead of an abusive husband and a child every year. I wanted to go to school instead of church. I wanted to be myself, find someone, raise my children, live in peace." Society *retires* women sexually (due to their loss of reproductive abilities) when they reach middle age, sometimes before they undergo menopause. Middle-aged women are made to feel physically undesirable after years of thinking that any physical desire was unnatural.

The same institutionalized thinking that ostracizes lesbianism and homosexuality penalizes heterosexual desire. In a civilization that is based on the worship of a disembodied, inimitable, misogynist god, we are taught to fear woman as creatrix, the being to whom we are all unquestionably and quite literally tied to at birth. In a better world in which we would embrace our undeniable births and our undeniable mortality we would rejoice in our sensual capabilities. Lesbianism would not be seen as a reaction to male dominance or as a rejection of men. Most lesbians do not hate men at all, they simply love women. Homosexuality would not be viewed simply as a rejection of patriarchy as well as outright contempt of woman. In the world which I describe, heterosexual society would no longer love men and hate women. In this same world, our sexuality would be truly free to express itself through our spiritual connections with all things on Earth.

Sexuality surfaces everywhere in our culture, albeit distortedly due to the repression of our primordial memories of what it truly is. We experience it in the hip-gyrating movements of our cumbias and the cheek-to-cheek twirling tension of the Tex-Mex polka (both dances are commonly danced by women together as well as men and women); in the mingling blood of our mestizo heritage, in the stifling of emotions by the church, its hymns and passion for the suffering of Jesus Christ (passion derives from extreme feeling and here it arises from repressed erotic and psychic sensations). Mexican erotica is charged by all our senses and reflected in the traditional costuming of the genders: low cut dresses, tight mariachi charro pants, open toed pumps and pointed, dapper cowboy boots. In sum, our culture is infamous for its intensities.

Sexuality has been denied to us to claim for ourselves; we have to go through various phases to explore our erotic selves while attempting to remain true to the Mexican/Chicana/Latina/India/mestiza aspects of our sociopolitical identity.

We will invariably play out dominance and submission roles with lovers of the opposite sex as well as our own sex, and with lovers of other races and class backgrounds. This polarity remains an overriding reflection of both public and private relations within our system. We will invariably try to objectify our lovers as we have been sexually objectified, lovers of the opposite sex as well as our own sex, lovers of different races and different class orientation. We will sometimes find it impossible to escape a sense of shame, regret, violation after expressing our sexual desire, so long have we been taught that sex is an unforgivable crime against divine mandates. In the past, an admittance of our sexuality demonstrated, at the very least, a lack of dignity and self-containment. It will take more than our generation or the next to free sex from male-legislated concept marriage. Nuns and priests taught us well with their two-by-four beatings, with their orders to get on our knees on cement floors and pray to statues of breathlessly beautiful suffering saints, whose pain we were to emulate in order to overcome our vulgar earthliness.

A woman who never marries but maintains multiple lovers at any given time, three lesbians cohabiting together, a mother who chooses not to co-parent with anyone, especially not a husband—these are all acts with social and political repercussions. Each of these alternative lifestyles is a challenge in the transformation of *our* culture. In the words of Aleticia Tijerina, "A radical is born with the will to survive and the strength to make trouble." When it is a question of survival, of struggling for our sanity, our self-gratification, the elimination of internal and external conflicts in our daily lives and in our homes, no act is insignificant.

As human beings denigrated by the Spanish Conquest and later made invisible and further commodified by North American Anglo dominance, the majority of us don't feel that our own lives have ample influence to make a "political" difference. While our sexuality has been a political issue for the men governing our societies since before the Aztec Empire, we don't have to follow exactly the model for resistance of Anglo and European feminists.[15]

Instead, we may begin by learning to listen to our own inner voices, to trust our "poet's intuitions," the visions of the dreamer. We can enjoy the titillated nerve endings of our bodies, bodies that white media tells us are inferior and ugly. We can celebrate our rediscovery of the orgasm of which women, a generation ago, were taught to deprive themselves.

We may start by casting from our bedrooms, homes, offices, factories, fields, classrooms, and streets, the ghosts of our mothers, fathers, nuns, priests, and even the Pope.

Since early childhood we are indoctrinated to believe in a great many sexually repressive tales. We must remind ourselves that these tales were told to us by men and women whose own lives may have been stunning contradictions: the priest who secretly has sex with his female confessioners (or alter boys); the Mother Superior who falls in love with her favorite female student; the father who rapes his eleven-year-old daughter, telling her that he is only doing it to "warn" her of what she will encounter with her husband; the mother who admonishes her teen-age daughter when she gets pregnant and does not reconcile with her own teen-age pregnancy; the husband who is so fixed on his wife as a holy virgin mother he will not permit her to express her sexual desire without seeing her as a "whore" and suspecting her of betrayal. These representatives of society, assigned the task of perpetuating sexual and spiritual oppression, were forced into hypocrisy because the asexual and anti-evolutionary God upheld by this civilization is inimitable.

Sex in and of itself has not caused woman sorrow. The way she has been used sexually as a result of her reproductive abilities has. Before the Conquest, Aztec women had become the spoils of war. As in other *advanced* cultures, our indigenous past was moving from an economy that had earlier developed self-sufficiency for women to one where men systematically took charge. It is impossible to "free" our attitudes about our sexuality in a society where we are not free as human beings. Moreover, women historically have been associated with the body, which we know is perishable and therefore of no value. Because of the degree to which religion has stigmatized women, it is understandable why women still do not see the link between eroticism and spirituality. But if we cannot claim anything for ourselves, let us at least begin to integrate the mind, soul, and body. Our principle struggle can be for an understanding of the beauty of our whole selves—an organic, unified entity rejoicing in our connection with all living things on Earth.

Seven

BRUJAS AND CURANDERAS
A LIVED SPIRITUALITY

Myths are not lies, but rather men's attempt to impose a symbolic order upon their universe.
—Sarah B. Pomeroy, Goddesses, Whores, Wives, and Slaves

WOMEN'S HISTORY IS ONE OF RELIGIOSITY

Men of Western Culture may have been the designers of cults over the past two millennia, but the women have long been relegated the task of preserving those cults, not often as official representatives but with daily rituals of popular culture and by passing faith from generation to generation. A growing trend among those of us who are pursuing non-traditional lifestyles is to return to long lost and non-Western ways in search of new direction for our lives; we have unearthed the ways of our Mexic Amerindian ancestors preserved by our mestizo elders, most often, women, in the form of curanderismo.

However, women must be cautious about our sources for spiritual regeneration. Even as we select from our Mexica (Nahua) and Christian traditions, it is only we today, who ultimately can define what is needed to give us courage. If we lived in an utopian society where adults were not daily faced with challenges in all facets of our lives, our personal strength might not be tested. But for the brown woman of limited means there is no utopia. Challenges in and of themselves are not negative. It is how we respond to life's tests that is important. So, as we begin to solicit spiritual guidance no longer from a paternal white god figure but from a brown or black symbolic mother, we must also return to her all her vital energies that were taken from her over the centuries.[1] We must take heed that not all symbols that we have inherited are truly symbolic of the life-sustaining energy we carry within ourselves as women; so even when selectively incorporating what seems indispensable to our religiosity, we must analyze its historical meaning. We must, if necessary give it new meaning, so that it validates our instincts to survive on our own terms. Moreover, survival should not be our main objective. Our presence shows our will to survive, to overcome every form of repression known to humankind. Our goal should be to achieve joy.

When we become knowledgeable about plants, we see proof that the traditional medicine of our ancestors indeed was curative. This knowledge again, was taken from us throughout recent generations and is still kept from most of us who are integrated in Western society, replaced by synthetic treatments for illnesses through drugs and Western medical practices. My point here is not to make a blanket condemnation of modern medicine and medical technology, but to recognize that its basis lies in very ancient practices which are not necessarily inaccessible to us. Society accepts the help of therapists or clergy. But the woman developing Xicanista conscientización may also find herself turning to the tradition of relying on community elders for guidance to interpret our experiences. She may follow suggestions from such community servants to participate in sweat lodges, to meditate, or to undergo some other form of "spiritual cleansing." This apparent synthesis of belief systems for mestiza consciousness is her way of coping in a society that does not give her humanity substantial value. It is not a contradiction of irreconcilable ideologies. At this juncture in her history, by recalling her blood-tie memories to the Americas and relying upon the guidance of her dreams and intuitions, she gradually reawakens her female indigenous energies:

WE DO WELL in developing our own ways, our own alchemy for cures, a combination of modern medicine and ancient practices. We take from the Eastern Buddhists even as we do from our grandmothers' American indigenous knowledge.

WE DO WELL in using our imaginations and intuitions and to speak of them to each other.

WE DO WELL by not being afraid to commit the taboo of same-sex touching. For our caresses have too long been reserved by men for themselves and for their sons.

WE KNOW WE DO WELL because those of us who are inventing that which has not been passed on to us, or using our new ability to read to learn from books, or our recent independence from the traditional roles of obedient daughter, young matron, and wife, to travel on our own, interacting with other cultures and learning to determine what is necessary for us to appropriate for our own survival, know we make ourselves *feel* better, that is, stronger willed and self-confident. We know that the ancient native practice of the sweat lodge is not only physically beneficial but does in fact give our emotional selves a sense of rejuvenation. In other words, we are reclaiming all that which was taken away from us by the particular direction civilization took. We will determine for ourselves what makes us feel whole, what brings us tranquility, strength, courage to face the countless—not for one moment imagined—obstacles in the path on our journey toward being fulfilled human beings.

So, if a woman decides that she still finds rewards in pursuing the rituals and mandates of the church, or simply by "meditating in the temple" of her own room, or if she constructs an altar in her home, (perhaps not like the one she knew as a child of a myriad of saints and crosses, but of articles that have special meaning for her); or if one day, she discards all religious icons and can embrace herself with self-acceptance and calls *that* her spirituality, she is continuously doing one and the same thing: maintaining her well being.

For this purpose alone, for us, who are often regarded with contempt in this society, whose entire people are regarded contemptibly, all and every attempt at peace and health should be seen as valid. We descend from a long and endless line of non-valued human beings, born to servitude and to pay homage to a higher order, and we fit into the present schema for the sole purpose of continuing that anonymous line of labor. Any act that we commit that does not serve that purpose is an act of insurrection to the system. As Xicanistas in our daily lives, in our work, we make very deliberate and courageous decisions daily to undermine that system. In this respect too, we must understand that in proclaiming our spirituality it must be to serve our needs, not necessarily those of our mothers, but of the next generation of women:

> We must address our spirit guides for clarity
> on the fact of abortion as we have been taught to do so
> with regard to conception and birth.

We must address our spirit guides on the needs to learn
to defend ourselves physically, to protect each other,
to provide for each other's material needs. Our paternal
religious teachings have served not only the male gender
but a certain class and race, and for the most part
leaves the vast majority of us
with a great and inconsolable sense of fallibility.
We must ask to not be afraid of the truth
of the extent of our sexual desire, not to fear it
even as it has been denied to us.
We must ask for the gift to communicate our needs,
to be eloquent and determined in our public articulation of
them.
We must search within ourselves and in each other
for the courage to challenge the misogynist
and otherwise unjust legislation imposed on us
by the lawmakers of the world.
We must, above all, search within ourselves
and grapple with the misogynist, racist, and
classist that has been planted in our own
minds and cast "her" out. She has turned
mother against daughter, woman against woman,
and woman against herself for too long.

The awareness that we have at times in our lives barely survived
the most trying and humiliating conditions is what makes our bodies
tremble, our minds flounder, and our emotional states fail in fear of the
present and future. When this happens, as it does to many of us, even
as we sheroically fight against it, knowing our responsibilities and our
loyalties to our immediate families and our communities at large, we
must not accept the long held premise that it is due to our inherent
weaknesses and that it is our own personal failure.

When one of us dies of cancer, loses her mind, or commits suicide,
we must not blame her for her inability to survive an ongoing political
mechanism bent on the destruction of that human being. Sanity remains
defined simply by the ability to cope with insane conditions.

Furthermore, our long-range objective in understanding ourselves,
affirming ourselves, integrating our fragmented identities, truly believing in the wisdom of our ancient knowledge is to bring the rest of

humanity to the fold. That is, today, we grapple with our need to thoroughly understand who we are—gifted human beings—and to believe in our gifts, talents, our worthiness and beauty, while having to survive within the constructs of a world antithetical to our intuition and knowledge regarding life's meaning. Our vision must encompass sufficient confidence that dominant society will eventually give credence to our ways, if the world is to survive. Who, in this world of the glorification of material wealth, whiteness, and phallic worship would consider *us* holders of knowledge that could transform this world into a place where the quality of life for all living things on this planet is the utmost priority; where we are all engaged in a life process that is meaningful from birth to death, where we accept death as organic to life, where death does not come to us in the form of one more violent and unjust act committed against our right to live?

BRAVE NEW WORLD

We live in a future once believed possible only in the minds of those with sardonic imaginations. Aldous Huxley, in his novel *Brave New World,* predicted a society in which human beings were created out of test tubes. We know today that such a scientific feat is possible and holds the possibilities of equally resultant horrors for humankind as those foretold in *Brave New World.* There were human beings in Huxley's world born only for the purpose of serving those considered genetically *superior* to them. However, we know that this concept was already implemented throughout recorded history, that slavery was based on this belief.

We live in an age in which we live with the potential of virtual destruction of the entire planet through the abuse of nuclear power. The twentieth century ushered in an age long awaited by male scientists: to have power over life and death in massive proportions.

If our history as women has been regulated by men because of our biological ability to reproduce the species, what does it mean that science now begins to think of dispensing with the womb? In fact, in terms of reproduction, it has already eliminated the need for direct male contact through intercourse with the process of artificial insemination (something the Hebrew God already did in both the Old and

New Testaments). With such questions weighing over humanity—the persistence of wars, ongoing poverty, and diseases for which we have no cures (events not so unlike those of the medieval age of Europe)—it is no wonder that so many Western thinkers are in search of a new truth on which they can explain their existences on the planet.

Along those lines, there is a strong rise of fundamental Christian Churches. They attempt to affirm some mythical moral past that above all was based on the regulation of woman's sexuality and spirituality. Furthermore, to return to that supposed time of unquestionable, stringent male serving morality would ultimately lead us back to where we are now, in search of meaning, of sensation, of connections.

In the White Woman's Movement, the attempt to re-appropriate woman's spirituality came via asserting a matriarchal time, said to have preceded recorded history, during which the Great Mother Goddess was worshipped. White feminist theologians, such as Mary Daly, have done strenuous research on behalf of these arguments. As non-white feminists in the United States became more visible, they expressed a contention to the WWM's emphasis on the White Mother Goddess. The white feminists' position was understandable in light of their own analysis since it was, to use feminist vernacular, "a healing process" for middle class, educated, white women. Audre Lorde stated in a published address on this subject, "An Open Letter to Mary Daly":

> So I wondered why doesn't Mary deal with Afrekete as an ex-
> ample? Why are her goddess-images only white, western-
> european, judeo-christian? . . . It was obvious that you were
> dealing with non-european women, but only as victims and
> preyers-upon each other. I began to feel my history and my
> mythic background distorted by the absence of any images of
> my foremothers in power. . . . What you excluded from *Gyn-
> Ecology* dismissed my heritage and the heritage of all other non-
> european women, and denied the real connections that exist be-
> tween all of us.[2]

If the white woman first saw her "oppression" in opposition to the dominant status of the white male, we understand that it was her obvious recourse to juxtapose her truths to his. That is, white man as master of the universe created a white god to justify his superiority over the human race. White woman as his mate, unearthed a white goddess who preceded the creation of the white god and therefore her power superseded that of the master.[3]

But non-white women draw on the various resources of our own continents for our spirituality. Peoples with strong African affinities have revived and are daily making more active the Yorubic religion brought to the American shores with slavery and driven underground by white masters, such as that which Luisah Teish proclaims in her book *Jambalaya*.[4] Most non-white feminist activists, however, are living fairly innocuous lives and the various ways by which their spirituality is exercised are personal and diverse.

The Chicana feminist, who is of mixed European and Amerindian origins is making similar attempts at reviving the credences of her ancestors, vis à vis, the traditional practices of curanderas. Such practices, some of which may be traced back to the Nahua people (Aztecs) and certainly to various other Mexic Amerindian peoples, such as the Huichol, also have similarities with European beliefs, which we discuss in part later here. Commonalities are what drive anthropologists all over the world in their attempt to understand humankind—since the further back we go, it seems, the more we can observe cultural universals.

The feminist-activist, who has been involved with the WWM to some extent through her work—for example, in rape crisis intervention and domestic violence—can be nearly as harmed by the dominance of white feminism as by the male based society that has systematically annihilated her sense of well being, body, mind, and spirit. These women are themselves, very often, what is termed by white feminism "survivors" of incest, child abuse, alcohol abuse, and other atrocities endorsed by the social structure in which we all live. They enter into this line of work out of a need to help others like themselves as much as the need to "heal" themselves. However, the modus operandi of the white feminist establishment is unsatisfactory as it does not speak to women of color culturally, but may always border on the condescension white well-meaning members of society tend to feel toward people of color. This kind of therapy does not recall anything from the collective memory of mestizas. One of the strongest characteristics of the Chicano Movement has been our collective memory, a sense of familia that has been like a membrane holding together those of us committed through conscientización.

So, certain feminists originating from that form of activism, are recalling the folkways of their grandmothers while altering the Catholic faith of their devout mothers. For example, they remain devoted to certain Catholic saints, giving a woman focused dimension to their symbolism. The Virgin of Guadalupe is a favorite. She is not only the patron saint of México, a cultural bond for all of us as "Guadalupanas," but also the "brown" mother goddess, Tonantzin. She, therefore, is an ancient indigenous maternal symbol for us.

One way in which Catholic saints are attended to by brujas and curanderas is in the form of inexpensive votive candles purchased in supermarkets with the picture of the saint and a petition painted on the glass. The rising cost of these candles is an indication of their increasing popularity.

The ritual of candle and incense burning used by the church as a very solemn affair is also advocated by spiritualists of all kinds. It is no less solemn for us, save for the fact that their use is often disassociated from an evocation of male power. "Aura sweepings," the cleansing of the spirit, is another practice, accomplished sometimes with the use of smoke, such as the burning of sweet grass (Native American), copal (Aztec), or tobacco (Native American/Yorubic).

The bruja and curandera might associate the fundamental betrayal of the church with her womanhood, with her devout Catholic mother. She, therefore, may be inclined toward her grandmother's beliefs, or the teachings of a community elder. Creating some distance from the last generation, from whom she is unlearning many lessons that have felt harmful to her well-being, allows her to recapture some of her spiritual orientation, and to adapt it to her own needs while still operating within her own culture.

In much the same way that the WWM sought an affirmation of womanhood through European goddess worship, the mestiza resurrects her own pantheon of indigenous goddesses, primarily Guadalupe/Tonantzin, and Coatlicue. This desire for what is popularly called "self-empowerment" is a most necessary process toward self-healing.

By healing we refer to recovering from the devastating blows we receive from society for having been born poor, non-white, and female in a hierarchical society.

Ritual may be used as a veritable healing method. As psychologists have noted, human beings must have some order in their lives to help them function in society. Ritual may be used to calm oneself and/or to reassure others when chaos seems at hand. It may be through an aura sweeping, tarot card reading, the construction of altars, or "channel" sessions, just to name a few of the alternatives to institutionalized religions women are practicing today for themselves. All methods employed by the spiritually oriented Xicanista in search of psychic rejuvenation are valid when utilized respectfully—that is, acknowledging non-hierarchical connection with all life energies. We may, as has been suggested by feminist-spiritual practitioners, assume the customs passed on to us through old beliefs or invent our own—which we see now more frequently.

Some feminist-activists in the mental health services are using these methods with their Latino/a clientele, which seems to respond more effectively to this treatment than to the alien mental health practices of the white establishment. This desire to heal our traumatized selves, as I say, is one step. Most significantly, it is an affirmative step toward the declaration of one's significance in the spectrum of all life force and what constitutes society. We may now become whole individuals in the larger picture of humanity. We now have voices. We may now be legitimate contributors to our world.

However, an attempt at obtaining such direction from our past simply by imitating or inventing ritual is not necessarily the clearest path or rather, does not guarantee an evolved spirituality. Many women have found just as many disturbing contradictions in ancient practices with regard to their womanhood as in the church that they have so recently come to question. Their disappointment should not be surprising given their new Xicanisma consciousness. Therefore, a synthesis of old forms with goals that aim to restore the feminine as a prominent component is required. Above all, our applications must correspond to our contemporary needs and concerns.

TRADITIONAL HEALING: THE ROAD TO SELF-EMPOWERMENT

Many of these things you must experience, before you understand them.

—*Un curandero,* Curanderismo: Mexican American Folk Healing

The history of curanderismo derives from ancient knowledge that spans all five continents. The methods of curanderismo which apply the use of mental, spiritual, and material expertise descend from Native American, European, Eastern, and Middle Eastern philosophies and knowledge.[5]

Arabic medicine (borrowed from Greek knowledge) was a great contributor to Spain before the reconquest of Spanish territories. Spaniards brought not only knowledge of the medical sciences with them to the Americas, but their own Judeo-Christian beliefs. Christian symbolism is an integral part of curanderismo. African beliefs, which came to the Americas with the slave market also merged. Most recently, Eastern philosophies are being adapted by Chicanas, in particular, Buddhism, although it may be acknowledged that there are deep parallels between the Native American and the Eastern perception of life.

The Arabic medical practice of utilizing herbal cures was re-adapted in the Americas with plants found on these continents and combined with Native American healing knowledge, which, in addition to herbal medicine, also has included baths, setting bones, and other remedies.

There is wide-spread acknowledgement of certain ailments so that various communities of curanderas are able to identify symptoms and treat them without necessarily being healers themselves. For example, when I was fifteen years old, I experienced "susto" as a result of being approached and followed on the street one night after work by a strange man. A good friend of my sister told her mother, who then sent over herbs for me to take as a tea. I suffered from this ailment for approximately two weeks and took the tea just as I would have taken a dose of medicine prescribed by a Western doctor for a bad cough. In Mexican communities, such prescriptions are respected. Based on traditional beliefs, our community, whether urban or rural in the United States, is close knit and gives a sense of tribal affiliations. Therefore, while I had never met the woman, her prognosis was accepted.

Susto (literally, fright) is among the most common afflictions from which we may suffer. Among others are mal de ojo, bilis, and empacho.[6] There are very common prescriptions for the ridding of these ailments. Their symptoms are physical and psychological in nature. Their causes may be physical and/or magical.

In terms of curanderismo, magic is directly related to the supernatural realm of our reality. I use the term supernatural loosely because supernatural implies a probable reality beyond natural forces. However, for curanderas the supernatural *is* a reality based on the natural forces of the universe. Another explanation is that curanderas believe that persons can cause physical and emotional illnesses in others by use of personal power or with the help of non-corporeal beings.

Not all curanderas work actively with spiritual elements. They may specialize in herbal and massage treatments. Most, however, do recognize to some extent the power of espiritismo. Quite often they attribute their divine power to the Supreme Maker of Christianity. Others, and this is a growing trend, are subscribing to a spiritual philosophy that is not necessarily Christian. These curanderas believe that we all are born with souls (a belief of all major religions) and that our corporeal beings are transient. We therefore, can solicit the aid of spirits who are no longer in their corporeal bodies. Although many curanderas claim to be Catholic, this, of course, is not what has been taught in Catholicism which believes in the death of a life as final while the soul awaits Judgement Day.

In any case, curanderas who mostly specialize in the spiritual healing approach, widely adapt Judeo-Christian symbolism in their rituals. For example, they may find the use of candles essential to the remedy. The material use of objects, such as candles, incense, and oils, are employed for the benefit of the solicitor as a reassurance that something concrete is being performed. Do not mistake this for a placebo. Einstein proved to the naïve scientific world that matter is energy. Through energy that treatment is made effective. The espiritista, who is not necessarily a curandera in the medical sense—that is, she may not prescribe medicinal herbs or give massages—may see her role as a diagnostician of physical ailments with a developed faculty that detects the cause and offers a prognosis that counteracts that cause.

Some espiritistas believe that everyone has an inborn faculty to communicate with transcended beings, although not to the same capacity. However, without being aware of one's faculties, one may be vulnerable when exposed inadvertently to negative energies. What I mean by negative here is debilitating forces, energies that deplete one's self-confidence or ánimo.

I would like to make a distinction here in the web of human resources that we have and are to each other as Xicanistas who seek spiritual, mental, and psychic guidance from each other. I have titled this chapter, "Brujas and Curanderas," which indeed, implies the discussion to be of women endowed with a range of wisdom. Again, I am limited to the use of popular idioms to clarify a portion of our identity. A bruja is not necessarily a curandera in the traditional sense. She falls under the rubric of a spiritual healer or psychic. The curandera, on the other hand, is a specialized healer, learned in the knowledge of specifically healing the body. However, in non-Western thinking, the body is never separate from the spirit or mind and all curative recommendations always consider the ailing person as a whole.

Curanderas may also be categorized according to their particular knowledge, for examples: sobaderas, those who give massages; yerberas who are expert in herbs; and parteras, midwives. A curandera may be expert in any combination or all of these healing aspects. She usually demonstrates a gift for healing at a very young age and by the time she is a woman, she is recognized by her community as a curandera.

As the granddaughter of a curandera, I understood as a child that such developed faculties are not to be exploited or capitalized upon. Anyone with any regard for life will agree that such knowledge should not be used except to reinstate Karmic harmony. If in fact, we release our passive faith from Christian doctrine and make use of recent *discoveries* we have acquired through modern physics, we cease to view life as linear, hierarchical, jutting up to heaven and making divinity in our lives increasingly remote. In its place, we instate a perception of life as being physically connected from atom to atom, no single part being more essential nor grander than the rest and that we are all vital to each other.

Today we are all convinced that we are helpless in the face of the unexplainable. Yet, on the contrary, there are no mysteries experienced in life that we cannot unlock from within our own imaginations. However, we must have as our rule of thumb the preservation of natural resources and the well-being of humanity. What this society has come to conceive of as progress threatens the annihilation of humanity. It has already begun with the steady genocide of certain peoples, in addition to the permanent extinction of certain vegetation and animals. This systematic annihilation until now did not seem to directly affect white people (who have controlled the world for many centuries), so it was not, until now, a major cause of alarm.

However, "control" of human and natural resources for the sake of profit notwithstanding, many people, those of color and white, female and male, have discovered a vast void in our daily lives even when subscribing to a major religion. Centuries-old religions do not directly address the demands placed on our lives by contemporary technological society.

This leads me to my reference to brujas. In Mexican culture, a brujo is someone to fear and to revere while a bruja is someone to hate to the point of killing if at all possible. However, I claim this term for women who are in tune with their psyches, allow their lives to be informed by them, and offer their intuitive gifts to their communities without fear of being seen as loathsome or mad. The key is to remember that historically woman, who is fertile and filled with the mysteries of reproduction, was hated and feared by men for that reason alone. If we dispense with that fear but retain or reinstate our insights and connections with all living things, we have a woman with developed psychic resources, a bruja.

Brujas also have their range of categories. They may practice the esoteric arts, for example, Tarot readings. But the key to remember is their inherent communication with the spirit world.

In my opinion, when I discuss espiritistas, they fall under the classification of brujas. If an individual elects to investigate further into the beliefs of espiritismo she must do so by first accepting some general premises. At this time, espiritismo, while a growing movement numbering in the thousands, is not an institution sanctioned by dominant society. Also, espiritismo, as it is practiced by traditional Mexicans, is still embedded with the seeds of male supremacy in the form of God the Omnipotent Father. We must always keep in mind that the institutionalization of beliefs is done for the benefit of the few who have invested interests in maintaining the status quo. Therefore, the decision to move toward espiritismo must be a personal one.

A final word of caution for those of us who elect to practice curanderismo, espiritismo, or to solicit the guidance of those who do. A curandera and a bruja should be seen as a specialized human resource and she should keep this in mind about herself, too. Modern society approves of people consulting a gynecologist, chiropractor, or a psychologist if we have an ailment that they have been trained to attend. However, training does not exempt these individuals from being susceptible to the ailments they know how to help remedy. Brujas, curanderas, or healing women also are just that, trained specialists, but keep in mind that no one is exempt from human frailties, from the potential of committing errors.

THE NEW AGE MOVEMENT IS MOSTLY WHITE AND AFFLUENT in its following. While it may be said that there are those among them who are sincere, the nature with which the New Age philosophy is executed, vis à vis capitalism does give rise to skepticism. There are, for example, great fees for sessions with "channels" said to communicate with spirits. There are New Age retreats (with high fees). There is New Age music. I do not disclaim the professed faculties of such channels. I do enjoy the music. However, I do take issue with the capitalization of spiritual faculties by certain New Age channels.

The development of this practice must not be used to profit the individual, neither through monetary gain nor personal aggrandizement, by exploiting the vulnerability of people, who despite their race, class, and sex privilege, are alienated from their spiritual selves, which is, in fact, *the* self.

The development of such faculties must always be viewed with a sense of humility, to recognize one's integration and dependency upon other life forms on the planet. The object of such practitioners should always be to reinstate harmony among life forms, which cannot be accomplished through hierarchical privilege. A blatant example of this abuse is seen with the monetary success of Lynn Andrews, self-proclaimed shamaness of Beverly Hills.

An espiritista of good intent does not utilize her don (healing gift one is born with) to compete with others of developed faculties. She does not employ it to control (another word for power) others. If an espiritista (using channeling) capitalizes on her faculties, either monetarily or by communicating to solicitors that her faculties are a personal power that can be used to control them, she is serving solely to perpetuate imbalance. Charging a fee for sharing one's spiritual gifts is a privilege granted by the free enterprise system under which we live today. It has no direct association with espiritismo. A channel who charges and gets large sums of money for her/his "services" (as some New Age channel celebrities do) does not prove that her or his abilities are of great worth. He or she simply proves a facility for being an entrepreneur.

While espiritismo is not necessarily feminist, it is egalitarian in that it sees all humanity, as well as animal and plant life, respectful of each other. It is an acknowledgement of the energy that exists throughout the universe subatomically generating itself and interconnecting, fusing, and changing.

While subatomic studies may serve as a theoretical basis for social change, on a more pragmatic and immediate level, they offer a personal response to the divided state of the individual who desires wholeness. An individual who does not sense herself as helpless to circumstances is more apt to contribute positively to her environment than one who resigns with apathy to it because of her sense of individual insignificance.

Espiritismo is not in and of itself the answer to the emerging threat of human annihilation that we live under. But the life that an espiritista leads and some of the decisions that she makes with regard to her environment will lead her to make the kinds of decisions that feminists, community activists, and environmentalists make. More importantly, it will not leave her feeling anonymous and vulnerable in the social schema. Her personal traumas experienced as a direct result of her femaleness, her brown skin, and her economic hardships, are understood as being part of the degenerating system we are obliged to live under. Once the causes for certain obstacles in her life are identi-

issue of
victimization

fied and worked through, she does not flounder about as merely a "survivor," such as one who has survived a plane wreck and awaits a rescue team (which may never be forthcoming) but uses the new affirmation, *that she is and has always been part of the intricate network of life on this planet,* to strengthen herself and to share her knowledge with others. Ultimately we seek to propel ourselves into a collective state of being, which is so ancient we will consider it new.

In the long run, spirituality will be a state of being that is not defined, but lived, as a unified self, and the concept of an inherent struggle between good and evil imposed on us for thousands of years will have been relegated to an unfortunate memory for all of humanity. We will nevertheless not want to forget, lest we return to it—and we, along with this, our planet, Earth, may not have a second chance.

POSTSCRIPT: A PRESCRIPTION FOR RELIEVING EMOTIONAL AND PHYSICAL ANXIETY

Baños are a remedy for both physical and emotional ills prescribed by curanderas throughout the ages in the Americas. There are also dulce baños to increase or maintain a joyful state (such as being in love). The following "recipe" may be used to cleanse the self of negative energies in the environment, to rid one of an unsettling feeling, or regularly, for chronic anxiety.

BAÑO

Baños may be taken on Tuesdays and Fridays. (Sundays are okay, too. Refrain from baños during menstruation.)

1. Several drops of Spirit of Ammonia
2. Several drops of Spirit of Camphor
3. Handful of eucalyptus (fresh is best, substitute in another form, if necessary, okay.)
4. Handful of sage (fresh is best, substitute in another form, if necessary, okay.)
5. Splash of Agua de la Florida
6. 3, 7, or 9 lemons or limes
7. 3, 7, or 9 garlic cloves (amount to correspond with number of lemons or limes)

Place and pour ingredients directly into one or two large pots and bring to a boil. Limes/Lemons must be cut open crosswise (+), squeezed and thrown in whole. Cover, simmer. When cool, sift, but retain lemons/limes. Baño may be taken standing up in the shower, or if preferred, in a warm bath. Using a small container, pour baño systematically over yourself, starting with the top of your head, back of the neck, across shoulder blades, etc., always in the shape of the cross of the four directions. You may want to rub the lemons/limes directly on your body, vigorously, before finishing. During the baño, concentrate only on its curative effects, do not let your mind wander. Afterward, do not dry yourself off, but patting dry with a towel is okay. Let your hair and skin air dry. Have a clean, preferably, white, or brightly colored garment (like a nightgown) ready to slip on until you're dry. If it is before bedtime, you may sleep in it. This treatment will be much more enhanced if you take time before the baño to prepare yourself with meditation. Use a white candle, incense of your preference, and/or a clear jar of water. It will help you to relax and to concentrate on your baño.

eight

UN TAPIZ:

The Poetics of Conscientización

I

Now i think i know how you saw me that first summer . . . i was part of the culture that wouldn't allow me to separate.*[1]

I left the church in tears, knowing how for many years I had closed my heart to the passionate pull of such faith that promised no end to the pain. I grew white. Fought to free myself from my culture's claim on me.#

Culture forms our beliefs. Culture is made by those in power— men.+

> dark women come to me
> sitting in circles
> I pass thru their hands
> the head of my mother
> painted in clay colors . . .#

We were drawn to each other by the Indian spirit of mutual ancestors.*

I am visible—see this Indian face—yet I am invisible. I both blind them with my beak nose and am their blind spot. But I exist, we exist.+

II

. . . [O]nce being born it would no longer be innocent, for being was to survive and to survive, one must hurt weaker beings. No, the end of harming another living being was not the destruction but the saving of oneself, which becomes the true objective.*

In the shed behind the corral, where they'd hidden the fawn, Prieta found the hammer. She had to grasp it with both hands.

She swung it up. The weight folded her body backwards. A
thud reverberated on Venadita's skull.+

Women do not coagulate into one
hero's death; we bleed
out of many pores, so constant
that it has come to be seen
as the way things are.#

Love? In the classic sense, it describes in one syllable all the
humiliation that one is born to and pressed upon to surrender
to a man.*

III

That power is my inner self, the entity that is the sum total of
all my incarnations, the godwoman in me I call Antigua, mi
Diosa, the divine within, Coatlicue-Cihuacoatl-Tlazolteotl-
Tonantzin-Coatlaopeuh-Guadalupe they are one.+

With this knowledge so deeply emblazoned upon my heart,
how then was I supposed to turn away from La Madre, La Chicana? If I were to build my womanhood on this self-evident
truth, it is the lover of the Chicana, the lover of myself as a
Chicana I had to embrace, no white man.#

IV

It is
my face, wanting
and refusing everything.

. . . I want to feel
your touch outside
my body on the surface
of my skin.

I want to know, for sure,
where you leave off
and I begin.#

V

We are afraid to look at how we have failed each other. We are
afraid to see how we have taken the values of our oppressor
into our hearts and turned them against ourselves and one
another.#

We needled, stabbed, manipulated, cut and through it all we
loved, driven to see the other improved in her own reflection.*

I will not be ashamed again. Nor will I shame myself.+

OURS IS A POETICS NO DIFFERENT than other literary movements throughout the ages. We are looking at what has been handed
down to us by previous generations of poets and, in effect, rejecting,
reshaping, restructuring, reconstructing that legacy and making language and structure ours, suitable to our moment in history.

What makes the Mexic Amerindian woman's literary expression
questionable (and indeed ours is often under suspicion as legitimate
literature) is essentially the same mechanism that has always kept us
invisible as human beings and suppressed our contributions to the
changing process of society. Supporters of the status quo doubt the
value of our cultural endeavors because they measure our efforts against
self-serving standards. If we learn to use language in such a way that it
conforms to these standards, then, of course, our work proves itself
worthy (though often deemed imitative). The *individual* who adopts
the prevailing standards will be rewarded, the one who refuses is
ostracized. This punishment and reward system for assimilation is not
just "the American way," it is the last resort when blatant rejection on
the basis of class, race, and sex are no longer considered acceptable by
society.

PRIVILEGE GRANTS LANGUAGE
WHICH ESCAPES ME

But what of the vulgar limitations of language? As a utilizer of symbols—
the written word—my dilemma is not only that of social marginalization from the language of dominant society, but also the diminishment

of my function as a poet who attempts to give some tangible interpretation of life's meaning. For there is one universal aim of poetry, it is the relentless attempt to free human desire: to inspire the will to live, to rejoice, to let the imagination flourish. Part and parcel of this endeavor is the poet's willingness to accept death, death with dignity, as part of life. The "political" poet is outraged at death without dignity, death caused by the insanity and greed of war instigated by special interest groups who have it in their hands to catalyze and manage such destruction. But all poets are as intimate with death as we all are with breathing.

The written word was historically the exclusive realm of a particular class of people: white, upper class, well-educated men. Over time a handful of "exceptional" women have been admitted to this exclusive circle. Women, who have had access to only mediocre and often inferior public or parochial institutions bent on the repression of the human will, were not meant to take on the pen as a way of life. Being of the generation that globally rebelled against authority, we have managed, remarkably, I think, to change that.

Choosing to be conscious transmitters of literary expressions, we have become excavators of our common culture, mining legends, folklore, and myths for our own metaphors. Ours is not Homer but Netzahualcoyotl, not Sappho but Sor Juana, not Athena but Coatlicue. Our cultural heritages were "discovered" in the era of our generation's rebellion. They were not directly passed on to us from the previous generation, which because of social ostracism, lack of education, migration, dispersion, and poverty, was not in a position to uncover and share such a rich and illustrious legacy.

What is most provocative and significant in contemporary Chicana literature is that while we claim and explore these cultural metaphors as symbols of rebellion against the dominant culture, we have also taken on the re-visioning of our own culture's metaphors, informed as they are by male perceptions. As an example, we need only look at the figure of Malintzin/doña Marina/La Malinche, traditionally seen as a symbol of betrayal of the indigenous race. In recent years, feminist writers have reinterpreted Malintzin in a variety of ways—from slave victim, heroine, and mother of the mestizo race to genius linguist and military strategist. By viewing her with compassion, we have attempted to clarify how the patriarchal conquest ultimately left this young Mexic Amerindian woman little choice but to obey in the name of God the Father.

Our early poetry, primarily intended to catalyze resistance and to stir the hearts of the pueblo, was a poetry that employed the language of daily life. The emergence and vitality of this poetry played an important role in the Chicano Movement's two primary goals: the gaining of legitimate acknowledgment by dominant society, thereby generating greater educational and economic opportunities, and the affirming of our unique cultural identity in an Anglocentric society.

We have, however, reached a new phase in our poetics of self-definition. As mestizas, we must take a critical look at language, *all* our languages and patois combinations, with the understanding that language is not something we adopt and that remains apart from us. Explicitly or implicitly, language is the vehicle by which we perceive ourselves in relation to the world. If we as writers no longer necessarily feel bound to a process engendered by the Chicano Movement, we are each individually accountable now for our use of language and the ideas communicated through it.

The vast majority of us were taught to be afraid of a certain type of English: the language of Anglos who initiated and sustained our social and economic disenfranchisement, who consciously or unconsciously instigated our traumatic experiences in monolingual Anglo schools, and who subscribed to and exacerbated the racism under which we have always lived in the United States even though we are U.S. citizens. At the same time, we were equally intimidated by the Spanish spoken by people of middle-class or higher economic strata who come from Latin America. For how could a language of those so different experientially from us, speak for those of us here who have so long been denied a sense of belonging, a sense of historical ties to this nation, and indeed, to any nation?[2]

On the one hand, we may choose to adapt standard English and white writing standards, using material from our cultural heritage as a "motif." This, in my opinion, would reduce our poetry to Oaxacan paper cuts strung from beam to beam: white standards the firm structures, with Hispanic "flourishes" lending the local color that sanctions the celebrated fallacy of the melting pot. By white writing, I refer to the current Anglophile trend being processed through workshops and M. F. A programs across the United States. Ivan Argüelles puts it succinctly:

> Evocative, finely crafted, witty, urbane, sophisticated, occasionally troubling, but always safe, White writing is easily the most pervasive literary fashion today . . . White writing can sometimes be politically correct, but sanitized and with only faint air-brushed innuendos of anger.[3]

On the other hand, we may equally limit our perceptions by refusing to explore the possibilities of language (therefore, ideas). One Mexican linguistic trait that we are heir to is the irresistibility of playing with language. Word-play for the Mexican Spanish speaker is contagious, a reflection of our sense of irony and humor about life. In the process of word play, of actively transforming one word into another and then another based on the similarity of sounds, we create new meaning, or give the original thought a fusion of multiple meanings.[4] In attempting to do this with English dominant speakers—especially, but not exclusively, white people—I am always disappointed to see that the unimaginative way they have been taught to hear language makes a complete disaster of my attempt at "word-play."

We are intimate with passion. Again, to illustrate my point I quote from Argüelles' definition of white writing to demonstrate what Mexican Spanish writers do *not* want to aim for: "White writing does not concern itself with Thanatos, the mystery of death, but with guilt feelings aroused in watching a close relative die. White writing ignores Eros, concentrating instead on 'relationships.'"[5] We, on the other hand, want to strike a balance between these two. We want to treat language with the fastidious attention of alchemists, changing base metals into precious gold. Of course, not all of our writers have suffered the "language trauma" I have described. Some have, in fact, been encouraged to read, to explore language, and to pursue higher education. But so many of us, *too* many of us, do suffer the anxiety induced by the pressure to speak "correctly" and therefore we come to doubt our writing skills.

And, whatever our relationship to language, all mestizas are products of the hegemony that has instilled in us self-contempt for our cultural identity. We have been immersed in a North American value system that honors the competitive spirit and the desire for individual recognition as the *sine qua non* of success. This frenzy for individual immortality is not my concern here. What *is* my concern is when the appetite for society's carrots inhibits the poet's initial instinct: her primary desire to reconcile with her *impermanence*. Existential angst, mortality, the sense of one's humble transience through life—whatever term one prefers for one's impermanence—has always been a vital motivation behind artistic creation.

Undoubtedly this has been a core concern since the early times of literary history. Woman has always known that she is connected to the cycle of birth and death of all living things. She experiences it organically. It was man who, feeling himself alienated from the birth process, marked out a spiritual split in his collective psyche and forced upon women irreconcilable dualisms, dichotomies, and polarized opposites. A profound anxiety about man's capability of creating and sustaining life generates an even deeper anxiety about man's death. If women now share this male anxiety about death, it is because they have been psychically and physically beaten into a denial of their primordial connection to the cycle of life and death.

This dominance of man over woman's psyche, the subsequent objectification of her existence, the alienation of his own connection to living matter, is the basis of man's view of woman as "other." And the dark-skinned woman (because it is in her form that archaeologists have found the first traces of early goddess worship) has become the epitome of the "other" for men.

It is, therefore, a misunderstanding of the psycho-historic dynamic, which gives rise to the concept of the "other," that can strip this term of its meaning. Woman is, most assuredly, the "other" of man. But a man cannot be the "other" of woman, and most certainly the white male image in power in the United States today is nobody's "other." As man shaped his phallic Sun-Father God world, he defined the other: as enigma, as his mysteries. Other is that which man has denied himself to be. But "other," when she comes to know herself, is truly not other to herself, and man is never an enigma or mystery to her. His thoughts, his fears, his deepest secrets, are plainly reflected in the civilization he has built around us.

As the post World War II generation, or the generation of the "Baby Boom," we were born when the United States was truly on top and projecting into the great, endless, fantastic future where nothing was going to stop it. We were literally *rocketed* to the moon with a mission to penetrate its virgin soil for the betterment of us all. Yet we are now living to hear quite the opposite message reluctantly being delivered to us by every kind of "expert" and authority (with the exception, of course, of politicians, who are not "experts" so much as keepers of the gate): that is, environmentalists and economists alike are affirming that the United States, along with the rest of the world is in deep trouble. Nations are not immortal, after all, and neither is our planet.

We must realize then, that not only are our own physical beings vulnerable but so is everything else, from nationhood (as we were taught as children to conceive of it), to the earth's resources. This to me is the work of the conscienticized writer: whether we choose to use cultural metaphors familiar to our elected audience (e.g., Chicanas) or to introduce images borrowed from other cultural legacies, we must remind ourselves and others that nothing is separate from anything else. Matter and energy are one in a constant state of flux: this fusion can only be expressed in our work if we allow ourselves to be open to the endless possibilities of associations.

If we continue, for example, to view the Virgen de Guadalupe as the metaphor for mother, traditionally the chain of associations follows thus: Virgen de Guadalupe = Mother = Woman = Nurturer = Fertility = Nature = Earth = Female = female. Not only is woman locked exclusively into the historically traditional role as procreator and nurturer, but given our Western orientation of dualism, we are automatically programmed to juxtapose the male as penetrator/protector. But imagine earth as not female, for earth is a planet. Imagine nature as neither female nor male, but as nature. Yes, nature is fertile and sustains our lives; but both woman *and* man are fertile. What may happen when we refuse learned associations, dualisms, metaphors? We may begin to introduce unimaginable images and concepts into our poetics.

"THE AUTHOR IS THE POEM'S FIRST READER"[6]

Language and ideas are our only points of departure, because they are, perhaps, the only elements that a poet is conscious of at the time she picks up the pen. At a subconscious level (and pardon the term *subconscious*, which I am the first to concede is only marginally descriptive), the poem is materialized from thought to hand to pen. Consciously, the poet gropes for the image or metaphor that "feels" right but she does not know what she is creating until it is done. At times, she doesn't know if it *is* done, or how to finish, or even what to make of it.

That is why, to use a popular analogy, like a child who has come of age and whom we have schooled to the best of our abilities, we are sometimes amazed at the stories we hear told about our literary creation. Critics and university professors go about their business then, evaluating, interpreting, measuring, comparing, and placing into social and historical context our "child," our poem, short story, novel. If we as poets like what we hear, we beam with pride at what we most surely *deliberately* instilled in our prodigy. If we don't like what we hear, we are quick to question the authority (the critic) or to doubt the author (ourselves), wondering if we have failed at our endeavors. But the construction of poetics and prose, the development of ideas, is not the achievement of any one individual writer of her generation. Together, we create a tapestry. At times it is vibrant with color and movement and during other periods, it is dull and redundant, and still at others— just poorly done. No one of us is infallible, no one of us alone always achieves the perfect confluence of elements in her creation.

Conscienticized Poetics, then, takes on everything and everyone at once—or at least, that is its mission. It is often difficult to persuade even those in our lives, one's male lover or sister (or female lover) that we are creating not only a new poetics with our own language but a new concientización.

I want to discuss three books that I believe are part of this new tapestry of concientización: Gloria Anzaldúa's *Borderlands/la Frontera: The New Mestiza,* Cherríe Moraga's *Loving in the War Years: Lo que nunca pasó por sus labios* and my own novel, *The Mixquiahuala Letters.*

"HER BODY HAD BETRAYED HER"[7]

Borderlands requires close reading in order to appreciate its schema of ciphering and deciphering, its interweaving of a journey of self-understanding and the challenges of the writing process itself. "This book, then, speaks of my existence," Anzaldúa declares in her preface and for her readers, *Borderlands* is a blood curdling scream in the night.

In the earlier days of Chicano literature much attention was focused on writers who explored social conditions. There was a tendency to exclude from academic or critical purview those writers whose work and life did not fit comfortably within the campesino archetype. Gloria Anzaldúa, a Tex-Mex with a background as a fieldworker, would seem, then, the likely successor to the late Tomás Rivera. His book, *Y no se lo tragó la tierra/And the Earth Did Not Part,* dealt with (from the "universal male perspective") the coming of age of a campesino, the role which achieved recognition as the "true" Chicano experience. However, Anzaldúa was not readily recognized within the Chicano literary milieu of the 1970s because of its male heterosexist dominance. Instead, to her great credit, she carved a place for herself in literature as a feminist Chicana writer.

Furthermore, her feminist writings influenced as much by her exceptional physical maladies (directly female related) lead us into remote labyrinths where she seeks psychic, not just social, understanding of the human condition. The inner self—though inseparable from her physical self—is the one Anzaldúa feels to be her truer representation. Inseparable from her story and vision is our knowledge that Anzaldúa began to menstruate at three months of age, and underwent a hysterectomy as a young woman. And this rare and painful condition, in my estimation, informs every aspect of the text, even as the author speaks of her development as a poet and a political activist.

One of the strongest taboos in Judeo-Christian theology has to do with woman's menses. While in some cultures, such as the Native American, woman's blood is still seen as potent and magical, the authors of the mythical texts of the Bible literally attack woman's blood, telling us that because we bleed, we are despicable and wanton. During puberty, at a time a girl usually begins to menstruate, she is immediately separated from the world of men, that is, from the world itself.[8] Thus, as her title insists, Anzaldúa's vision is one based on marginalization; this marginalism, she professes, is her vision of the future. The masses of people who are forced to live on the borderlands of dominant culture as well, she believes, have a sixth sense, developed as a strategy for survival. They, therefore, have an edge on the average citizen who conforms to the status quo.[9]

In addition, in accordance with the religious orientation of Chicana culture, Anzaldúa feels an inherent sense of "otherworldness." Her spiritual informants are Mexican, specifically Mexic Amerindian. Her guide is Coatlicue, multiple deity and mother of the gods of the Mexica pantheon. In Mexica culture, Coatlicue is both creator and destroyer, both exalted and denigrated. Anzaldúa, like some feminist historians of religion, believes that the Aztecs disarmed Coatlicue of her greatest endowments as mother goddess and reshaped her role according to the needs of the imperialist patriarchy.

I would venture to add that Anzaldúa's spiritual affinity for Coatlicue serves as a resonant reflection of her desire for disembodiment that would free her from a tremendous physical and emotional anguish. "She felt shame for being abnormal. The bleeding distanced her from others. Her body had betrayed her," writes Anzaldúa. Though specifically Anzaldúa's experience, this desperate desire to distance oneself from one's body is not unusual for women. So many of us have been taught by the church and our Mexican background, that our bodies are sin-ridden, untrustworthy, and in any event, do not belong to us.

Cherríe Moraga's *Loving in the War Years,* contrary to Anzaldúa's *Borderlands,* reflects an acute connection with her physical self and sexuality. Anzaldúa struggles with the acknowledgement of her physical self:[10] "Tallo mi cuerpo como si estuviera lavando un trapo. Toco las saltadas venas de mis manos, mis chichis adormecidas como pájaras a la anochecer."

I scrub my body as if I were washing a rag. I touch the protruding veins of my hands, my sleeping tits like birds at nightfall.[11] Anzaldúa's sexual preference is a conscious decision, "*I made the choice to be queer"* but maintains the controversial opinion that, "for some it is genetically inherent." Moraga, on the other hand, says of herself in her preface:

My mother's daughter who at ten years old knew she was
queer. Queer to believe that God cared so much about me, he
intended to see me burn in hell . . . Todavia soy bien catolica-
filled with guilt, passion, and incense, and the inherent Mexican
faith that there is meaning to nuestro sufrimiento en el mundo.

For the political activist, sexuality has been the last frontier to liberate.
It is for this reason that an open dialogue about lesbianism is so crucial
to the understanding, affirmation, and recognition of our personal and
public selves.

Loving in the War Years, like *Borderlands,* using autobiography,
along with essays, journal entries, and poems, represents one woman's
attempt to unravel the conflicts facing and within a conscienticized
writer. In an essay entitled "A Long Line of Vendidas," Moraga ex-
plores the various influences that control the lives of poor and working
class women of color in the United States in order that we may begin
to understand what we need to do in response to them, instead of "in
reaction to."

Moraga also grapples with the identity issues shared by those of
"mixed blood." This "mixed blood" reference, usually applied to Native Americans and Anglos, is troublesome to me since as Mexicans,
we are already mestizos—of mixed blood—and perceived as such by
both Mexic Amerindians and Native Americans, as well as the rest of
society. The term mestizo means mixed blood. The very basis of the
ongoing social and political polemic of the mestizo/a is imbedded in
our mixed blood status. Nevertheless, because Moraga's Mexican
mother married an Anglo, Moraga feels neither "fully" Mexican nor
"fully" Anglo. And yet, Moraga also wonders, has she betrayed her
mother's culture by opting to reject the mandated roles of wife and
mother?

Gloria Anzaldúa takes on another task; she feels she has no reason
to question her mestizaje, and indeed, she reaffirms the long denigrated
blood of her Indian heritage, yet claims:

So mama, Raza, how wonderful, no tener que rendir cuentas a
nadie. I feel perfectly free to rebel and to rail against my culture. I feel no betrayal on my part because, unlike Chicanas and
other women of color who grew up white or who have only

recently returned to their native cultural roots, I was totally immersed in mine (21).

Roughly translated, the Spanish expression Anzaldúa employs here
means "one does not have to be accountable to anyone." In fact, none
of us "tenemos que rendirle cuentas a nadie," but the unfortunate truth
for us is that we are all, in one way or another, compelled to explain
our motivations at the instant we set pen to paper and declare an "I" or
even the implied collective, "i." I believe this is due to our unconscious and sometimes conscious sense of colonization. That is, as "un-
official" members of society, we do not presume a right to our
perspective.

But of course, an Anglicized brown woman always walks a deli-
cate tightrope. Denial of her mestizaje does not change what she is.
The point for *us* in our identity analyses—through prose, poetry, and
essays—is a self-evaluation that brings us closer to the truth about
ourselves in an affirming way. Carmen Tafolla, in her publication on
and for "la Chicana," *To Split a Human,* tells us as much:

> Don't play, "Will the Real Chicana Please Stand Up?" Much as
> we have heard different groups compete for "charter member-
> ship" in the Most Oppressed Club, Deep in the Barrio Bar,
> Pachuca of the Year Award, Mujer Sufrida ranks, and Double
> Minority Bingo, we must admit that membership dues must be
> continuously paid and advertised. It is irrelevant to try to justify
> how "Chicana" we are or to criticize others for being
> "Anglicized."[12]

If Moraga did not affirm her Chicana affiliations until she was an adult,
she had long given consideration to the agonizing conflicts generated
by the sexual proscriptions of "proper" Catholic society and her own
desires. Self-reflection and the complexities of identity are both shown
to have been part of these two authors' lives long before they took up
the pen to dare attempt any analyses.

Spirituality, a material analysis, and a re-vision of sexual mores
regarding women are three main issues Moraga contends are necessary
when addressing a particular blend of feminism applicable to our culture. While the order of priority or the degree of emphasis on any one

of these factors may vary—all observations and conclusions that depend on the personal experience of the writer—Moraga's perceptions and proposals are not so different from those of Gloria Anzaldúa's.

AN INTERLUDE ON CHICANA FEMINIST LITERARY CRITICISM Our literature, perceived by dominant society as a "minority literature," has primarily been supported by academic Chicano Studies, or more specifically Chicana scholars. As opposed to the literature of African and Native Americans, until now, except for a current handful of exceptions, we have not seen our publications distributed widely to the general public. Furthermore, much of our writing has been directed to our own people—and the texts we are discussing, I believe, were intended to contribute to the discourse of our ongoing struggle for self-definition and a sense of place in society. Female literary critics are also taking up the task of interpreting imaginative works with a desire to identify theory—ideas which may be applicable to the Chicana experience as a whole. In a paper entitled, "The Politics of Poetics: Or, What Am I, A Critic Doing In This Text Anyhow?" Tey Diana Rebolledo takes a critical look at *herself* in order to carry on the critic's role as speaker, thinker, voice of her Latina community, which she elects to address. Rebolledo, it becomes clear in this essay, who was trained as a "structuralist, semiotic critic," has become increasingly suspicious of theory "which turns the vitality and the passion of those texts of our writers into an empty and meaningless set of letters." Her proposal as an academician is that we recognize that our literature does not need legitimization by the academy, that the most important aspect of the critic's analysis are the texts themselves.[13]

"Releas(ing) her readers from what could be referred to as her personal biases or subjective interpretations" is Alvina Quintana's succinct description of the goal of this, my first novel.[14] Quintana is referring to my two deliberate ploys used to dissuade readers from interpreting the novel as autobiography. The first was a disclaimer at the beginning of the novel. The second was the construction of the novel in a series of letters, accompanied by my suggestion that the reader read them in a variety of different orders, thus producing diverse interpretations beyond my narrative control.

Subversion of all implied truths is necessary in order to understand the milieu of sexist politics that shape the lives of women. Moraga and Anzaldúa suggest this in their texts and Teresa, the main character of *Letters,* as much as she does not always see it, is an insurgent.[15]

CHICANALOVE

Teresa is a Chicana of working class background. During a summer of study in México she befriends, Alicia, to whom the letters are addressed. Alicia is of mixed Latina/white middle-class background and a burgeoning feminist. Thus begins Teresa's confrontation with herself as a conventional married woman from a conservative Mexican upbringing.

Whereas male writers may be critical of the institutions such as the church and state that have controlled our lives, they do so with the benefit of male privilege. That is, they write on the premise that even as brown men of little economic means, the world has been defined by other men for the benefit of men as a discussion among men. On the other hand, women *know* they have little, if anything to do with society's signs. That is why, I believe it is equally painful and important to read of Anzaldúa's search to claim the "wound" that is the symbol of her existence, as it is to read Teresa's self-admonishment as she writes to Alicia in Letter 32: "You had been angry that i never had problems attracting men. You pointed out the obvious, the big·breasts, full hips and thighs, the kewpie doll mouth. Underlining the superficial attraction men felt toward me is what you did not recognize. i was docile" (113). We so often go for our own jugular.

While Anzaldúa would have us see her physical self as indistinguishable from her spiritual image of duality, Moraga concludes the opposite, that is, she claims the spiritual through the physical. She sees her religious indoctrination inextricably tied to her sexuality, stating, "Simply put, if the spirit and sex have been linked to our oppression, then they must also be linked in the strategy toward our liberation" (132). Teresa, too, takes a stance against the institutionalization of spirituality and its direct connection to her sexuality in Letter 4. Yet, in Letter 24, we listen to her draw on the resources of folklore, Catholic mythology, and woman-identified beliefs to combat a negative energy force that threatens her and her friend. Her gesture of wrapping her rosary around the fingers of her non-believer friend (which in this passage seems to suggest that the source of danger may be male as much as it is supernatural) is a demonstration of her loyalty to woman. Throughout the book Teresa is both protector and nurturer. As Teresa evolves as a feminist, she is placed in the dangerous position of being viewed as a traitor to the male-dominated Chicano Movement. As Cherríe Moraga explains in her essay, "A Long Line of Vendidas": "The woman who defies her roles as subservient to her husband, father, brother, or son by taking control of her own sexual destiny is purported to be a 'traitor to her race' by contributing to the genocide of her people—whether or not she has had children. In short, even if the defiant woman is *not* a lesbian" (p. 113). Ultimately, however, Teresa, like many other women characters in contemporary Chicana poetry and prose, is emphatic in her refusal to be viewed as Malinche, a betrayer of her race. In a section of *Loving in the War Years* entitled "La Malinchista," Moraga claims that

> Chicanos' refusal to look at our weaknesses as a people and a movement is, in the most profound sense, an act of self-betrayal. The Chicana lesbian bears the brunt of this betrayal, for it is she, the most visible manifestation of a woman taking control of her own sexual identity and destiny, who so severely challenge the antifeminist Chicano/a (p. 112).

After making similar statements, Anzaldúa declares, "Not me sold out my people but they me" (p. 21). In Letter 22, Teresa plays a verbal chess game with a mexicano who hopes to have her in bed that night:

> He began, "I think you are a 'liberal woman.' Am I correct?" She replies . . . "What you perceive as 'liberal' is my independence to choose what i want to do, with whom, and when. Moreover, it also means that i may choose *not* to do it, with anyone, ever."

It may be said (and indeed, it has) that neither the character of Teresa, nor the works of Anzaldúa and Moraga are representative of the thoughts or lives of the majority of women. Yet in the history of civilization, when can it be claimed that a poet is the typical citizen marching in step with the times? Poets and artists are dreamers who weave stories out of their dreams, which *are* reflective of their times, but which most people do not, cannot, or refuse to see during their times.

I see *Borderlands, Loving in the War Years*,[16] and I would like to see my own *The Mixquiahuala Letters* as meaningful examples of public risk-taking. The woman writer cannot fail to be crucially aware of the possible consequences of her cultural interpretations and her claims as feminist, both within her own culture and within the dominant one in which her works are received. The ideological problem that the personal is political does not include a formal, theoretical solution. As Sigrid Wiegel states "Love, pain and happiness, the desire to overcome personal boundaries and self-assertion cannot be distributed according to rules: that would result in the collapse of human relationships."[17]

Thus, in all three texts discussed here, the principal thematic concern is that of relationships or connections, with all their seemingly irreconcilable complexities: woman with man, woman with woman, woman as daughter, woman as mother, woman with religion, woman with Chicano/mexicano culture, mestiza with Anglo society, among many others. As writers, as Chicanas, as conscienticized women, we must live with the very problems presented in our narratives. Each of us, as Wiegel states, "must learn to voice the contradictions, to see them, to comprehend them, to live in and with them, also learn to gain strength from the rebellion against yesterday and from the anticipation of tomorrow."

nine
TOWARD THE
MOTHER-BOND PRINCIPLE

During the early evolution of the human race, motherhood was the only recognized bond of relationship.
—The Woman's Encyclopedia of Myths and Secrets

According to Nahua legend, the tonalpohualli, calendar and cosmic constitution of the Aztecs, was designed by the grandmother goddess, Ozomoco along with her consort, Cipactonal. The goddess is thus seen as the real author of the almanac.
—The Fifth Sun: Aztec Gods, Aztec World[1]

The secret of fatherhood can only have been revealed to men by the women themselves, because women were the keepers of calendrical records, another traditionally female skill that most men thought beyond their comprehension. Before the advent of monogamous marriage, a late development in human history, there would have been no reason or inclination to correlate copulations with births.
—The Woman's Encyclopedia of Myths and Secrets

Generally when men took over control of agricultural work, developing the plough, and other large-scale earth-working tools, they also began to develop ideas of the male as the cosmic generative principle. Watching grain seed germinating as if of itself in the Earth, they could conceive of the male seed as containing already, in itself, the whole germ-energy of life. (Long into the Middle Ages, people believed that a drop of male semen contained a complete miniature fetus). . . .

The female ovum, or egg, wasn't discovered until 1827. So for two thousand to four thousand years of patriarchy all religious, philosophical, biological, and medical theories were based on the assumption of the male as the sole generative physical and cosmic force.
—The Great Cosmic Mother: Rediscovering the Religion of the Earth

Woman, what have I to do with thee?
—Jesus to his Mother, John 2:4

*While the Vatican proclaims that the Virgin Mother of God always
existed, the Jungian determines that all men want a virgin mother, at
least in symbolic form, and that the symbol is so powerful it has a dynamic and irrepressible life of its own. . . . Nothing it seems, even to non-
Catholics, could be more natural than this icon of feminine perfection, and
submission . . .*
—Alone of All Her Sex

*When a Mexican American woman becomes a healer, her status within her
circle of devotees surpasses that of any man. It is as if her role of mother is
expanded to include all those who are in need of her nurturing
ministrations.*
—Twice a Minority: Mexican American Women[2]

*As a mother, even at the risk of her own life, protects and loves her child,
her only child, so let a man cultivate love without measure toward the
whole world . . .*
—*The Buddha,* Discourse on Universal Love

A LONG, LONG TIME AGO,
MOTHER WAS NOT A DIRTY WORD

The sexual implication surrounding Mother in association with giving
birth and sex being viewed as contemptible by society has stigmatized
mothers. Mother is a woman, she has had sex. This must mean that
some man has violated her, has had his way with her. She is a used
thing now. "Puta madre," "chingada madre," "a toda madre," "pinche
madre," "son of a bitch," "motherfucker." We fight when we hear
these words because deep down inside we fear they contain some
truth: our mother *had* to have sex in order to give us birth, and sex is
bad. But hasn't she also been our primal source of tenderness and
comfort? If only she were the Virgin Mary. But she is not. She is
human. She is human and she is very far from perfect, as we come to
believe shortly after we leave childhood and enter puberty when,
along with the rest of society, we learn to resent Mother for having
such power over us.

There must have been a time, long ago, when Mother was not seen
as every woman's vocation, as motherhood is now. Going back earlier

than tribal times when men provided protection against predators—there must have been a time in human history when men too, were naturally nurturing, gentle, and bonded to the infants and children of their kinships.

Jesus of Nazareth did not invent love for humanity. Muhammad did not, neither did Buddha. Such was the violence of their times that their voices rose up to remind men of their humanity. While all such "wise men" had something to say about woman on behalf of women, none was inclined to listen to woman; or rather, such rare moments were not emulated by the men that became their followers. And so, woman's voice was lost and human spirituality became imbalanced.

LIKE THE RINGS A STONE CREATES WHEN CAST INTO A POND that widen and multiply, la hembra first submits to parents, next to extended family; if she belongs to the church, she then defers to that institution, deeming its mandates sacred and unquestionable. She ultimately must surrender her will to all of society: school, a husband and, of course, always she is aware of the watchful eyes of the all-knowing Father in the sky. Through this rigorous training she is yet not una mujer completa until the day she becomes Mother. Then she is at once transformed into a visible and valued entity and becomes an institution in and of herself, a source that at times must be deferred to and paid homage and of which there are always many expectations, a considerable number which are humanly unrealistic.

This idealization is simultaneously juxtaposed with equal denigration of her Mother status. Within the context of our high-tech society, and as the gap grows wider between the few haves in this world and the multitude of have-nots, denigration of Mother eventually penalizes humankind as a whole. Without a society that considers the needs of mothers above all, the world's future citizens suffer and consequently, society as a whole suffers.

Throughout this book it has been impossible not to discuss Mother as dictated by society within one context or another because it is, in fact, a synonym for woman within our culture; or at least, it is the only unequivocally approved definition of our reason to exist. I have discussed the historical symbolic relevance of the Virgin Mary in our lives in "Eva," referred to our respected roles as curanderas and brujas in

"Spirituality," have rebelled against the Virgin/whore dichotomy in the "Leftist Oriented/Catholic Paradigm," and cited the economic hardships of Mother in "A Countryless Woman," as well as the connections we make as mothers as a result of political activism in "Watsonville." In the essay on sexuality I have noted the only traditionally accepted reason for our having sexual relations, which is to become mothers, or more specifically, to reproduce. I remarked on the anachronistic and neurotic regulation of Mother by men in "Machismo," and have suggested the philosophical dilemma we have undergone because men identified our reproductive abilities with nature and excluded man from the cycle of all living things on this planet in "Poetics."

In Mexica society, women who died in childbirth were honored in the same way as warriors who died in battle. Mexica mothers were considered to be giving birth to future warriors. Even at the present time, women are serving the needs of la patria when giving birth, producing labor and brain power for global corporations and fodder for the wars that protect their interests. When, as a result of the refusal of profit-motivated corporations to adequately provide for the vast majority of the human population, there is poverty, starvation, and rampant disease (as there is in the United States); women, whose bodies are controlled by legislatures and modern medical technology, are held responsible and punished with unwanted pregnancies, traumatic abortions, and sterilization programs.[3]

In our many-tiered world of social privileges, religious and secular practices have customarily established a child's social status as that of his mother's, this includes race identification. In the United States, we can recall slaves raped by white men, whose children were then born into slavery as mulattos, the color of their mothers and not the free fathers. However, in New Spain political power, racism, and sexism together were legislated with a very complex breakdown of castes. Shortly after the Conquest marriage between Europeans and Amerindians was illegal. All mixed bloods were called castas. While castas could eventually breed themselves back into the white race, apparently it could not be done with a European woman and a non-white male; the idea apparently seemed unthinkable.[4] This is due to it being a patrimonial and patrilinear system: the white woman had no real power to pass on to her children. The repercussions of the racial caste system implemented throughout the Americas during colonial times are still felt today. In the United States as recently as the 1960s, marriage between whites and non-whites in some states, such as Arizona, remained illegal.

NEW KINSHIPS TO NURTURE OUR CHILDREN

Family, in the sense of blood relations, is under pressure due to the demands of professions at one end of the scale, and for many when labor migrations force families apart at the other end. In México, the sheer need to survive drives indigenas from their villages to the cities. In the United States for some of us in the work force the WASP values of individual achievement override those of our Mexican/Amerindian background. And for a variety of reasons, in the United States, more so than ever in the past, mexicanas and Chicanas are leaving their hometowns to start new lives elsewhere.

What may be retained as the family unit undergoes restructure, are the roles of "nurturer" and "provider/ protector." Nurturer has been associated with role of mother, while provider/protector has been associated with men. While these roles provide security and a sense of well-being for a child, they do not have to be restricted to gender or to the child's biological parents. Any caring adult in the household may assume these roles.

Characteristics such as nurturing, serviceability, and selflessness are valued within the context of Mother. While encouraged in women, such traits are denigrated, deemed worthless, seen as liabilities within the value system in which we live. That system lauds competitive and aggressive behavior for the sake of individual achievement, and above all, sees these qualities as inherent in man's nature.

New Familias:

Women are heads of household.

Lesbians and gay men are pursuing parenthood through adoption and/ or artificial insemination, as are single heterosexual women. While Catholicism seems to be synonymous with our culture, the use of contraceptives and present legalization of abortion allow some women to choose to have fewer children or none. They form non-traditional, nurturing kinships with other adults.

Families are forming out of second marriages. One or both spouses are parenting children that are the products of previous marriages. This includes gay couples.

There is no evidence of the "maternal instinct" being inherent in woman; although women who reject mothering may be stigmatized with the "Llorona Complex," that is, they may be shunned as a result. Just as Freudian analysis—that also stigmatizes female behavior to a great extent—is steeped in classical Greek mythology, the Llorona story also derives from patriarchal mythology and scorns women who deviate from society's expectations of being all sacrificing for the sake of their children.

It is true that a woman can bond with the child in her womb, that she lactates at the baby's feeding time or when she hears its hungry whimpers, and that she can distinguish that kind of cry from one that signifies something more serious. Mother-bonding when the fetus is in utero and during the early stages of infancy is necessary to ensure the child's survival. By the same token, the unexplained phenomena of spontaneous abortion may be a woman's way of preserving the species by not bringing another human being into the world that she is not prepared to care for, put another way, that might not survive in this world.

Although the responsibility of mothering is placed on the biological mother, anyone can be motherly. An incorporation of mothering qualities into our value system would radically change our world. Government and media alike have bandied about the need to return to our values as if any reasonably sound member of society had ever deliberately chosen a life for herself and her children that is unsafe, unhealthy, and a shameful dead-end.

According to the 1990 U.S. Census most *Hispanic* (government label; apparently Mexicans comprise the largest group among this population) poor families are working families. Female Hispanic median earnings are less than white and African American female earnings. One out of three Hispanic households were maintained by women only, and one out of two female headed households live in poverty. While new laws attempt to make non-custodial fathers financially accountable, the burden of maintenance falls for the most part on the mothers.

Elvia Alvarado, a Honduran mestiza campesina organizer—Honduras being the second poorest country in the Western hemisphere, tells us this:

> Campesina women are terrific administrators. With the measly
> dollar a day the men give us, we buy corn, beans, sugar, salt,

rice, oil, and coffee. If we can run our homes on a dollar a day, we'd do a better job of running our country than these rich guys can. . . . It's the rich who need the U.S. aid, not the poor. We've lived for years with only our beans and tortillas. If the U.S. stopped sending money, it would be the rich who'd be hurt not us. They're the ones who live off the dollars.[5]

If we believe in a value system that seeks the common good of all members of society, by applying the very qualities and expectations we have placed on motherhood to our legislature and our social system—to care selflessly for her young, to be responsible for her children's material, spiritual and emotional needs—we are providing for the future. Indeed, we may be contributing toward the insurance of a future for our planet.

MOTHERS WHO ARE DAUGHTERS OF MOTHERS

Many of us are daughters of women who may not have wanted to be mothers but who believed that they had no choice, and in fact, may have had none. We may be daughters of women who thought they wanted to be mothers because they believed that was what they had to be to be seen as grown women. In either case, because of the exultation of the Virgen de Guadalupe in Mexican society, almost no mother would say she did not want to be a mother—that she did not want the children she received from God. In practice, however, women may nevertheless have practiced abortion to limit childbearing. We can't guess how many or how often because the church's mandate against abortion and contraception would keep women from making family and even husbands privy to such decisions.

Most of us are daughters of formidable women. They are formidable in the sense of prevailing over every kind of seemingly insurmountable obstacle that society can impose on its members. They prevail or they get sick and die. That is usually the alternative. Heart disease; high blood pressure; AIDS; mental disorders; breast, uterine, ovarian, lung cancers, and tuberculosis are among the many illnesses that affect our women in disproportionate numbers as compared to white women. It isn't because we are biologically more disposed to disease, of course, but because poverty, which includes lack of health care and proper diet and excessive ongoing stress, make them more vulnerable to illness. Often our mothers have been recipients of poor, if any, health care; and women who have had no resources for psychotherapy, if indeed they sought it. So, of course, they are and we, their daughters, have become formidably strong women. Surviving such hardships toughens us generation after generation.

Many of us are daughters of mothers who married because it was the only option open to them to leave their parent's home, which may have been an abusive or/and impoverished environment. Some mothers married because they were really in love yet others may have thought that is what they were supposed to do—fall in love, get married, have children, become grandmothers, die—if not happy, at least guilt-free—with the knowledge that they fulfilled their role in life as God-fearing women. Some women discovered after marriage that they were no longer in love. But they stayed because of economic necessity, fear of reproach from their family, prohibitions against divorce by the Catholic Church, or any number of reasons long ago established to keep our mothers "in their place."

The above are only some examples of what many generations of women who precede us have lived through. My point in citing some examples is to say that we are daughters of women who have been subject to a social system—compounded doubly by Mexican traditions and U.S. WASP dominance that prohibited them from opportunities that may have challenged their creative and intellectual potential in more ways than being wife, mother, and assembly line worker. To explore the web of our mother-daughter relationships under ongoing colonization would be a worthwhile and essential study for our self-comprehension as Xicanistas. Unfortunately, this would require an ambitious and lengthy mapping that would extend beyond the focus of this essay. By observing the repressive conditions under which many of our mothers became mothers, I mean to emphasize that as we become mothers, biologically or otherwise, because of our new Xicanista consciousness, the definition of Mother is altered from the one we experienced as daughters.

DAUGHTERS OF FATHERS AND DADDYS' GIRLS

No less significant regarding our self-identification as women is how we have internalized male authority during our upbringing. A woman, because she feels disowned by her mother or because she cannot relate to the role her mother offers, may become more identified with the masculine within her. Jungian Maureen Murdock explains, "Many high-achieving women are considered *daughters of the father* because they seek the approval and power of that first male model. Somehow mother's approval doesn't matter as much; father defines the feminine, and this affects her sexuality, her ability to relate to men, and her ability to pursue success in the world."[6]

Another kind of father-identified woman learns to get approval and attention in the world when she has been "daddy's girl." Unlike the father of the daughter who takes on traditionally male behavior (i.e., seeks to be the family provider, shows little vulnerable emotion in public) the daddy's girl gets power through seduction, that is, playing on her femininity. Daddy's girl wants to be pampered but she rejects the Mother inside her and cannot give of herself to her community as a responsible adult woman. She identifies traits associated with Mother, such as listening, caretaking of children or the old and sick with her first female model, whom she has rejected. On the other hand, the daughter of the father formerly mentioned, wants nurturing but has also rejected her first female model and therefore does not allow herself to express her need to be taken care of. In both cases, the issue is the way the father-related daughter has responded to the actual mother and to her own subsequent disconnection with the mother archetype. However, in all of society, the masculine has dominated so that there is a collective and individual imbalance of masculine values permeating our lives. Regardless of the dynamics of our personal experiences, we all—male and female—must find our way back to the feminine.

NOW, if per chance we believe ourselves in full control of our faculties, economically stable, generally experiencing a fulfilling life when we become mothers, we may indeed make some very conscious decisions on what being a mother will mean for us and to our children. Generally, the polemic of defining mothering is twofold, social and psychological. Neither is ever separate. We are informed through society—our culture, the church, and state—what Mothers are or should be. How a mother personally manifests this conditioning affects her children in a very personal way. Among each other, in our private discussions, we may discover that we have experienced our mothers in similar ways because of class and race commonalities. However, there are always some crucial differences which, as we become women, we find have affected us in crucial ways. For example, while there are mothers who indeed preferred their sons over their daughters, there are also some mothers who want to see their daughters reach full potential. Furthermore, there have also been mothers who rejected the self-sacrificing tortilla-making image that we often assume comes naturally to Mexican women and instead, despite the dismal consequences they (and their children) may have had to pay—they leave, with or without their children. Still, other mothers "leave" symbolically and are not, for whatever reason, there at all for their daughters or for themselves.

MOTHERLESS DAUGHTERS— MOTHERLESS MOTHERS

In a society in which church and state concur that male authority must be deferred to, as has been discussed in other chapters here, the female as Mother has been delegated the task of nurturer. However, she has been assigned the role of nurturer of *man*—who will grow up to be mythical hero and warrior (Quetzalcoatl), divine savior God incarnate (Jesus Christ), bread-winner husband (Joseph), sire of the family blood-line (king), heir, protector, social mediator for his wife and children—*something important.*

On the other hand when many female children reach puberty (at the very onset of breast development and menstruation), they are already in training to be nurturers—from coddling dolls to baby-sitting younger siblings. However, while the father may begin to re-frain from affectionate demonstrations with his pubescent son, the mother will often continue such behavior with her male children well into adulthood. Again, I make general statements here regarding traditional Mexican culture. Therefore, while girls are taught that they must be givers of affection and caretaking, they are not always given the message that they are deserving of receiving nurturing. In defining for ourselves what kind of mother we will be, we must keep in mind that many of us were symbolically orphaned at the age of puberty. For those of us who may feel this way—as we take on the new role of mothering, where the caring of a child may become the single most important responsibility we have, we must find ways in which we ourselves get nurturance. By doing so, by having others sometimes care for us—even in small ways—it replenishes our energy and positive feelings about ourselves that we need as mothers.

Many, many women, heterosexual, lesbian, in long term relationships and single, experience a great sense of alienation from dominant society. We almost never see women reflective of ourselves (except usually in stereotypes) on television, in Hollywood productions, popular U.S. literature, or anywhere in mass media. Nothing in dominant society mirrors our experiences, so even when we have a lover/partner and family in our lives, the loneliness does not entirely go away. For the woman who is a mother of young children, her alienation is intensified by the various ways society restricts mothers from participating in the world. So sometimes, our only real affirming source is a close friend. Many, not all, heterosexual women have been trained to reserve their tenderness for men. (Most lesbians have been taught this too, but they don't practice it.) Therefore, *comadres* may be a splendid source for companionship, spiritual uplifting, positive affirmation. By comadre I am not limiting the definition to solely the woman who has baptized our child or vice versa, but to mean close friend.

The comadre has often served as confidante and social ally. She is loyal to you in your ongoing struggles with lover, family, society, and that is a special relationship to have indeed. Sometimes she is the only person in our lives who understands us because, in fact, she experiences many of the same struggles we do.

But because of this, these comadre relations may also unfortunately slip into unproductive and even self-destructive relationships— drinking or taking drugs together, going out together and leaving the children alone, obsessing about unsatisfying lovers, or in fact, mutually holding on to the anguish that comes with experiencing racism, sexism, and economic burdens as part of our daily lives. A comadre that encourages us in negative behavior and attitudes can be seen as an alcahueta and should be avoided. The role of alcahueta in Mexica society was greatly frowned upon because she encouraged women to behave licentiously. If caught, she was cruelly punished in public but the woman who contracted the alcahueta's assistance suffered even greater punishment.[7] While the alcahueta in Mexica society was seen as a go-between for adulteresses, our definition may expand itself to any supposed friend who encourages us, intentionally or not, to be dishonest—first and foremost with ourselves.

Under healthy circumstances, however, the comadre can be our ideal source for sensitive demonstrations of affection and concern. A comadre can massage your feet, wash your hair; she can read out loud to you from a novel or poetry. She can come over and cook a meal or rock you to sleep. And this all may and should be done out of sincere and unconditional caring. Not only can we hope that our comadre may occasionally baby-sit for us or lend us a little money for food or other expenses when we need it—as comadres have traditionally done—we can learn to be each other's mothers, even for one day of the month. Comadre means just that: co-madre.

THE YIN/YANG OF THE MOTHERBODY

As young as eight years of age, a girl child may begin to develop breasts. Soon after she may start menstruation. Henceforth she is no longer an asexual being simply existing in the world; her body has distinctly defined her as female. In many societies for thousands of years, her reproductive abilities have determined her whole existence. This function of our bodies to prepare each month for the possibility of pregnancy takes its toll on our bodies and on us emotionally. For the next three to four decades of her life, every month will be marked by her moon-time. Indigenous people in the Americas recognize a woman's moon-time (referred to as such because in fact women's menses *are* affected by the moon's cycles) as a time when she is especially powerful. However, in Western society, a woman's moon-time is derogatorily summed up as "the curse." The hormonal effects of a woman's menstruation can affect her in many difficult ways both physically and emotionally. Bloating, depression, cramps, and breast pain can be part of a woman's life for as long as two weeks of every month for most of her life. Women are always aware of their bodies.

When a woman's menses begins to slow down and menopause nears, her body begins new changes. In Eastern thought, she would now begin to have more "yang" (interpreted as masculine) quality because her estrogen level is dropping. In early societies, when a woman reached menopause, she was reaching the age of wisdom.[8] In Western society, however, she is still regarded negatively, because she can no longer reproduce. Along with the end of her menses come many other physical and emotional changes. Osteoporosis, hair loss, vaginal drying, hysterectomy (there has been in recent years a notable rise in practice of this severe surgical procedure by the medical profession), mastectomies, weight gain, night sweats, and hot flashes are among the changes that may affect a menopausal woman.

Although women are always aware of their bodies because of reasons mentioned above and elsewhere in this book, women are not always in tune to their bodies. Or rather, the negative connotations contemporary Western society gives to women's reproductive abilities have caused women to feel everything but in tune with their bodies. Moreover, a woman is made to feel that what she looks like and what she feels like is shameful if it at all is reflective of her hormones. While the younger woman is pressured to act and look sexy, she must also desire to embrace the Virgin Mary's posture of sexless motherhood. On the other hand, the older woman is often ridiculed if she feels or thinks of herself as "sexy." Since she can no longer aspire to be "blessed with child," the older woman has lost her raison d' être. At no time in a woman's life today is she given reprieve from being aware of her motherbody, a body that the modern medical profession has made her feel alien from and a body that is often so far from perfect—according to mainstream aesthetics—even she does not want it.

WASP society renders the indigenous looking woman invisible; and if she does not conform in appearance and dress to the standard of beauty set by white culture or at least conjures a dark exoticism (Indian princess look), she is further treated in a demeaning manner. However, Chicana Jungian therapist, Clarissa Pinkola Estés, remarks, on discovering the Tehuanas of the Isthmus of Tehuantepec, "lo! . . . a tribe with giant women who were strong, flirtatious, and commanding in their size." She goes on to conclude that from such powerful people outside the United States she learned "to refute ideas and language that would revile the mysterious body, that would ignore the female body as an instrument of knowing".[9] Furthermore, Estés tells women how society conditions us to loathe our bodies, but I think, it is especially important for us as mestizas to keep in mind that: "To attack a woman thusly destroys her rightful affiliation with her own people . . . In essence, the attack on women's bodies is a far-reaching attack on the ones who have gone before her as well as the ones who will come after her" (203).

Inherent to our intellectual and practical concerns as Xicanistas should be our attention to our motherbody. Currently older and younger women are learning about, caring for, and regarding their bodies in such an ancient way it seems radically new. We are learning to accept ourselves: our chaparrita stature, our Nahua straight black hair, our Olmec lips, our Mongoloid skin color and fold in the eyes, Nayarit protruding tummies, and our flat Chichimec bottoms. In addition to biannual checkups, learning to do breast check-ups at home, finding what treatments best suit us during especially difficult stress and hormonal related times (from over-the-counter medication to acupuncture), claiming "quiet time" for ourselves to rest, meditate, or cry if so inclined, and working some form of exercise into our lifestyle, acceptance of our bodies is an important first step toward self-love.

Among the Mexica nobility much pressure was placed on the woman to comport herself and present herself with great dignity. Women who did not bathe three times a day were publicly reprimanded as being both dirty and lazy.[10] But her ancestors, the Toltecs, to whom the Mexica woman prayed, in addition to being credited for their beauty, among the nobility dictated authority. The Tolteca women were also warriors and went out to battle. All our lives we are also called to battle. Regardless of what society tells us about our bodies, we must remember that how we personally feel about ourselves and how we take care of ourselves is the ultimate determinant as to who we are.

MOTHERGUIDES PREPARING THE NEXT GENERATION

Parents, but in particular mothers, are blamed for the "failings" of their children and yet children are being taught everyday by the world around them. It is a world that women did not create. The impoverished, the working poor, and single mothers have lifestyles with their children that most did not elect intentionally. In fact, many mothers did not get pregnant intentionally.

While mothers are responsible for their children, they alone do not teach their children. Today, in the United States, the media heavily influences children. As individuals we can't control what is produced by the television and film industries and by the present popularity of video games, but we can monitor what our children view and experience as "entertainment." By doing so we can minimize some of the brutal male violence, sexism, and racism that children are exposed to in life.

We can be vigilant about the kinds of toys our children play with. As in so many societies, Maya children are given toys which allow them to simulate grown up behavior and prepare them for their roles as adults. Because maíz is a main staple for the Mayas it is considered sacred and children are shown early on to regard it as such. The toy older boys are given, which is not a toy but actually a smaller version of the one that grown-ups use, is a tool for weeding the fields. It is called a *loob-che'*.[11] What role do we prepare our little boys for when we give them toy guns, supermacho figures, and when we show enthusiasm for such combative sports as football and wrestling?

Although many of us sometimes lack the energy to play with our children, even on week-ends, or to always be attentive to what they are experiencing at home, we can make some effort to teach our children about the simple joys in life, that is, to maintain a general positive outlook from day to day. We can play music, all kinds of music (on the radio if that is all we have) while we are doing other things at home. We may sing to them and with them. And don't forget laughter. When they're small they like to learn to help with chores around the house and, patiently, we can show them how. (Unfortunately, this enthusiasm usually wanes as they get older.) If we don't have a garden we can start a flower box, some avocado plants, a window sill cactus garden. We can color with the little ones, take walks, plan an outing: to a museum (on the day when there's no entrance fee), the park to play catch, a free mariachi concert—something relaxing, enjoyable, doable—and take friends along, yours and/or theirs. The point is to just spend a little time with them on their turf. Try not to announce

plans that you are not sure of to avoid disappointment. These suggestions are by no means meant to imply that caretakers of children don't
think of these kinds of activities and many more, on their own. I
mention them here as a way of reminding and encouraging us to do
them. Our other responsibilities are often so pressing, we tend to think
of playing with our children as something of a luxury rather than to
integrate it into our lives.

Approximately one fourth of today's high school graduates are techni-cally illiterate. Reading to our children at an early age is invaluable. There are now children's books that are culturally sensitive to children who are not middle-class Anglos from heterosexual nuclear families. We do not have to resort to the traditional fairy tales that portray monarchical world of princesses who are rescued by Prince Charm-ing and live happily ever after in a castle. I recommend going to book-stores and carefully choosing books for our children. Books are expen-sive but there are paper editions and we can ask friends and family to give our children books instead of toys at gift giving times. Books may also be found in thrift stores and second hand bookshops, not to mention at the library.

Story telling, especially to small children at bedtime can be invalu-able for many reasons. First, it is an opportunity to spend time with our children. We give them personal at-tention that we may not have been able to give throughout the day, and comfort them, which may lead to a

My son
listen to our words with good
judgment
look at things
look long and wisely ask yourself
what is real?
what is true?
that is how you must work and act
in a secret place the elders
the-wrinkled-faces-and-the-white-hair
left us these words:
look long and wisely ask yourself
what is real?
what is true?
listen to their words
Listen!
my son
you will act
you will cut wood
you will work the land
you will plant cactus
you will sow maguey
you will have food
you will have clothing
you will grow straight
and tall
you will be spoken of with praise
one day
you will tie yourself to a
life companion
you are your loved one's support
you are the eagle
you are the tiger
—ancient Nahuatl canto[12]

more restful sleep and calm child. To my mind, the best story telling comes spontaneously. We do not have to "make up" stories. We can share our own lives with our children through story telling about our childhood and family history. As children grow older and become more aware of themselves as people in the world, I think it is reassuring to them to have a sense of connection with their family past, a connection between their own childhood and yours, a sense of who they are and how they fit in the world. Heed the advice in the ancient Nahuatl verse about the Talquetzqui, "the storyteller uses words of joy/flowers are on his lips/his language is strict/his language is noble/the bad storyteller is careless/he confuses words/he swallows them/he says useless words/he has no dignity."[13]

Remember that children do not have the capacity to listen objectively to a lot of what they hear from adults. They may end internalizing or assimilating impressionable accounts they hear from parents. Children ought not to be our confidantes. Taken to an extreme, telling our children about our own emotional traumas and disappointments is now identified as a form of incest.[14] Children are not there to hear your woes, your fears of life. In time, they will grow up and meet their own challenges. Spare them of your pain when you

My daughter
my necklace of precious stones
you are my blood
you are my color
you are my image
now listen!
now understand!
you are alive
you have been born
Nopiltzin has sent you to earth
here on earth there is
heartache
fatigue
a wind blows
it is obsidian
it is sharp
it is cold
we are burned by the sun
we are burned by the wind
but our god has given us
food
sleep
strength
laughter
my daughter
watch for the dawn
raise your face
raise your arms to the sky
wash your hands
cleanse your mouth
you will spin
you will weave
you will learn what is Toltec
the art of feathers
how to embroider in colors
how to dye the threads
my daughter
now listen!
now understand!
you are noble
you are precious
you are turquoise
you have been shaped by the gods

can. Don't cry on your child's shoulders. You are the adult. Your hardships are yours. Children should be spared of your anger and frustration regarding your life. They don't have to be there for you. Your children are your responsibility at all times and they are at no time responsible for your problems.

Very often in Mexican families, our children are made aware of our marital problems or our indiscreet behavior causes them to be exposed to our other problems. We know about our parents' extramarital relationships, if they exist. We are blamed by a disappointed parent for the acts of her or his unfaithful, alcoholic, or otherwise irresponsible spouse. While we may not be fated to repeat a pattern of such behavior when we become adults, it is very difficult to separate ourselves from the pain of having had such "models" or authority figures during our upbringing.

In the United States today, about one out of three females and one out of four males have been sexually molested as children. This is what has been reported but the actual figures may be higher. The heterosexist macho stigma attached to males who have been sexually abused, especially by other males, has kept most males, until very recently, from reporting their victimization. If you are not the one out of three, then you may have a sister or brother who has been the victim

see that you do not dishonor them
do not act common
do not become ordinary
you are precious
you are turquoise
my daughter
pay attention
be strict with yourself
you were not meant to sell
vegetables
wood
handfuls of chili
pots of salt
in the doorways of the houses
on the street
you are noble
you are turquoise
you are not common
you must not cheapen yourself
choose your life companion
with care
you must go to the end of life
together
even though your companion
be poor
only a very small eagle
only a very small tiger
do not neglect your loved one.
my daughter
with these words
my duty is done
may the gods give you
a long and happy life
my turquoise one.
—Mexica mother to daughter[15]

of sexual molestation or incest. Do
not hold this in for the rest of your
life. Do not protect the offender.
Seek outside help. This may be the
hardest thing you ever do and it
may be the most important. If by
chance you are aware that a child in
your life is being abused in this or
any other unforgivable way, do all
that you can to stop it. If you are
the offender, remove yourself from
that child's life and get help.

We must be vigilant about child care. Very little research has focused
on child care patterns and preferences among U.S. Latinos. According
to the U.S. Census Bureau Hispanics are more likely to use child care
provided by relatives than are whites and Blacks.[16] This information of
course may be interpreted in a number of ways, not least among them
being cost but also the lack of cultural sensitivity that many facilities
show toward Mexican parents and their children. Twenty-five years
after the initial activism of early feministas calling these problems to
the public's attention they continue. In fact, many of the bilingual and
bicultural community-based child care centers started in the seventies
have been closed down because of lack of funding. Child care for
many of us is virtually unaffordable. And yet, we must have it in order
to hold down jobs to provide for our families.

Obviously, the obligation of having child care for our children
does not end with cost. We must stay attentive to the kind of child care
our children are receiving. We must not hesitate for a moment to
express concerns we may have regarding the facility or the child care
staff. If our concerns are not addressed satisfactorily, we must take
suitable action. Our children depend on us for this.

At this writing, the United States federal government is finally
considering providing a national health care program for its residents.
Most parents, as much as they can afford it, try to be attentive to their
children's health care. Some who are impoverished must make decisions between a booster shot for a baby and food for the family.
According to the Centers for Disease Control, low income persons

and minority populations, especially African Americans, Latinos, and Native Americans, are more likely to fall prey to infectious diseases like AIDS and tuberculosis. As much as we can, we must find ways to provide a healthy lifestyle for our children. This must be a priority in our lives. Our children depend on us. The best health care, of course, comes through prevention. We cannot prevent all diseases but we can stay healthy to some degree by being diet conscious, staying attentive to our emotional needs, and keeping active. Part of being a good parent means being informed. Go to health food stores and peruse the literature about diet and food. Educate yourself about the beneficial effects of herbs, vitamins, and minerals. Understand that what passes for good food in the supermarket is very often not. The Food and Drug Administration, which is supposed to be looking out for our health, so that we feel assured of its safeness (for example, when we buy a package of ground beef stamped FDA approved), is regulated by a bureaucracy that ends up delivering us a mixed set of goods. In actuality, that beef may be injected with hormones that go into and are harmful to our system. Another example, there has been an FDA proposal to regulate dietary supplements (vitamins, minerals) as drugs, which would mean that they could only be taken by a doctor's prescription.[17] Because the pesticide-dependent agricultural industry squeezes out small organic farmers, organic food products are comparatively expensive. But we must remember with regard to what we put inside our bodies that your family's health in the long run is worth more than cutting corners on the food bill. Cancer in children, high-blood pressure in adults, and hysterectomies performed on younger women are all examples of possible diet-related illnesses.

Addictive behavior may be learned or it may be inherited. In any case, we do teach our children by our own behavior. We must try not to pass on to our children our own learned bad eating habits, such as junk food addictions and compulsive eating. Along these lines, the list of addictions is probably endless. Alcohol and other drugs, as well as cigarette smoking, are not only addictions that we do not want our children to grow up and take up themselves, the damage we do to children because of our own addictions, can be irremediable, even tragic.

In addition to the degradation and hardships we may experience living and working in a society that penalizes us because of our race, class, and low economic status, if we come from abusive homes, we obviously do not have the skills ready at hand to be parents who are always patient and nurturing and prepared to meet all our children's needs and wishes. There have been limited support services to turn to help us overcome some of the trauma, stress and addictive behavior we experience and to which we expose our children. Nevertheless, when we know we need outside support, we must not hesitate to seek it out. This is as much for ourselves as for our children who depend on us. If you do not know where to turn, start by calling a woman's health clinic for references.

There is the ongoing problem of finding support that is relevant to our cultural experience, however. The world of psychoanalysis has its roots in white male thinking. It is almost impossible when seeking counseling to find someone—male, female, Latino/a or otherwise— whose training is not affected by assumptions that do not pertain to the mestiza reality. Support groups also tend to be dominated, run by, and geared toward a white, middle-class perspective. Consequently, when we do have the courage to attempt to break the silence of our pain and preoccupations, we are often quickly discouraged because we are so horribly misunderstood. It is not only a matter of custom that we hesitate to talk about our "problems" with strangers, but we imme-diately know that people outside of our cultural experience truly do not have the same point of reference.

Nevertheless, we cannot always make it alone. As stated, above, mothers of young children especially, who find themselves without a ready support network, such as loving blood relations, can suffer in-credible isolation and anguish. The demands of caring for a small being, however voluntary or fulfilling as we may tell ourselves they are, are still demands. In addition to the time and energy child care takes, our anxiety may be aggravated by financial worries, health issues, work or family related problems, and so on. Therefore, as mothers, we must recognize the point at which we simply cannot carry it all on our own shoulders and we must, for the sake of our children, and our own well being, seek outside assistance.

Men and women who are not parents do not always comprehend fully the extent to which women raising children are stretched. My own baby did not sleep through the night until he was about fifteen months old. When he was turning two and being weaned and potty-trained, we moved from Chicago to California where he soon became very sick with pneumonia. I did not have health insurance and nursed him at home. In California, he developed allergies and asthma and for several years we had many difficult days and nights that went into weeks when he suffered from this condition. Caring for healthy children is demanding but caring for sick children—and all children get sick—is particularly stressful for their primary caretakers.

Women and men who are friends of mothers sometimes want their mother-friends to spend time alone with them, give them attention, go out and play, make love, get drunk, do the things they can do without having to consider child care first. Things like a full night's sleep or making plans for Saturday night are taken for granted. Many mothers would like to have time out, too, but that is not always an option. Women and men who do not have children, who have friends who do, can learn to be supportive. It may be a question of saving a mother's sanity by just committing to baby-sit her child or children one evening or one day a week, or just once a month. The mother-bond principle has to start somewhere.

Brown mothers (especially but not limited to low-income), deal everyday with antagonism against them that is pervasive in society— from the police officer who stops her on the pretext of charging her with a traffic violation but questions whether or not she is a citizen, to employment where she may have worked her way up to management but is harassed by resentful co-workers as if her position is owed solely to Equal Opportunity Employment policies, to shabby treatment by salesclerks and snubbing from neighbors in her new neighborhood. In addition to her own experiences, negative attitudes also affect her children such as through school desegregation programs, gang rivalries, neighbors and their children who pick up on their parents' disapproval of people of color living nearby. Therefore, as brown mothers, we are not only dealing with education, health, and economic burdens, but with ongoing experiences that degrade us and our children.

We must not only be vigilant about the education that our children receive once they are on their way to learning the three Rs in elementary school, but the kind of education they receive in many schools primarily still run by white-dominated administrations and faculty. Today, gross stereotypical assumptions continue about our children by those who presume to be educators. We may not have the time to join PTAs but we must make the time to let teachers and administrators know we care about our children's curriculum. There is a current attitude among school officials that parents must also be held accountable for their child's education. I concur wholeheartedly; by the same token, we, of a marginalized culture must hold our schools accountable for the kind of education they are giving our children. Examine your children's textbooks, talk to your children as often as possible about their day at school, keep attentive to what is going on. When and if you feel something should be questioned, question it.

Not only in large urban environments but also in smaller cities and towns throughout the United States going to junior high school and high school has become a dangerous activity, even for those of our children who do not want any part of drug or gang violence. Some high schools have metal detectors at the entrances and students are checked for weapons. Young men and women who have done nothing more than strive to do well in school have been shot and killed intentionally or by "accident" as a result of the pervasive violence among the youth.

Equally frightening, while we may do all that we can to teach our children about the dangers of drugs, they are a fact of life in society. When my son was in the third grade, in a small parochial school in Albuquerque, I received a notice issued by the principal. Parents were being alerted to the fact that it had been discovered at his school, as well as at others, that cartoon figure stick-on tattoos laced with hallucinogens were being passed out to children. By who? Who knows.

Protecting our children from the day we decide we are going to be mothers to the day they are of legal age and have assured us that they are responsible for themselves requires incessant daily and nightly vigilance that quickly becomes second nature. If anything can be defined as mother instinct it is this demand placed on mothers to care for their offspring. Since society places that expectation as a demand foremost on the mother, she is forced to accept this commitment. As mestizas of a tenaciously traditional culture, even in the 1990s, our daily reality remains that even long after adulthood, mothers are still held accountable for their children's behavior. In fact, this applies to most women in contemporary society, irrespective of race.

The mother-bond principle requires us all to be responsible for all children. But we can't do that successfully, of course, unless we are also attentive to our own needs. Being mothers puts real demands on our time, finances, and nurturing skills, but mothering by any definition does not have to mean self-sacrificing or the martyr sufrida madre that tradition has often mandated. As Xicanistas, female and male alike, whether we are biological mothers or not, we can learn to incorporate qualities customarily seen as inherent in mothering and apply them to how we treat ourselves, our relationships, and of course, our children.

ten
RESURRECTION
OF THE DREAMERS

In an infinite universe, every point can be considered as the center.
—*Stephen Hawking,* A Brief History of Time

In compiling these essays, I sought to speak about millions of women who live on both sides of the border, whose lives for generations have been reduced to the level of dehumanized utilities. I have not always spoken from my personal experience because I know that unlike millions of women, I as a writer have a voice that can be heard. And this fact has marked my life as indisputably distinct from those who do not. I spotlighted that which has been deemed traditional and therefore, sacred in most of our lives, the Christian God, mothers, men, the preservation of Mexican customs; ideas that we still must challenge while we stand at the threshold of the twenty-first century.

In doing so, I also found that our lives are guided by a deep religiosity that transcends male constructed theologies, although the latter have ruled us for more than the past five hundred years. What Europeans added to the subjugation of certain populations, including women, in Mesoamerica was racism. Ethnocentrism already existed among the Pre-Conquest nations. However, the Mexica, the most powerful people in Mesoamerica at the time of the Spanish Conquest had already entered the systematic process of subjugating women inherent in imperialism. We have only to remember the most famous india in Mexican history, Malintzin. Born of royalty, she was sold by her own mother into slavery so that her inheritance would be given to her brother instead. Malintzin was not just a symbol of mestisaje, she was a woman (according to some sources, a girl of fourteen) in the flesh and she was sold into slavery and later given as a gift to Cortés because the imperialist social scaffold of her times permitted it. She not only had a son by Cortés, but he also married her off to one of his men; therefore, her life at all times was one of property—to be sold and given away.

THE BLACK HOLE OF EMPIRICAL DATA

Throughout Western history two schools of thought have rivaled each other to help society make meaning: the rational and the intuitive. The first relies on the premise that an individual can be detached from his subject and can make empirical conclusions based on measures, qualification, and linear deductions. The subject is therefore objectified—must be objectified—and the investigator maintains the position of being detached.

Intuitive thought (the realm of the poet) is associated with mysticism and is devalued by Western culture. Faith (evoking powers that cannot be rationalized) was legitimized by rational society in the way of institutionalized religion (giving credibility to faith by offering material evidence: i.e., the Bible). Intuition in scientific and academic research is often referred to as a "hunch" but is only valid when qualified by external measurements.

In poetry (which relies on intuition), any statement may be made and go undisputed. Irrational-seeming verses can be explained as metaphors, whimsies of the poet, or simply too esoteric to decipher. Although the essay form doesn't forgive such deviations from what most people accept as basic truths, a reliance at times on intuition has been necessary for me, since there are so many aspects of our lives that at any given moment only we acknowledge, and yet no "legitimate" source verifies our perceptions. Nevertheless, as the authors of *Hispanic Women's Theology* state, "The self-definition of a vast number of persons is an intricate element of reality." In our experience with dominant intellectual society, both within and outside of academia, women—especially women of color—are often dismissed for our attempts to use our personal experiences and perceptions as the basis of our theories. Because of the pretenses of "objectivity" in traditional scholarship, our deductions are viewed as biased and therefore invalid when we base them on our experiences and perceptions.

By the same token, liberal attitudes toward the philosophical beliefs of indigenas that rely heavily on oral history, mythology, and dreams are often patronizing. The "noble savage" in tune with nature is for some white intellectuals the mystical, dark other of their alienated souls. They understand that their own kind has gone so wrong and is so far from any useful meaning for humanity that they are finally attempting to relinquish their own ethnocentricity to "learn" from primal peoples. Learning is okay, appropriation is not. Appropriation occurs in academia when scholars study cultures outside their own, objectify their subjects, and use their findings for professional advancement. Learning happens when the investigator does not see herself entirely separate from her subject and is open to incorporating, at least in part, some of the other culture's world view into her own life, not just in her work.

Mestizas in academia are not interpreted as noble savages. Most of us do not lay claim to any specific Native American group. As Chicanas, we are seen as inferiors who ultimately aspire to "steal" from white people all that which they insist is rightly theirs in the United States. Of course, from a historical perspective the facts are that:

> of all the ethnic groups in the United States, Mexicans and Indians have passed from conquest, annexation, purchase, and into economic colonization. For Mexicans, their subject population status is the result of having provided land and labor for [140] years to a national dominant subcultural group of Anglo-Saxons.[1]

Despite the history and present status we share with Native Americans (although not exactly the same, of course) we are sometimes looked upon with suspicion by those who claim Native American blood and our indigena heritage is questioned.

We may call ourselves what we prefer but we are mestizas, Mexic Amerindian women, mixed-blood, and in our individual genetic makeup we reflect our mestisaje. Some of us "look" more Amerindian than others of us. In this color-conscious society, shade and hue will obviously cause each of us to experience our indigenous lineage differently. In other words, the more india we look the more poor we look (and often are), the more gravely we suffer from the differentiated negative treatment of white dominant culture.

I would like to note that indigenas have and continue to suffer the ethnocentrism of their respective countries throughout the Americas. While México boasts a superficial pride regarding its native populations, other governments such as Brazil, Paraguay, Argentina, Venezuela, Guatemala, and the United States have set upon eradicating their native populations. While there is no recognition of the mestizo, per se, in the United States, the mestizo in México became the national model; however, there, too, economic privilege and color are crucial criteria for determining the social status of the individual.

THE STALINIZATION OF CHICANO/AS IN ACADEMIA

My own experience with teaching in higher education began in 1975 at the age of twenty-two, when I had just finished state college in Chicago. I became a college instructor, just as I have fallen upon my life as a writer, by doing it. After moving to Northern California, I was offered a part-time teaching position in an Ethnic Studies Department at a junior college. The classes I was asked to teach were called "Pre-Columbian Civilizations of Mexico" and "Racism, Sexism, and Political Power in the United States." Not unlike the curriculum offered at most institutions of higher education today, such classes were not offered where I went to school and therefore, I had to go out and research as much as I could on both subjects in order to get to the business of lecturing on them. In terms of the latter course, although I used a text and held class, as part of the grade requirement, students were expected to spend a given amount of time volunteering in the community project of their preference, from working with juveniles at the YMCA to tending to a community garden.

Indeed, the growing state university that I attended in Chicago had not had a single Chicano/a instructor, much less offered Chicano Studies courses. Due to the demands made by the Chicano Student Union, a group newly organized for just such purposes, a young Chicano instructor was hired and held the first and only Chicano/mexicano related course I had ever experienced in my life just before I finished my B.A. degree.

In 1975 Viet Nam veterans were returning from the war, and invariably I have always had at least one vet in my classes over the years. My first one verbally attacked me in class and accused me of being part of the "system." As far as I know he was the only vet who has been disrespectful to me in class but he was not the only student who was ever confrontational. He was a young, long-haired white guy, from the suburbs, undoubtedly shell-shocked and I was a young, dark Chicana from Chicago, the kind of person he had probably not given much thought to before. When he accused me of collaborating with the "system," I explained to him about my part-time status. I didn't have so much as a contract with the college. And I offered to march right down to the Dean's Office and back up any complaints he had against the school.

Since then I have taught at numerous colleges and universities throughout this country. In all cases the very reason I have been hired is the very reason I have been dismissed at the end of the year, if not after one semester: pressure on a department to hire a "minority," usually from students, sometimes an influential faculty member. The manner in which I conduct my courses may not vary greatly from my other colleagues, except that, for example, instead of choosing *Moby Dick,* I might have students read García Márquez' *Erendira.* Unless the course calls for it, I don't talk about Chicanos or other repressed groups. When requiring a book by a Latin American or a woman, I've been accused of including too much about them. One feminist chairperson reprimanded me for reading the word "lesbian" aloud out of an Anaïs Nin diary after a female student complained. It seems that the mere presence of a brown woman in front of a class has often been menacing enough to students used to seeing authority personified by a rather conformist looking older white person. My intent in the classroom is to conduct a class that meets the criteria of the particular course, as laid out in the college catalog and by previous instructors. However, I have taken opportunities to express my own views while on campus by giving public talks for students groups, such as MeCha or women's groups, for example. If taking a glance at my books were not enough, it isn't long before the administration and my colleagues are aware of my sentiments about the white male hegemony of our society.

Since the eighties, many people are convinced of a big white lie that there is an advantage to being a woman of color seeking a position in the university today. Many individuals (certainly not women of color) are under the misconception that because of Affirmative Action and E.O.E. policies, white men are being driven away from any new university posts they are qualified for, disregarded because of their race and gender. While it is true that some universities have succumbed to pressure to provide one or two slots especially earmarked for token hiring of people of color, they are usually conditional hirings. They are offered as a one year visiting professorship, an artist residency, a revolving-door contingency plan: no sooner are you in, then you are out. Now and then, there is a tenure-track position and even more rarely a Chicana is given it. The retention of minority (I feel comfortable using that term here, where we truly are in the minority) faculty remains low. The administration and/or department can then claim to have fulfilled a certain requirement and thereby relieve themselves of further obligation along those lines of hiring. At the same time, no real change has taken place within the department since the temporary hire has had none of the privileges or power given permanent faculty.

Despite my extensive teaching experience, publications, and degrees, as recently as this writing I have never been offered so much as a tenure-track position at a state college. It is also important to note that it hasn't always been solely white faculty and administration that have ultimately refused to have a woman like myself as a potential permanent colleague. On several occasions over the years I have had the experience of receiving a lot of lip service from Latino/as (including notable writers as well as some professors who use my poems and novels in their classes and for their own work) expressing their desire to have me at their various institutions and yet ultimately, when it came time for the vote, I did not receive their support.

My point here is that as a woman of color in the United States, a politically controversial educator, a brown woman who is intensely private but admittedly free-willed with regard to how she manages her private life, in a hierarchical institution I am made answerable to everybody. Because such a woman stands at the bottom of the pyramid of institutional power, she is first made answerable to those who have "brought her in" (usually claiming to be taking the reins into their command on the bases of fighting racism). And when such a woman does not see herself indebted to anyone and/or is unwilling to participate in the intrigue of in-house politics—she's out. The subtle ways in which "power over" are played out in politicking within any institution blow a great big hole in the general view that because of Affirmative Action, a woman of color today is the most attractive and likely candidate to be considered by any department. A certain kind of woman of color, perhaps, one who will not make most of her colleagues too uncomfortable with her presence (such as one who is not U.S. born, and whose personal history is unencumbered by U.S. race and class experiences), and then she must contend over the next six years as to whether or not they will find her tenurable.

Despite the lip service against racial and sexual discrimination espoused by some feminists and some women and men of color who hold tenured positions (and there are all too few of those to begin with), there is no guarantee that they are sincerely concerned with doing much more than being self-serving. Very few among those very few will do very little toward challenging their institutions in any way. Or they will do it when there is clear personal advantage to be gained or when there is little to no risk, not a moment before. As for the rest whose interests are clearly invested in their careers and not social change in or out of the institution, there are far too many. If you cannot toe the line for somebody—which will ultimately be everybody— but still depend on a teaching position for your livelihood and as a career, best to persignarte and proceed without self-deception.

Because I am now known first of all as a poet and writer, however, I would like to think that the example of Ana Castillo is the exception; and I have shared my experiences only as a personal example. The experience of women who devote themselves exclusively to a career in academia is a somewhat different, if not always a more encouraging story.

Many of us who travel within academic circles are looked down upon because we are seen primarily as the daughters and lovers of mongrel bandidos. We descend from parents, grandparents and ancestors who lived as beasts of burden. Institutionalized racism, no stranger to academia, insists that our labor backgrounds indicate mental deficiency, physical inferiority, or at the very least a cultural tendency toward lack of ambition.

While early white feminists were caught up in the discourse of the "body," women of color (who derive from non-Western traditions) and working class women integrated the equally crucial, elements of class and race. But we are not allowed to make universal statements as women because we are not part of dominant culture. Anglo women speak of "woman" referring to all women, just as white men for thousands of years, have spoken of "man" to represent humankind. However, when the gringa scholar is not speaking of the Anglo woman, she adds the ethnic qualifier, such as, "Black women, Jewish women." Perhaps, she may delve further into otherness to the point of daring to observe "Native American" women or "Japanese" women but those obscure groups such as "Chicanas" or "Filipinas" (who have contributed to the functioning economy and social order of the United States since the beginning) are often viewed as much too ambiguous and ultimately too insignificant to her inherent perceptions to consider for too long or in depth in their feminist analysis. But Chicanas and Filipinas do not perceive ourselves as obscure, nor our cultures as nebulous. Our histories are long and rich and real indeed.

A Chicana is a whole onto herself.

Being placed at the bottom of society's social strata, we are dependent upon representatives who may or may not make authentic statements about our lives. But the statements are made only if our reality is perceived at all and considered noteworthy.

In these reflections, while I have made some general statements about our experiences, I have also refrained from being emphatic; while millions of women share certain social experiences, not one lives a duplicate life of another. In addition, we must be aware that nothing is static; just as society changes (albeit reluctantly) the individual changes throughout the course of her life. Not only are the deductions made by one generation challenged by the next, but we ourselves reevaluate our perceptions from one decade of our lives to the next.

THE DANGERS OF ARMCHAIR FEMINISM

It is no longer solely the Chicano male, other men of color, and white women who aspire to acceptance into the elitist realm of academia. There was a brief period when men of color and *white* women joined leagues against the "old boys" network; some of these men of color were bewildered when all too abruptly their white feminist colleagues became interested instead in women of color. Such is the inevitable and endless succession of tenuous loyalties in an institution founded on exclusion.

The National Association of Chicano Studies (NACS) has been in existence for over twenty years, holding national and regional conferences annually. However, Chicano Studies remains a field largely unrecognized by universities throughout the United States. Unlike other scholarly associations whose members clearly participate solely out of professional interest, NACS membership, which includes many students, is largely comprised of Chicanos. In these gatherings participants are engaged as much in the polemic of self-identification as an intellectual dialogue on the discipline. In the nineties, due to their insistence, the views of feminists and lesbians are finally part of that dialogue.

And what of the Chicana in academia? In the words of the authors of *Hispanic Women's Theology*, what are the "moods and motivations" of the Chicana seeking an academic career? By entering academia, one may argue, women can participate in social change. This has been the philosophy of the scholars and students who participate in MALCS (Mujeres Activas en Letras y Cambio Social), an organization founded in 1981 in northern California dedicated to Latinas in academia. An important support system, its annual meeting serves to further educate and connect women in need of affirmation and exchange. MALCS has grown from a mostly nationalist Chicana constituency based in California to a largely Latina feminist membership which holds its annual institute throughout the United States.[2] Its willingness to allow for self-evaluation (an inherent quality of Xicanisma), has helped it to expand and endure as original founders prepare a new generation of scholars and women active in the community committed to addressing the needs of women like themselves. Not all scholars and students who are Latinas share this philosophy simply because they are Latinas, to be sure.

In the mid-1980s Chicana and mexicana feminists entered into dialogue with a series of colloquia that took place along the border. Institutions that have expressed prominent interest in Chicana feminism include the Colegio México in Juárez and most recently the Universidad Nacional Autonoma de México in Mexico City. Dialogues among mexicana feminists and Chicana feminists have paved the way for a greater understanding among Mexican intellectuals of the actual colonized status of people of Mexican origin in the United States. The customary attitude of Mexicans toward the Mexican born in the United States was denigrating, seeing us as either "traitors or trash" for being born of nationals who "fled." The renowned Mexican writer, Elena Poniatowska, has now made several public statements regarding her appreciation of Chicana writers and our authentic Mexican identification.

Mexicana feminists are coming to realize that despite American citizenship and certain gringo acculturation, the mestiza in the United States has been prevented from benefiting from many of the privileges available to gringos due to racism, sexism and their poor to working class backgrounds. In this sense, her experience is more akin to the Mexic Amerindian woman than the mexicana of middle class background. Since racism is an international fact, many intellectual mexicanas are white and come from comfortable backgrounds, not too unlike gringa feminist scholars. Moreover, due to the extent of poverty in México, middle class mexicanas have enjoyed the benefit of housekeepers and nannys, which most middle class women in the United States can't afford. Many Chicana feminists, who often come from working class backgrounds or have worked full time to maintain a middle-class status, have observed that they believe they have more in common with the mestiza domestics that serve these women than with their intellectual mexicana colleagues. Be that as it may, there is now a deliberate effort among feminists on both sides to reach across the border to each other for an unprecedented understanding of the very particular ways sexism has affected all of us.

But on what terms does the Xicanista get in step once back and on her own at her institution? By the time she earns her doctorate, she is well versed in Western philosophy and letters, having succeeded in a rigorous program under mostly white mentorship in an androcentric context. She is often jaded by the competition as well as by the experience of being courted for being Chicana and then often "dropped" for being Chicana by administrators and faculty. She may be accepted for her ethnicity but rejected for her gender, or accepted for her gender and ethnicity but rejected if she is lesbian or any of a combination of these parts of the whole that she is but which at no time have ever all been fully accepted by society. Any Chicana who joins the institution and is in a position in which she may determine the acceptance of another Chicana knows full well that she too applies that divisive strategy and will invent some of her own, if she is that ambitious to succeed within the institution. It comes with the territory. And while this new territory is conquered, the territory of indigenista philosophy (which does not see the world in hierarchical terms of power) once compromised, is forsaken. No amount of copal burning or number of sweats will change that fact.

Nevertheless, after so much effort, the potential rewards of the career are tempting and seem ever so close. Indeed, by then she is convinced that she has not only earned the glory but must have it. But to get it she must play by the university's rules, even if she has convinced herself that she will beat it at its own game. In other words, the careerist Chicana has become what the white woman scholar was permitted to be two or three decades ago.[3] She is articulate in meetings, the classroom and in her writing. She usually minds dress codes, carries herself well in social functions, attends conferences, presents papers. The newest member permitted in the world of higher education once reserved exclusively for well-to-do white men and only recently his female counterpart, the new Chicana scholar is well on her way.

And there are some worthwhile results:

- Chicana sociologists work fastidiously at assessing the Chicana labor force, her behavior and attitudes within the family and all related aspects of her participation in society.
- Psychologists, educators and those in related fields educate their colleagues on how our children and people in general have been misunderstood, disregarded and even mistreated in society because of cultural differences.
- Literary critics interpret the works of Chicana creative writers in a language shared by their colleagues helping to legitimize it as literature worth studying.
- Chicana feminism is becoming a credible field of study as are Gay and Lesbian studies,[4] although neither are yet widely accepted.
- Historians (of which we have fewer than ten Chicanas with doctorates at this writing) have the most unfortunate task of either examining our past using sources that obviously either omit or distort us and employing white male methodology, not writing about us at all, or, still using Western arguments and

language try to make a revisionist case with what they do find.
Failing all that, she may try to walk the tightrope: take the arguments of radical feminists of color and buttress them for
good measure with sources sanctioned in academic discourse.

In all cases, most scholars are engaged in discussion almost exclusively with others in their own fields. Scholars in the whole melange of disciplines supported by present academia invest years of work and financing into projects that ultimately make or amputate their careers. *Sometimes* such studies serve to change policy. *Sometimes* they persuade people in power to do something. But in day-to-day terms the motivation for this kind of work may be simply career-based. I am certain that many a woman has asked herself about the probable ineffectiveness of her "feminism" within male dominated, racist, hierarchical academia. In the interim, do we enjoy the institution's benefits, privileges, its elitism, and its distancing from the blood, passion, and misery of the people to whom we claim blood-ties and in some cases, even claim to represent?

Will we ever admit to ourselves, if not to each other, that our competitive drive may be due in part to white patriarchy, so entrenched in our nerve endings and brain cells that internalized racism, sexism, and gynephobia is embedded in our unspoken thoughts, if not at times actually exuding from our own lips? And yes, like an animal who has a taste for blood, once power is tasted, we want more.

We may eventually ascend to the higher echelons of the academic elite when we adhere to its supposed empirical methods for fact finding, systematically exclusive bureaucracy, and the glorification of competition, which not only makes us compete with men on *their* terms, but eventually with women like ourselves on *white men's* terms. Then our studies serve not so much the betterment of our communities as the enhancement of our own professions.

Yet Xicanisma in order to be a viable alternative to stratified society cannot be elitist. It is not a woman-identified ideology mirroring patriarchy, a grab for material power when white people or men are not looking. It is not free from the consequences of its actions. To borrow from the lyrics of Bernice Reagon in her song "Are My Hands Clean?" we must consider the irony for us of the following:

For three dollars a day my sisters make my blouse.
It leaves the third world for the last time
coming back into the sea to be sealed in plastic
for me.
This third world sister
and I go to the Sears Department Store where I
buy a blouse
for sale for 20% discount.
Are my hands clean?[5]

ACCORDING TO THE NATIONAL INSTITUTE AGAINST PREJUDICE and Violence in Baltimore, an information clearinghouse, "partial surveys indicate that 20–25 percent of all students of color are victimized by bigotry at least once in an academic year".[6] Most of the schools we attend in heavily Mexican populated areas from preschool to college are vastly deficient in supplies and staff. Curriculum that is relevant to our reality by teachers who are also from our communities still is largely absent in the educational system throughout the United States at all levels, in both public and private institutions. And if there are not enough qualified educators to fill the occasional slots allotted for a person of color it is because the educational process is often hostile to his or her needs.

Consequently, there seem to be three principal demands that student activists have been placing on their institutions since the late 1960s: recruitment and retention of Latino/a students, more U.S. Latino/a faculty (in many cases there are none to begin with), and Chicano/Latino Studies or one required course in non-Western cultures. In 1993, over twenty years after the establishment of a Chicano Studies Department at Berkeley, most universities and colleges throughout the United States fail to recognize Ethnic Studies as a legitimate curriculum. Certainly not isolated examples by any means the following are examples of current struggles of Latino students in education:

Han de saber although nearly a quarter of the population in California is Latino, Chicano Studies in that state are not considered to be relevant to the curriculum, while European and Anglocentric history remains so. In spring of 1993 Chicano students at the University of California at Los Angeles went on a hunger strike to demand a Chicano Studies

Department. As a result the university conceded only in granting the students the Cesar Chávez Center but no official Chicano Studies Department.

Han de saber in September 1993 at Fullerton College, California, two hundred students from local high schools joined about one hundred in a march through Fullerton California State University, "chanting about the need for more Chicano Studies courses, in both high schools and colleges." Six people were arrested.[7]

Han de saber at the University of Vermont in Burlington, a ninety-five percent white institution in an almost all white state, students of color have been fighting against racism in its various manifestations on that campus since 1969. In spring, 1991, a group of multiracial supporters of this struggle set up a shantytown on the campus called "Diversity University" (DU) to protest the Board of Trustee's failure to act on its commitment to "cultural diversity." DU offered courses like Native American History, Racism in the Women's Movement, Radical Sexuality, and Visionary Art. In November DU was fire bombed and destroyed one night, while a group of unidentified men nearby sang "God bless America." Authorities found no suspects.

Es más In January 1992 student activists at Vermont went on a twenty-one-day hunger strike and in February eight students of color had a hearing before the U.S. Civil Rights Commission to present their complaints and experiences against racism. Anthony Chávez, assistant director of the Office of Multicultural Affairs received three death threats by telephone as did several students during the period of the fire bombing of DU. "Right now," Chávez said in an interview, "the university is run by custom, not by the Constitution. It's a plantation."[8]

Han de saber that some African American faculty at Mills College in Oakland, California, have also referred to that campus as a plantation. Mills, a private women's college, in the past provided a liberal arts education to young wealthy white women. Today it is recognized for a certain openness to feminism, lesbians, white working-class and middle-class women. It still has a disproportionately white faculty. In 1992 students of color came together to protest white supremacist perspectives in some of their courses, the scarcity of and lack of retention of faculty of color, among other related issues.

Han de saber at the University of Illinois at Champaign-Urbana

Latino student demands date back to the 1970s. On Cinco de Mayo, 1992, over six hundred students of all races marched in solidarity with Latino/a students to the Administration Building. Instead of negotiations with the administration, the seventy-five students who staged the sit-in were forcibly removed by the University police, Champaign police, Urbana police and the sheriff's department in riot gear using stun guns and billy clubs. As the students were being removed they were asked for identification cards and photographed. "Weeks after the protest, they received letters of reprimand, warning them of the consequences of any similar activities in the future."[9]

Es más In December 1992 about two hundred fraternity members pelted the Latino cultural center at UI-Champaign-Urbana with snowballs as they shouted, "Ya . . . I'm RACIST!" Apparently, there were two local police cars with officers who witnessed the incident and did nothing.

Han de saber in the 1990s neo-Nazi youth have been organizing White Student Union groups and openly advocating white supremacist violence on U.S. campuses. Numerous White Student Unions that organized to end alleged discrimination against whites, including Affirmative Action, reportedly existed across Louisiana, also at the University of Minnesota and the University of Florida at Gainesville.[10]

Student protest movements are often multiracial. They not only include the ethnic groups traditionally subjugated in U.S. society— Latinos (particularly Puerto Ricans and Chicanos), Native Americans, various Asian nationalities, and African Americans—but also sometimes progressive whites. Whereas homophobia was not always seen as a priority issue for activists of color, gay and lesbians of all races are gradually being permitted to participate in the struggle against the hierarchical elitism of the university system with those in protest against racism and sexism. It is crucial for students to keep aware that the old strategy of "divide and conquer" is one of the first employed by the administrations of their respective campuses. (It was certainly shrewdly employed by Cortés in his conquering of the indigenas and the main reason for his success despite the odds against him.) While it is crucial for individual groups to caucus and decide for themselves what their specific needs are, only with alliances will they have any hope to have them met.

BASIC ELEMENTS FOR A RESURRECTION

When we die, it is not that we die, for still we live, we are resurrected. We
still live, we awaken. Do you likewise.
—*Aztec mourning prayer*[11]

NO SEMEAGÜITEN

In Mesoamerica, before the Spanish Conquest people throughout the
Americas relied largely on maíz as their food staple. This gave rise to a
myth of how the first kernel came to be given to the people. There are
variations of this myth. But with the Conquest, the Catholic Church
condemned the peoples' stories and beliefs, and in popular culture they
were eventually altered or forgotten. Early socioreligious indigena
thought became diluted with Catholic and European indoctrination.
In Chinantla (northeast of the state of Oaxaca), some chinantec stories
suggest now that the far off land from which maíz came might be
Europe, others say that Christ brought maíz.[12] Just as the present day
indigenas were aggressively disconnected in many ways from their
own ancestors most mestizos have no way of knowing which indigena
group they descend from in México. Such is the result of the systematic annihilation of a people's history, if not the people themselves.

Therefore, as Xicanistas (no longer just obreras culturales pero
guerrilleras culturales) we must simultaneously be archaeologists and
visionaries of our culture. Our mestiza conscientización contains within
itself the elements for an unthreatened planet; we can contribute that
collective vision toward the development of an alternative social system. Our Mesoamerican indigenous ancestors developed advanced
societies that rivaled that of the Greeks. Our legacy has mostly been
vanquished and is kept out of the educational curriculum but we can
seek it out. From our indigenous background, we can draw examples
to understand the endless possibilities and the connections of all things
in the realm we perceive as the "universe."

Our Spanish heritage and its ongoing dynamic in our lives, not
only connects us with the Eurocentric ideology of dominant society of
all of the Americas, but as mestizas, it serves to grant us a sophisticated
and complex perception of dominant society.

The bilingualism (indeed in some cases, multilingualism) that many, although not all, of us have practiced since early speech is not only a powerful communication tool, it allows for the diverse dimensions that each language brings to our psyches. We have been stigmatized for not speaking English correctly and not knowing proper Spanish; but language is more than a fixed set of verbal standards, it is a way of seeing the world. By having these two languages as part of our daily dynamic, we have a unique comprehension of society. The supposed stigma may be converted into an asset. As Francisco X. Alarcón, the poet, has written in one of his poems, "A beso is not a kiss." Words reflect conceptions of reality and do not simply translate literally.

Our forced labor under exploitative and even fatal conditions endured for hundreds of years proves us to be physically, emotionally, and psychically able to withstand any challenge to our survival. To survive in a society that considers us dispensable utilities and yet, to care for and lovingly raise generation after generation, expect and even demand love in our lives, work under sometimes arduous conditions and yet find it within ourselves to appreciate flower and song, despite endless degradation to put on our red lipstick and walk down the street with our heads high like Queen Nefertiti, in my estimation, makes us quite formidable, thriving thick stemmed and aromatic as a calla lily. In the frank words of the Chicana-Apache religious studies scholar, Inez Talamantez, "We are a god-damn walking miracle." We do not simply survive, that would imply that we were no more than drones. We live lives full with meaning. Now that we know that we can endure any circumstances and that daily we prove that we must be reckoned with by dominant culture, we must have faith in our vision.

Our social conditioning prompts us to proceed through life "on faith" in a hierarchy. Indeed, Christianity teaches that a hierarchy exists beyond death. We now must base our faith on the fact that the meaning of life is not organically dependent upon a higher order. We are made of the same molecular structures that make up all life forms on this planet and all that makes up this planet is interdependent for survival.

Let us allow for the speculation that matriarchy existed for much longer than patriarchy itself has been the rule. Let us also consider that a hypothetical matriarchy was equally sophisticated, equally complex as anything that has been known since recorded history; and let us remember that archeological findings show that fertility-based cultures did initiate the understanding of the arts and sciences that we have to work with now. Consider for example, that as recently as the eleventh century A.D., there appears to be considerable evidence pointing to traces of a matriarchal society in the "mysterious" Toltec Empire. "In former times women had held the supreme power, as at Tula, for example, and it even appears that a woman, Ilancueitl, was at the origin of the royal power in Mexico."[13] Further investigation in this area might lead us to speculate that the very source from which the Aztecs claimed their magnificent accomplishments was in fact, if not matriarchal, matrilineal. We must consider that perhaps matriarchy was not a primitive way of life that through linear time had to be replaced by imperialist patriarchy. There may well have been an ongoing conscious decision to not pursue the route toward human exploitation because matriarchal aims were quite different: the rejuvenation and regeneration of earth's life sources. Matriarchy was *not* like patriarchy, except run by women, women in control, women subjugating men, exploiting men, clubbing men on the head and dragging them by the hair back to the cave. It was also *not,* I am convinced by the preponderance of archaeological proof,[14] some long-term period of fruit and berry gathering preceding early agriculture. At some point it was undoubtedly that, but we might consider that there is much, much more that we do not know or do not want to accept about pre-recorded history, because we have for too long been seeing humanity through the eyes of patriarchy. In our case, as women of Mexican descent, the severity of the Conquest destroyed much of our more recent history.

Indigenous people, among the most significant of our "endangered species," throughout the planet have belief systems in which they (like the Christian Bible) foretell the end of the world, such as the prophesies of the Mexica, Hopi, and the people known as Aborigines in Australia who refer to their history as "Dream Time." While the concept of the world may have been restricted to mean each people's particular way and land, the *final* end (because mythologies usually discuss several ends of the world and beginnings) is usually "related to the willful destruction of nature, the disturbance of cosmic balance, the declining respect for nature, and a deterioration of humankind's proper relationship with it."[15] The ultimate objective for us all now is not a question of man vs. woman, nor people of color vs. whites, nor rich against poor. Today it is a question of a unified global consciousness for the sake of salvaging what we have left of our Earth's resources, rejuvenating and regenerating them, and taking care of its residents.

We, mestizas, heiresses of Christianity, have been alienated from our intuitions and dreams, our same-sex lovers, and our umbilical tie to the Mother-Bond Principle by over four thousand years of spiritual oppression, not only five hundred years of relentless racism. We have all come to suffer the fate of "The Massacre of the Dreamers" whenever we have dared to utter the prediction of the inevitable fall of the Omnipotent God in the Sky. Macuilxochitzin (Tula poet), doña María Bartola Ixhuetzcatocatzin (Ixtapalapa, first chronicler of the Conquest), Sor Juana Ines de la Cruz (New Spain), Rosario Castellanos (México), Veintimilla de Galindo (Ecuador), Federico García Lorca (España), Gabriela Mistral (Chile), Alfonsina Storni (Argentina), Julia de Burgos (Puerto Rico), to recall only a sand-like sprinkling of poets who ached with primordial dream prophecies for a world much different than the one they were forced to live in and were killed for desiring so desperately.

The violent repression of our spirits and sexuality has gone against our molecular connection with the Earth. We continue on this mummified track because the process of alienation and denial that has been violently imposed on humanity has existed for so long, we're numbed into apathy. We have forgotten but it is not too late to remember.

The Hopi people's belief in an apocalypse is not a dogma. They believe that their world will not end if the people return to the Way of the Great Spirit. Many Hopis are also very protective of their prophecies, among other reasons because they believe that the divinations are only relevant to their Way: their lives and culture. For this reason, too, I have attempted to restrict my discussion to mestizas of Mexican descent. Our world, our Way, our communion with our spirit guides, our relationship with society is deeply rooted in our particular reality and history, which has brought us to this social status at present.

The current trend of el Movimiento is, by all accounts, acknowledged by all those concerned to rest in the hands of the women.

However, as long as we adhere to any kind of hierarchical ideology, our Xicanisma will wane. Our woman's consciousness should not be so superficial as to be used as a genital right to wave like a banner against men in that same "old boys" club fashion as has been done to us. It is not an "armchair" ideology to be eloquently espoused within the sacred halls of phallocentric and racist institutions. It is not a ready slap in the face of machismo for every male or white person who has been alienated from his or her spirit as much as we have.

Han de saber at all times that we are gente. Each of us is a valuable human being, to ourselves and to our communities.

Más han de saber that we must keep attentive to the needs of our bodies, minds, and spirits. Our bodies provide a vehicle for us throughout this life and we must be attentive to their needs. Our minds must be equally nourished. The life we live is a brief one; each of our spirits has a bigger plan, but while in this incarnation, for each of us to fulfill our purpose here we must be as fit as warriors.

Han de saber that our actions have consequences. Xicanisma, therefore, includes an ongoing awareness of our responsibility to ourselves, to those in our personal lives, to those we make alliances with, and to the environment (with all that the word implies).

However, when we have a vision in which brown women refuse to work for a system that renders us ineffective and invisible except to serve it, this appears as a threat to everyone (except others who see themselves at the bottom of the totem pole with us). Because our vision appears as a threat, we as individuals will be regarded antagonistically. Our vision is labeled male bashing, reverse racism, "limited" because we are primarily focused on a mestiza perspective to guide us, or any number of absurd allegations made in defense of the present system first by those with the firm conviction that the American Dream exists for all: If only we were willing to compete, if only we would quit whining and pull ourselves up by our bootstraps, if only we would all learn to be ambitious (read: think and act like white men) and make use of the opportunities that are presumably available to all American citizens, more of us would realize our goals. Second, entrenched in that American Dream ideology is a firm faith that God is male and a brown woman ought not to be so arrogant and demanding regarding traditions. Extreme cases are seen in the rise of fundamentalism. And finally, there are those others who take issue with us because they distrust the society in which they are invested, and yet we challenge that world view in ways they don't understand. Their cynicism causes them to resent us for many reasons. One is that because as society continues to malfunction and fall apart, they blame current policies, such as Affirmative Action programs, suspecting that one of us has gotten whatever sliver of the pie they believe they may have managed to get for themselves.

When we profess a vision of a world where a woman is not raped somewhere in the United States every three minutes, where one of every three female children do *not* experience sexual molestation, where the Mexican female is *not* the lowest paid worker in the United States— we are not male bashing or hating whites because overall they live a healthier life than we do, we are trying to change the facts of *our* conditions.

More facts: Latinas account for 20.4 percent of reported female AIDS cases in this country, yet we constitute only about 8.6 percent of the female population.[16] Our elderly are also among the poorest elderly in the United states with least support services available to them. Their median income is less than two-thirds that of whites. While it is true that because of our prevailing extended family structure, our elderly are usually at home with adult children and their families, we must remember that a large percentage of our families are not only among the poorest in the United States, but increasingly headed by women with children.[17] Our vision must call society to accountability for these disproportionate figures.

Everyday there is a war going on somewhere in the world and we live in an age (no less than several thousand years old) that accepts this as a fact of life. *Our* vision as Xicanistas expects peace. Again, our vision is seen as a threat because most people believe fervently in a socioreligious philosophy based on dualisms that make our society a complex system of irreconcilable opposites that are inherent in each other, i.e., the notion that we must "fight for peace." But peace is not the opposite of war, peace is the achievement of balance.[18]

One out of every four males in this country has been sexually molested at some time during his life (the number is probably higher but heterosexism has kept most men silent on this subject), the spread of AIDS has left no one exempt as a potential victim, and most people in this country are suffering the repercussions of a serious economic recession. Our vision inherently includes a better quality of life for all. But if we live in a stratified society it seems inescapable, even natural, that society must operate like the animal world's food chain. And there is always justification—if not some "sound reason"—found for why some people suffer more than others.

If we replace the term Chicana Feminism with Xicanisma or give it any other label, it should not be a term that excuses nationalism as a way of self-identification. Nationalism throughout the history of civilization excludes certain groups that will inevitably feel intimidated and react in like manner. Through territorial invasions, ethnic divisions, racist contempt for others, and ongoing oppression of women, nationalism always finds justification for manipulation for power.

IF XICANISMA IS NOT A NATIONALIST POLITIC, then what is it? Xicanisma is an ever present consciousness of our interdependency specifically rooted in our culture and history. Although Xicanisma is a way to understand ourselves in the world, it may also help others who are not necessarily of Mexican background and/or women. It is yielding, never resistant to change, one based on wholeness not dualisms. Men are not our opposites, our opponents, our "other." Many of us are as alienated from our true "feminine" spirit as men are, and men are just as vulnerable to the phallic mechanism of this society as we are—except for the barebone fact, of course, that as women, we do experience more subjugation than most men. As Chicanas we are excluded more than white men and women from mainstream society and from being eligible for many of the opportunities this country offers its citizens. This is an arguable fact.

What we have been permitted to be without argument in society is the compassionate, cooperative, yielding, procreator of the species, india fea, burra beast of burden of society. Viewed as ugly and common as straw. We know that we are not. Let us be alchemists for our culture and our lives and use this conditioning as our raw material to convert it into a driving force pure as gold.

Han de saber, mis comadres, tigres, águilas, and turquoise ones—bellas, sanas, y fuertes—that here lies the crux of our Xicanisma.

NOTES

INTRODUCTION

1. In Mexico, a Criollo is a Mexican-born individual of full-blooded Spanish lineage. Despite the Spanish descent, a Criollo in the Colonial period was not granted the same status as a Spanish-born subject.

2. First published in *River Styx* 7 (Big River Assn., MO, 1980). It is also in my book, *My Father Was a Toltec and Selected Poems (1974–1988)* (New York: W. W. Norton, 1994).

3. Please note that this is how this term is also applied by Gloria Anzaldúa in her book, *Borderlands/La Frontera: The New Mestiza* (San Francisco: Spinsters/Aunt Lute Press, 1987).

4. Michael D. Coe, *Mexico: Ancient Peoples and Places* (New York: Praeger, 1962).

5. T. R. Fehrenbach, *Fire and Blood: A History of Mexico* (New York: Bonanza Books, 1973), 104–5.

6. I considered it a personal failure; the thesis was completed and accepted by the Latin American and Caribbean Studies Department, Social Sciences Division, University of Chicago and I was conferred a Master's Degree in December of 1979.

7. Miguel Leon-Portilla, *Trece Poetas Del Mundo Azteca* (Mexico: Sep/Setentas, 1972).

CHAPTER ONE

1. As a young poet in 1974, I wrote something similar to this in "Our Tongue Was Nahuatl," in *New Worlds of Literature,* ed. J. Beaty and J. P. Hunter (New York: W. W. Norton, 1989).

2. T. R. Fehrenbach, *Fire and Blood: A History of Mexico* (New York: Bonanza Books, 1973), 234.

3. Fehrenbach, *Fire and Blood,* 238 and 162.

4. Hispanic Link Weekly Report, Nov. 6, 1989.

5. Please refer to John Glubb, *A Short History of the Arab Peoples* (New York: Dorset Press, 1969).

6. *Encuentro Femenil: The First Chicana Feminist Journal* 1 (1974): no. 2. (CA: Hijas de Cuauhtemoc). I can't recall how, but it seems fortuitously for me, this document came into my hands in Chicago around this time.

7. Please read their essay in *This Bridge Called My Back: Writings by Radical Women of Color,* edited by Cherríe Moraga and Gloria Anzaldúa (Watertown, Mass.: Persephone Press, 1981).

8. Anna Nieto-Gomez, "La Feminista," *Encuentro Feminil: The First Chicana Feminist Journal* 1 (1974): no. 2, 38.

9. See Angela Davis, *Women, Culture and Politics* (New York: Random House, 1989).

10. Thomas Shapiro, *Population Control Politics: Women, Sterilization and Reproductive Choice* (Philadephia: Temple University Press, 1985), 91–93.

11. I am reminded of two stories I have heard from U.S.-born Spanish-speaking women who went to public schools in the United States. One was sent with her sister, upon starting school, to the class for the hearing impaired. Another, attending a school with a majority Chicano population was sent to "girls' math" class. For further reading on the education of Chicanos please refer to Fernando Penalosa's *Chicano Linguistics.*

12. Marlene Dixon, "Chicanas and Mexicanas in a Transnational Working Class," in *The Future of Women* (San Francisco: Synthesis Publications, 1980).

13. Susan Tiano, "Maquiladoras, Women's Work, and Unemployment in Northern Mexico," *Aztlan* 15, no. 2 (1984): 341–78.

14. William C. Gruben, *Economic Review,* January 1990.

15. Figure quoted as of Dec. 1988 by International Trade and Finance Assn., Laredo State Univ., Tx. I will also note that maquiladoras suffer exposure to deadly chemicals due to lack of health regulations. Please refer to "The Maquiladoras and Toxics: The Hidden Costs of Production South of the Border" by Leslie Kochan, published in a report by the AFL-CIO, 815 Sixteen St., N. W., Washington, D. C., 20006.

16. Michael Jackson being crowned king in Africa comes to mind.

CHAPTER TWO

1. Heidi Hartmann, "The Unhappy Marriage of Marxism and Feminism: Towards a More Progressive Union," in *Women and Revolution: A Discussion of the Unhappy Marriage of Marxism and Feminism* (Boston: South End Press, 1981), ed. Lydia Sargent. According to Heidi Hartmann, "The Problem in the family, the labor market, economy, and society is not simply a division of labor between men and women, but a division that places men in a superior, and women in a subordinate position." Further, she contends that housework, relegated to women, "is crucial to the reproduction of capital."

2. NAFTA was passed and went into effect January 1, 1994. In protest, the indigenous rebels Zapatista National Liberation Army started an armed rebellion on that day against the Mexican government.

3. Juliet Minces, *The House of Obedience: Women in Arab Society* (London: Zed Press, 1982).

4. For example, when undergoing a writing exercise of one's first menstrual period, she alone, felt "empowered" by this experience, and stated that she had been told by her family that she the become a full member of her community as a result. Also, although she had been married to a Mexican for many years, she never quite understood the unquestioning subservience she observed among many of the Mexican women in her community to men.

5. Minces, *House of Obedience.*

6. Minces, *House of Obedience.*

7. Marilyn French, *Beyond Power: On Women, Men, and Morals* (New York: Simon & Schuster, 1985). See the final chapter, "The Long View Forward: Humanity."

8. By "community" Cruz is referring to Watsonville, Chicano issues, and women.

9. *Forward: Journal of Socialist Thought* 7(Jan. 1987): 1.

10. *Labor Notes,* no.98, June 7, 1987.

11. *San Francisco Examiner,* "Image," June 7, 1987.

12. Ibid.

13. *Forward,* Ibid.

14. *Forward,* Ibid.

15. Peter Shapiro, "Watsonville Shows 'It Can Be Done.'" *Guardian* 39, no. 24 (March 25, 1987): 1, 9.

16. Elizabeth Martínez, *Z Magazine.*

17. *MS Magazine,* March/April 1993, 92. Annette Fuentes and Barbara Ehrenreich, *Women in the Global Factory* (Boston: South End Press, 1983).

CHAPTER THREE

1. However, racism and converting the Aztec caste society into a class system accelerated the ongoing process of indigenous female subjugation. Please refer to "Aztec Women: The Transition from Status to Class in Empire and Colony" by June Nash in *Women And Colonization: Anthropological Perspectives,* ed. Mona Etienne and Eleanor Leacock (Westport, CT: Bergin & Garvey Publishers, 1980).

2. T. R. Fehrenbach, *Fire and Blood: A History of Mexico* (New York: Bonanza Books, 1973), 90.

3. Mariana Hidalgo, *La Vida Amorosa en el México Antiguo* (México: Editorial Diana, 1979).

4. Please refer to the fictionalized version of this experience in Letter Twenty One in *The Mixquiahuala Letters* (Tucson: Bilingual Press, 1986; Anchor Books/Doubleday, 1991).

5. Gloria Anzaldúa, *Borderlands/La Frontera: The New Mestiza* (San Francisco: Spinsters/ Aunt Lute Press, 1987).

6. For figures on this report please see *Working Woman,* April, 1993.

7. Nawal el Sadaawi, *The Hidden Face of Eve: Women in the Arab World* (Boston: Beacon Press, 1982/Zed Press, 1980).

8. Please see chapter 5, "In the Beginning There Was Eva" for further discussion on this subject.

9. Germaine Tillion, *The Republic of Cousins: Women's Oppression in Mediterranean Society* (Al Saqi Books, distributed by Zed Press: London, 1984). I am indebted to this text in particular for providing much of the information on Arab culture that I have connected with my own in this chapter.

10. For a further reading on this subject, please see, "Neighborhood and Social Control: The Role of Women in Maghrebian Communities in Southern France," Sossie Andezian and Jocelyne Streiff-Frenart, in *Women of the Mediterranean* (Zed Books, London: 1986).

11. Myrna M. Zambrano, *Mejor Sola que Mal Acompañada: Para la Mujer Golpeada—For the Latina in an Abusive Relationship* (Seattle: Seal Press, 1985).

12. Tillion, *The Republic of Cousins,* 100.

13. Tillion discusses several such cases in her study, as do many other authors, including Nawal el Sadaawi, who have written about women in the Arab world and in the Mediterranean. Please see, *Women of the Mediterranean,* ed. Monique Gadant (Zed Press; 1986).

14. Gadant, *Women of the Mediterranean.*

15. "Notes on Women in a Southern Italian Village," *Women of the Mediterranean,* 173.

16. Luce Irigaray, *This Sex Which Is Not One* (New York: Cornell University Press, 1985). Regarding her title, Irigaray says, "Woman 'touches herself' all the time, and moreover no one can forbid her to do so, for her genitals are formed of two lips in continuous contact. Thus, within herself she is already two—but not divisible into one(s)—that caress each other" (24).

17. Ibid, chapter 8, page 172.

CHAPTER FOUR

I would like to thank Elizabeth "Betita" Martínez for her time and feedback on earlier drafts of this chapter. As a woman who was there and is still there, her valuable input helped me think through my ideas in this essay. As testimony to her long-time commitment to Chicano/a activism, please see her publication *500 Años del Pueblo Chicano/ 500 Years of Chicano History in Pictures* (Albuquerque: Southwest Organizing Project, 1981).

1. Octavio Paz, *One Earth, Four or Five Worlds: Reflections on Contemporary History* (New York: Harcourt, Brace, Jovanovich, 1984).

2. See Jeanette Rodriguez, *Our Lady of Guadalupe: Faith and Empowerment Among Mexican-American Women* (Austin: University of Texas Press, 1994).

3. Fernand Braudel, *The Perspective of the World: Civilization and Capitalism, 15th-18th Century* 3: 393 (New York: Harper & Row, 1984).

4. Olga Rodríguez, *The Politics of Chicano Liberation* (New York: Pathfinder Press, 1977).

5. See Armando Rendon, *Chicano Manifesto* (New York: Collier Books, 1972).

6. Hayden Herrera, *Frida: A Biography of Frida Kahlo* (New York: Harper & Row, 1983). As a personal observation, with regard to Kahlo's fashion statements, it seems that when she desired to rebel against class, family, and husband she donned a man's suit and cut off her braids.

7. Lorna Dee Cervantes, "You Cramp My Style, Baby," *El Fuego de Aztlán,* 4, (Summer 1977): 39.

8. Andrés Guerrero, *A Chicano Theology* (Maryknoll, NY: Orbis Books, 1987).

9. Ada María Isasi-Díaz and Yolanda Tarango, *Hispanic Women: A Prophetic Voice of the Church* (San Francisco: Harper & Row Publishers, 1988).

10. A much cited text on the subject of the colonization of Nahua society through the Catholic Church is Jacques Lafaye's *Quetzalcoatl and Guadalupe: The Formation of Mexican National Consciousness, 1531–1813* (Chicago and London: The University of Chicago Press, 1976).

11. Witness similar reports of military abuse of Catholic clergy who symphathized with Mayan indians during the January 1994 uprising.

12. Isasi-Díaz and Tarango, *Hispanic Women.*

13. See *The Great Cosmic Mother: Rediscovering the Religion of the Earth* by Monica Sjöö and Barbara Mor (San Francisco: Harper & Row, 1987).

14. *Eros and Ethos: A Comparative Study of Catholic, Jewish and Protestant Sex Behavior,* Enrique Hank López (Englewood Cliffs, NJ: Prentice Hall 1979).

15. Toni De Gerez, *2–Rabbit, 7–Wind: Poems from Ancient Mexico, Retold from Nahuatl Texts* (New York: Viking Press, 1971).

CHAPTER FIVE

1. Alfonso Caso, *The Aztecs: People of the Sun* (Norman: University of Oklahoma Press, 1958).

2. Paula Gunn Allen, *The Sacred Hoop: Recovering the Feminine in American Indian Traditions* (Boston: Beacon Press, 1986).

3. Caso, *The Aztecs*.

4. In this paper I have relied frequently on the analysis found in John A. Phillips, *Eve: The History of an Idea* (New York: Harper and Row Publishers, 1984).

5. Phillips, *Eve,* page 39.

6. Robert H. Hopcke, Karin Lofthus Carrington, and Scott Wirth, eds., *Same Sex Love and the Path to Wholeness* (Boston & London: Shambhala, 1993).

7. Hopcke, Carrington, and Wirth, eds., *Same Sex Love,* page 39.

8. Monica Sjöö and Barbara Mor, *The Great Cosmic Mother: Rediscovering the Religion of the Earth* (San Francisco: Harper & Row, 1987), 276.

9. An accessible translation in English is Dennis Tedlock's *Popol Vuh: The Definitive Edition of the Mayan Book of the Dawn of Life and the Glories of Gods and Kings* (New York: Simon and Schuster, 1986).

10. The fruit, in this case, is aphrodisiacal.

11. Burr Cartwright Brundage, *The Fifth Sun: Aztec Gods, Aztec World* (Austin: University of Texas, 1979), 161.

12. Antonia Castañeda Shular, Tomás Ybarra Fausto, and Charles Sommers, eds., *Literatura Chicana: Texto y Contexto* (New York: Prentice Hall, 1972).

13. Fehrenbach, *Fire and Blood,* 104.

14. An analysis of the story of Malintzin Tenepal or "la Malinche" was taken on in *Encuentro Femenil* 1 (1974): No. 2 in an excellent essay entitled: "Malintzin Tenepal: A Preliminary Look into a New Perspective," Adelaida del Castillo. Norma Alarcón also published an examination of the Malinche stigma in Chicana literature in *This Bridge Called My Back,* entitled: "A Revision Through Malintzin: Putting Flesh Back on the Object."

15. Caso, *The Aztecs*.

16. Fehrenbach, *Blood and Fire,* 94.

17. Brundage, *The Fifth Sun,* 164.

18. Brundage, *The Fifth Sun,* 155.

19. Jacques La Faye, *Quetzalcoatl and Guadalupe: The Formation of Mexican National Consciousness, 1531–1813* (Chicago and London: University of Chicago Press, 1976). Also see, Eric Wolk, "The Virgin of Guadalupe: A Mexican National Symbol," in *Journal of American Folklore* 71, 1958.

20. Mariana Hidalgo, *La Vida Amorosa En El México Antiguo* (Mexico: Editorial Diana, 1979).

21. Sandra L. Orellana, *Indian Medicine in Highland Guatemala: The Pre-*

Hispanic and Colonial Periods (Albuquerque: University of New Mexico Press, 1987).

22. Barbara G. Walker, *The Woman's Encyclopedia of Myths and Secrets* (San Francisco: Harper & Row, 1976), 290. "Medieval theologians said Adam was forgiven. Christ descended into hell and rescued Adam along with other biblical patriarchs. He escorted Adam into heaven, saying "Peace be to thee and to all the just among thy sons."

23. See Walker, *The Woman's Encyclopedia*, 610–11.

24. Marina Warner, *Alone of All Her Sex: The Myth and the Cult of the Virgin Mary* (New York: Alfred A. Knopf, 1976), 35.

25. Arthur Evans, *God of Ecstasy: Sex Roles and the Madness of Dionysos* (New York: St. Martin's, 1988).

26. Warner, *Alone of All Her Sex,* 331.

27. Warner, *Alone of All Her Sex,* 335.

28. Warner, *Alone of All Her Sex,* 335.

29. Jerome, Comm. in Epist. and Ephes., III . 5, quoted in Mary Daly, *The Church and the Second Sex* (New York: Harper & Row, 1968).

30. Translation and introduction by Margaret Sayers Peden, *A Woman of Genius: The Intellectual Autobiography of Sor Juana Ines de la Cruz* (Con.: Lime Rock Press, 1982). See also the biographical notes in *The Defiant Muse: Hispanic Feminist Poems from the Middle Ages to the Present,* ed. Angel Flores and Kate Flores (New York: The Feminist Press, 1986).

31. See Sjöö and Mor, *The Great Cosmic Mother,* 276.

CHAPTER SIX

1. Monica Sjöö and Barbara Mor, *The Great Cosmic Mother* (San Francisco: Harper & Row, 1989). This book was of great assistance to me in the final stages of this project. I congratulate both authors on their successful undertaking of such a tremendous endeavor.

2. *Third Woman: The Sexuality of Latinas,* ed. Norma Alarcón, Ana Castillo, and Cherríe Moraga (Berkeley: Third Woman Press, 1989).

3. Olivia Espín, "Cultural and Historical Influences on Sexuality in Hispanic/Latin Women," in *Pleasure and Danger: Exploring Female Sexuality,* ed. Carole S. Vance (San Francisco: Pandora Press, 1984).

4. "His Favorite," *Third Woman.*

5. John Stoltenberg, *Refusing To Be a Man: Essays on Sex and Justice* (New York: Breitenbush Books, 1989).

6. Sjöö and Mor, *The Great Cosmic Mother.*

7. June Nash, "Aztec Women: The Transition from Status to Class in

Empire and Colony," *Women and Colonization: Anthropological Perspectives,* ed. Mona Etienne and Eleanor Leacock (Westport, CT: Bergin & Garvey, 1980).

8. For the special issue on Latina sexuality that I co-edited in the late 1980s, it took two years to gather sufficient material that was non-academic and non-male authored. *Third Woman: The Sexuality of Latinas,* ed. Norma Alarcón, Ana Castillo and Cherríe Moraga (Berkeley: Third Woman Press, 1989). For further reading on the subject please see the subsequent issue on sexuality, *Chicana Lesbians: The Girls Our Mothers Warned Us About,* ed. Carla Trujillo (Berkeley: Third Woman Press, 1991).

9. *Compañeras: Latina Lesbians,* ed. Juanita Ramos (Latina Lesbian History Project: New York, 1987).

10. *Esta Puente, Mi Espalda: Voces de mujeres tercermundistas en los Estados Unidos,* ed. Cherríe Moraga and Ana Castillo (San Francisco: Ism Press, 1988).

11. My translation.

12. Since the writing of this essay, Third Woman Press has published the well-received issue on Chicana lesbians, *Chicana Lesbians: The Girls Our Mothers Warned Us About,* ed. Carla Trujillo (Berkeley: Third Woman Press, 1991) in which an earlier version of this essay first appeared. For further reading on the subject, please refer to this excellent source.

13. Please see *Compañeras: Latina Lesbians* for testimonials to this effect from all the women who early on attempted to assimilate into white, middle-class, North American culture.

14. Victoria Alegría Rosales, "To All Women Who Have Traveled the Same Road as I," in *Third Woman,* ed. Alarcón, Castillo, and Moraga.

15. Read June Nash's article, "Aztec Women: The Transition from Status to Class in Empire and Colony" in *Women and Colonization: Anthropological Perspectives,* ed. Mona Etienne and Eleanor Leacock (Greenwood Press, 1980). It appears that at the time of the Conquest, woman's status was on the decline in society, although she still exercised certain amount of autonomy and wielded some power in certain areas as priestess or merchant. Racism complemented the new class structure of Colonialism, and approximately thirty years after the Conquest, Aztec women had lost all social status in México. She was most useful as a "reproductive" agent of slaves rather than a productive agent in the economy.

CHAPTER SEVEN

1. For practical purposes, I will limit the discussion here to those models that directly effect our lives. That is, while I believe that prepatriarchal traces

of goddesses are essential in our forming a holistic sense of woman, what effects us most directly comes by way of our patriarchal models.

2. Audre Lorde, "An Open Letter to Mary Daly," *This Bridge Called My Back.*

3. In *The Great Cosmic Mother,* Monica Sjoo and Barbara Mor suggest that "It is possible that the religious ideas of ancient Crete and Egypt originate in black Africa (21).

4. Luisah Teish, *Jambalaya: The Natural Woman's Book of Personal Charms and Practical Rituals* (Harper & Row: San Francisco, 1988).

5. For further reading on curanderas please refer to *Medicine Women, Curanderas, and Women Doctors,* Bobbette Perrone, H. Henrietta Stockel, and Victoria Krueger (Norman: University of Oklahoma Press, 1989).

6. Please see my novel *So Far From God* (New York: W.W. Norton, 1993), chapter three, for one description of the meanings of these maladies.

CHAPTER EIGHT

This essay was first undertaken in 1988.

1. The following passages are a tapestry I have created from the following texts: Anzaldúa, *Borderlands/La Frontera: The New Mestiza* (San Francisco: Spinster's/Aunt Lute's Press, 1987), Moraga, *Loving in the War Years: Lo que nunca pasó por sus labios* (Boston: South End Press, 1983), and my own novel, *The Mixquiahuala Letters* (New York: Doubleday, 1992/AZ: Bilingual Review Press, 1986). An * indicates that the excerpt comes from *The Mixquiahuala Letters,* a # will refer to a passage from *Loving in the War Years,* and a + will indicate that the passage comes from *Borderlands.* I want to thank the other two authors of this *tapiz* for their unique voices, which I have borrowed here to illustrate my arguments regarding the multiple obstacles that Chicana literature aims to overcome.

2. Gloria Anzaldúa discusses this point in an excellent chapter called "How to Tame a Tongue" in *Borderlands/La Frontera: The New Mestiza* (San Francisco: Spinsters/Aunt Lute Press, 1987).

3. Ivan Argüelles, in "Contributors' Advice," *Caliban* 4, 1988.

4. An excellent example of this is found in the work of poet, Alurista. He further imbues language with ancient and contemporary meanings; I would refer to him as a "mytholinguist."

5. Argüelles, "Contributors' Advice," *Caliban* 4, 1988.

6. Octavio Paz, *Children of the Mire: Modern Poetry from Romanticism to the Avant-Garde* (Cambridge: Harvard University Press, 1974).

7. Anzaldúa, *Borderlands.*

8. This subject is further discussed in chapter 6, "Toward an Erotic Whole Self."

9. I was intrigued by the "sapo" metaphor used by Chicano writers with regards to our "borderland" psyches. In my novel, *Sapogonia,* I invented a fictitious land where all mestizos reside. In Arturo Islas's novel *Migrant Souls: A Novel* (New York: William Morrow, 1990), he made an anagram of his hometown El Paso and called it "Del Sapo." Anzaldúa, too, referred in *Borderlands* to our people as toads: "We are the people who leap in the dark, we are the people on the knees of the gods" (81).

10. Please read her essay in *This Bridge Called My Back.*

11. Page 71 in *Borderlands.* My translation.

12. Carmen Tafolla's effort is to be commended. In my opinion, she has sincerely attempted to reach out to the Chicana who is entrenched in our culture. *To Split a Human,* Mexican American Cultural Center, San Antonio, 1985.

13. *The Americas Review* 15: No. 3–4, Fall/Winter, 1987.

14. *Criticism in the Borderlands: Studies in Chicano Literature, Culture and Ideology,* ed. Jose David Saldívar and Hector Calderón (Durham, North Carolina: Duke University Press, 1991).

15. For further discussion on Moraga's and Anzaldúa's text, please see Lourdes Torres' essay, "The Construction of the Self in U.S. Latina Autobiographies," *Third World Women and the Politics of Feminism,* ed. Chandra T. Mohanty, et. al. (Indiana: Indiana University Press, 1991).

16. For an update on many of the views discussed in *Loving in the War Years* please refer to Moraga's most recent publication *The Last Generation* (Boston: South End Press, 1993).

17. Sigrid Weigel, "Double Focus: On the History of Women's Writing," *Feminist Aesthetics,* ed. Gisela Ecker (Boston: Beacon Press, 1986). In 1987 I found this article immensely insightful and helpful in viewing my own works and my life as a woman writer.

CHAPTER NINE

1. Burr Cartwright Brundage, *The Fifth Sun: Aztec Gods, Aztec World* (Austin: University of Texas, 1979). "It is even probable that her own date-name was exactly this first day of the tonalpohualli and that in time it was separated from her and worshiped as a connected divinity; ultimately, with a change of sex, the transfiguration became her consort." (page 20f)

2. *Twice a Minority: Mexican American Women* ed. Margarita Melville (St. Louis: C.V. Mosby Company, 1980).

3. For a specific case regarding sterilizations of U.S. Mexican women see, Carlos G. Velez-Ibañez, "Se me acabó la canción: An Ethnography of Non-Consenting Sterilizations Among Mexican Women in Los Angeles." In *Mexican Women in the United States: Struggles Past and Present,* ed. Magdalena Mora and Adelaida del Castillo (Los Angeles: Chicano Studies Research Center Publications, University of California, Los Angeles, 1980), 71–93. Also, regarding sterilizations of women of color see Angela Davis, *Women, Race, and Class* (New York: Random House, 1983).

4. Fehrenbach, *Fire and Blood,* 227–44.

5. Elvia Alvarado, *Don't Be Afraid, Gringo: A Honduran Woman Speaks From the Heart: The Story of Elvia Alvarado,* ed. and trans. Medea Benjamin, (San Francisco: Food First Publishers, 1987).

6. Murdock, Maureen, *Heroine's Journey* (Boston, London: Shambhala Books, 1990).

7. Mariana Hidalgo, *La Vida Amorosa en el México Antiguo* (México: Editorial Diana, 1979).

8. Murdock, *Heroine's Journey.*

9. Clarissa Pinkola Estés, *Women Who Run with the Wolves: Myths and Stories of the Wild Woman Archetype* (New York: Ballantine Books, 1992), 201.

10. Hidalgo, *La Vida Amorosa.*

11. Elmer Llanes Marín, *Los Niños Mayas de Yucatán* (Merida, Yucatan, Mexico: Maldonado Editores, 1983).

12. Adapted from Toni De Gerez, *2-Rabbit, 7-Wind* (New York: Viking Press, 1971).

13. De Gerez, *2-Rabbit, 7-Wind.*

14. Ken Graber, *Ghosts in the Bedroom: A Guide for Partners of Incest Survivors* (Deerfield Beach, FL: Health Communications, 1991).

15. De Gerez, *2-Rabbit, 7-Wind.*

16. "On My Own: Mexican American Women, Self-Sufficiency, and the Family Support Act." Washington D.C.: The National Council of La Raza, December, 1990.

17. *Better Nutrition for Today's Living,* Vol. 55, No. 10, October 1993 (6151 Powers Ferry Rd., N.W., Atlanta, GA 30339–2941). See "Editor's Desk."

CHAPTER TEN

1. Carlos G. Velez, "Se me acabó la canci Sterilizations Among Mexican Women in Los Angeles," *Mexican Women in the United States: Struggles Past and Present* (Los Angeles: Chicano Studies Research Center Publications, 1980).

2. Beatriz M. Pesquera and Denise Segura, "There is No Going Back:

Chicanas and Feminism," *Chicana Critical Issues: Mujeres Activas en Letras y Cambio Social* (Berkeley: Third Woman Press, 1993).

3. Read Adrienne Rich's "Toward a Woman-Centered University (1973–74)," *On Lies, Secrets, and Silence: Selected Prose 1966–1978* (New York: Norton, 1980).

4. A whole retinue of feminist scholars throughout this country and abroad have based their critical arguments on *This Bridge Called My Back,* a document consisting mostly of free verse and personal essays. Again, we see the realm of intuitive thought being accepted as a legitimate form of argument but only once it has been translated into academese.

5. "Are My Hands Clean?" recorded by Sweet Honey and the Rock, lyrics and music by Bernice Johnson Reagon, 1985.

6. Elizabeth Martínez, "Campus Racism: Tip of an Iceberg," *Z Magazine,* April, 1992.

7. Martínez, "Campus Racism."

8. Martínez, "Campus Racism."

9. Elizabeth Canelo, Jason Ferreira, and Osvaldo Morera in "University of Illinois: El Movimiento and the Politics of Repression," *Z Magazine,* March 1993.

10. Elizabeth Martinez, "Campus Racism: Tip of an Iceberg," *Z Magazine,* April 1992.

11. Bernardino de Sahagun, *General History of the Things of New Spain (Florentine Codex),* trans. Arthur Anderson and Charles Dibble, Vol.10:192 (Santa Fe: School of American Research, 1950–1976).

12. Roberto J.Weitlaner, *Relatos, Mitos y Leyendas De La Chinantla* (Mexico D.F.: Instituto Nacional Indigenista, 1977).

13. Jacques Soustelle, *Daily Life of the Aztecs: On the Eve of the Spanish Conquest* (Stanford: Stanford University Press, 1961).

14. Ferdinand Anton in his book *Woman in Pre-Columbian America* (New York: Abner Shram, 1973) states, "Although statements concerning the matriarchy, which apparently was established in the Antilles and in the southern hemisphere, are extremely rare and sporadic, all chroniclers who mention it agree that it existed (without realizing its importance); it seems therefore that their statements can be accepted."

15. Rudolf Kaiser, *The Voice of the Great Spirit: Prophecies of the Hopi Indians* (Boston & London: Shambala Books, 1991).

16. National Council of La Raza fact sheet: Center for Health Promotion: HIV/AIDS, June, 1993.

17. *The Hispanic Elderly: The Community's Response,* National Council of La Raza, Washington, D. C. , July, 1989.

18. I credit muralist, activist Judy Baca for this definition.